SKYSCRAPER

THE LANDMARK LIBRARY

Chapters in the History of Civilization

The Landmark Library is a record of the achievements of humankind from the late Stone Age to the present day. Each volume in the series is devoted to a crucial theme in the history of civilization, and offers a concise and authoritative text accompanied by a generous complement of images. Contributing authors to The Landmark Library are chosen for their ability to combine scholarship with a flair for communicating their specialist knowledge to a wider, non-specialist readership.

SKYSCRAPER

DAN CRUICKSHANK

HEAD
of ZEUS

An Apollo Book

This is an Apollo book, first published in the
UK in 2018 by Head of Zeus Ltd

Copyright © Dan Cruickshank 2018

The moral right of Dan Cruickshank to be
identified as the author of this work has been
asserted in accordance with the Copyright,
Designs and Patents Act of 1988.

1 3 5 7 9 10 8 6 4 2

A CIP catalogue record for this book is available
from the British Library.

ISBN (HB) 9781786691187

Designed by Isambard Thomas
Printed in Spain by Graficas Estella

Head of Zeus Ltd
First Floor East
5–8 Hardwick Street
London EC1R 4RG

WWW.HEADOFZEUS.COM

PREVIOUS PAGE
Chicago: the city of towers. View from the north edge of the
Loop, with, left foreground, the Gothic pinnacles, buttresses
and lantern of the Tribune Tower, of 1923–5, designed by
John Meade Howells and Raymond Hood. This view was
taken in 1920.

Introduction

This book is about buildings I've long known and admired, and explores the ways in which they are intimately connected. Some of the connections are obvious, others more subtle and obscure. Some are even speculative because the story the book tells is so extraordinary, so full of human drama, of soaring ambition, descents into despair and – especially – untimely deaths that it has proved impossible to avoid excursions into the seemingly fantastic. In essence, what the book deals with is the emergence, in the late nineteenth century in Chicago, of a distinct American architecture, one that took inspiration from history but which also grasped the technical potential of the age and had a huge influence on the evolution and identity of world architecture for the next hundred years.

This story starts about twenty years ago, when I first visited Chicago. I was there for a specific purpose. It has long been agreed that the epic building type of the early twentieth century – the commercial 'skyscraper' – first came to fruition in Chicago. By common consensus this miraculous event took place in the early 1880s – although this seemingly obvious fact depends on a series of judgements. These include the basic question: what exactly is a skyscraper? This question not only relates to height, but also to technical and artistic issues. If the term skyscraper is, at least in part, synonymous with the notion of pioneering, 'cutting-edge', avant-garde construction and design, and the application of 'state-of-the-art' technology, then the definition must include techniques of construction, methods of servicing and physical appearance. When all these things are part of the debate then the nomination of the world's first skyscraper can be surprisingly difficult to agree. But what is universally agreed it that this birth took place in Chicago, even if the precise identity of the infant can be contested. And that is why I went first to Chicago: to look, to explore, to ponder and to decide – to my own satisfaction – which building is the prime contender. In a sense

Life flows in State Street, Chicago around the ground floor of the newly completed Reliance Building, which – when opened in 1895 – was arguably the first fully realized skyscraper of the modern age.

I've been pondering ever since and this book is, at one level, a record of my quest.

Two decades ago I took the view that the Reliance Building takes the prize. This is not a radical statement since many historians have taken a similar view, and this book reviews and ultimately reiterates the case. Virtually all the key elements of the Reliance Building – completed in early 1895 – are an echo of slightly earlier buildings – the steel-frame, 'fire-proof' construction and terracotta cladding, the use of Otis safety elevators. Its originality has more to do with art and with ideology than with methods of construction, but it is these that give it the edge, and suggest that it is the epitome – the first and finest expression of what we now take to be the skyscraper of the modern age. The Reliance Building is more minimal and clearly functionalist than its fellows, it is far more liberated from the late-nineteenth-century obsession with history-based ornament, and far more than any earlier skyscraper it embraces the potential offered by modern technology. It is clad with a curtain wall made largely of glass, and most of the elevation that is not glass is formed by beautiful white-glazed terracotta that helps to imbue the building with something of an ethereal quality. This simplicity, the swathes of glass, the pristine white terracotta – the fact that the material and means of construction and the demands of function are the building's most characteristic ornaments – make the Reliance appear astonishingly modern. It anticipates – indeed helps determine – buildings to come far more than most of its high-rise contemporaries. And who was responsible for this remarkable, epoch-making building? Strangely enough we are not quite sure. John Wellborn Root and Charles B. Atwood between them no doubt played key roles, with perhaps some input from Daniel Burnham. But – as so often happens in this tale – death intervened at crucial moments to baffle and obscure particular creative contributions. But of these three architects Root gripped and held my interest and imagination and it is his character and career that I examine in particular detail.

But the real star of this story is not a single building. It is Chicago, one of the world's great cities. It is great for many reasons: because of its location beside the inland sea of the vast Lake Michigan and within the loop of the Chicago River that defines the 'Downtown' area; because of the vigorous life and short but sensational history of the city, based on trade, markets, staggeringly energetic entrepreneurship (both legal and illegal), and because its history includes the music of African-Americans – the Blues – that found its urban voice in Chicago. And, of course, there is the architecture.

I have returned to Chicago several times since my first visit, most recently in October 2017. Of course I needed to consult archives, organize photographs, meet people, revisit the Reliance and other key buildings but also – and especially – to look once more at the city.

Only when the buildings mentioned in this book are placed in the context of the city and in physical relation one to the other is it possible to see them fully for what they are – the remarkable and inter-related products of a thriving, thrusting and ambitious community with a hunger for culture, in which business aspired to be dressed in the raiment of art. The most dramatic expression of this infant city's yearning for recognition and beauty was the World's Columbian Exposition of 1893 that created the ephemeral 'White City', which had at its heart a collection of vast, classically detailed, white-painted palaces that embodied the hopes and pride not only of Chicago but of the whole nation.

The relationship between the functionalist 'Chicago School' architecture of the 1890s, with its pioneering steel-framed skyscrapers and the classical fairyland of the 'White City' is extraordinary. Together these two bodies of architecture represent a seemingly strange paradox – the skyscrapers rising in

Downtown Chicago were to become the emblematic architecture of the United States, yet in the early 1890s the vast, low-rise classical palaces of the 'White City' were hailed by many as defining the national style. And what makes the relationship stranger still – as well as stronger – is that many of the same men were involved in the creation of Chicago's skyscrapers and in the building of the 'White City'. And many of the same people were involved – as clients, financiers, developers, engineers or architects – in the creation of the city's early skyscrapers, for example W. E. Hale, the client for the Reliance Building, and his ex-business associate Lucius Fisher, the merchant Marshall Field, the real estate magnate Potter Palmer, and the architects John W. Root, Charles B. Atwood, William Le Baron Jenney, Louis Sullivan, Dankmar Adler and – of course – Root's partner Daniel H. Burnham. All of which explains why it is essential to consider the skyscrapers in relation one to another and in the context of Chicago, and all in relation to the 'White City', to get a fuller understanding of this inspirational architectural legacy.

As with all great commercial cities, Chicago has repeatedly remodelled itself and – despite often impassioned conservation battles – many of its seminal buildings have been swept away. But on various walks around the city it is still possible to experience the architectural power of Chicago's Gilded Age, which started a decade or so after its Great Fire of 1871 and continued into the early decades of the twentieth century when the hunger for innovation and almost unbridled scale moved to New York, not returning to Chicago until the 1960s.

Exploration of Chicago's Downtown – where the key early buildings are located – can start in many places, but there is a route that brings together virtually all the major surviving buildings mentioned in this book. This route starts where the city itself began. On the corner of West Lake Street and North Wacker Drive is the site of the Sauganesh Hotel, which stood

Chicago's Elevated Railway – the 'L' – as it makes its way along Lake Street. The story of its creation from the early 1890s is fantastical and it does much to define the physical character of the city's 'Downtown'.

on the banks of the Chicago River. Built in 1831, the hotel was the scene for a meeting in 1833 during which the makeshift riverside trading community of Chicago was incorporated as a town, which in 1837 became a city. This site – now a busy and characterless traffic interchange – evidently remained something of a sacred site for the new city because it was here in 1860 – in a temporary 'convention centre' known as the Wigwam – that Abraham Lincoln was nominated for president.

From this interchange head west along Lake Street, over which crouches the crude, tough and utilitarian steel structure that supports the city's Elevated Railway. The people of the city take this outlandish creation in their stride, as if it was perfectly normal to build an urban railway system down the middle of major streets at first-floor level. It casts whole areas of the city into perpetual gloom, robs building occupants of prospect and light and fills their buildings with noise and dirt as trains rattle by. Other cities provided their citizens with city-centre trains by

burrowing underground, but not in Chicago where the 'L' – as the elevated railway is known – not only girdles Downtown (and thus earns it the colloquial name of 'the Loop'), but runs down its sometimes narrow streets. Other cities that experimented with high-level railroads strictly controlled the number and locations of routes. In London in the 1830s steam trains entered the city centre on brick-built viaducts, but these were few in number and cut across or ran parallel with existing streets. And most cities with mass public transport systems similar to Chicago's 'L' long ago decided that they were, on balance, more trouble than they were worth. Liverpool's Overhead railway opened in 1893, initially to serve the docks, was closed in 1956 and virtually all traces of it have been swept away, and New York's West Side elevated railway closed long ago and its raised route has been turned into the High Line linear park.

The story of the creation of Chicago's 'L' is predictably fantastical. Work got underway in 1893 – as the World's Columbian Exposition was opening (which had its own elevated railway) – and one of the earliest tracks was built along Lake Street. This unlikely, and in many ways anti-social, enterprise was driven by hard-nosed entrepreneurs who saw that a great deal of money was to be made. The most notorious of them was Charles Tyson Yerkes. State law required that property owners neighbouring the track had to give their permission for its construction, and these permissions Yerkes obtained by bribes, guile and deceit – and when he obtained agreement from the majority of owners he simply went ahead, leaving objectors to flounder in impotent rage. Outrageous but, human nature being what it is, the 'L' is now one of the best-loved symbols of the city, giving the place a distinct and rumbustious visual character and an extraordinary sense of bustle and energy; it's a late-nineteenth-century vision of the city of the future brought to life. Yerkes grew tired of Chicago and in 1900 moved to London to help finance the extension of

London's underground railway and so became one of the key figures in the growth of London's public transport system where – of course – trains were buried decently underground.

Moving west along Lake Street, below the shadow of the 'L', look out for the block of buildings on the corner with Franklin Street. These are a rare survival – a group of buildings constructed immediately after the Great Fire of 1871. They are worth remembering – four-storey, brick-fronted with ornately ornamented window lintels and cast-iron columns at ground level. They represented the architecturally unexceptional context within which the Reliance and its fellow metal-framed skyscrapers were to be created.

And then you come to State Street. This, arguably, is the spine of Downtown, and certainly more of Chicago's major late-nineteenth-century buildings are located on, or near, this street than any other in the city and most of the Chicago buildings described in this book can be seen by strolling down and around State Street. The street is long and straight and follows a grid laid out in 1830; central Chicago is, like most of New York, a gridiron city. And as in Manhattan, skyscrapers and high-rise buildings have, during the last hundred and thirty years, risen from the pavement's edge to create canyon streets. The prospect looking south is most impressive. Look hard and about three blocks away, and on the west side of the street, you will see the Reliance Building – a fourteen-storey giant that once towered over its neighbours, but is now all but engulfed by later high-rise buildings.

The Reliance Building records something about the social history of State Street because part of it was originally designed to accommodate medical doctors in small consulting rooms. State Street was a place of business, in all its many forms, and among the early doctors in practice in the Reliance was the extraordinary Ben L. Reitman, whose consulting room was on the eighth floor. Known as the 'hobo doctor', Reitman was a physician to the poor, to prostitutes, to social outcasts and, in particular, to the sexually diseased. He was also the lover of the radical anarchist and proto-feminist Emma Goldman – once, presumably, a regular visitor to the Reliance.

Almost opposite the Reliance is a solid block of building that represents one of the other early and dominant uses of State Street. From the start it was a major shopping street and this building was once part of the massive Marshall Field's Department Store. The evolution of this store from the mid-nineteenth century is virtually a potted history of commercial Chicago. Its first manifestation was a dry-goods store, opened on State Street in 1852 by Potter Palmer – a merchant who became the real estate force behind the creation of State Street and latterly an art collector who plays a significant role in the story told in this book. In 1865 Palmer went into partnership with two Chicago storeowners – Marshall Field and Levi Z. Leiter – and a few years later sold his interest so that the ever-growing store became known as Field, Leiter & Company. The store burned to the ground in the Great Fire of 1871 but this was little more than a temporary inconvenience for the remarkable Field and Leiter. They had been able, by pluck and determination, to save much of their stock and were back in business, in new accommodation, only a few weeks after the fire. By 1873 the store, ever thriving, was back on State Street and in 1881 Field bought-out Leiter to create Marshall Field & Company and to oversee the growth of his wholesale and retail enterprise into the most successful department store in the world. Field wanted to make shopping into a joyful experience, with customers feeling free to browse without pressure to buy in architecturally delightful surroundings, and created a retail model for international emulation, with Harry G. Selfridge – who worked for Field for a quarter of a century, rising from 'stock' boy in the wholesale department to junior partner – opening Selfridge's in London in 1908. This prime example of American

The Sullivan Center on State Street, built between 1899 and 1904 in two phases as a department store to the designs of Louis Sullivan, with additions in 1906 by D. H. Burnham & Company.

merchandizing in London's West End was, almost inevitably, designed by Daniel Burnham because it was D. H. Burnham & Co. that had given architectural expression to the Marshall Field flagship store that survives – now as a branch of Macy's – on State Street. In fact this store is, from the architectural point of view – and certainly in the context of the Reliance Building – most revealing. The existing store is a complex combination of five different phases constructed between 1892 and 1914, with the first of these phases designed in 1892 by Charles Atwood – then the lead designer in D. H. Burnham & Co. – and opened in August the following year. This was just after Atwood had began work on the Reliance Building, appointed by Burnham to complete the project started in 1890 by John Root and left incomplete at his death in January 1891. But while the Reliance is pioneering in its architectural simplicity and sense of utility, with its astonishing curtain wall of glass combined with a smaller proportion of white-glazed terracotta, Atwood's near contemporary work for Marshall Field is largely traditional. It is classical in its details – as were the buildings Atwood was soon to design (also under Burnham's control) for the World's Columbian Exposition – with its steel frame clad with granite to suggest that it is of conventional masonry construction. Chicago in the early 1890s was an artistically extraordinary place, tottering on the edge of dramatic change, with old and new architectural worlds existing in parallel.

On a block immediately to the south of the Reliance Building is the last major building designed by Louis Sullivan, an architect who plays a large role in the story of Chicago – and American – architecture in the 1880s and 1890s. It was designed in 1899 for the retail firm Schlesinger & Meyer, and then in 1904 became the flagship building of the Carson, Pirie and Scott department store chain which in 1901 was the first tenant of the ground floor of the then less than half completed Reliance Building. Sullivan's building – now known as the Sullivan Center – was completed in his troubled later years and has been altered and extended, yet it still embodies the power of his earlier epoch-making architecture. In 1896 Sullivan argued that architecture should follow the pattern offered by nature – or by nature as he observed it – where 'form ever follows function'. As far as he could see, in nature form only changes when function does, so in this building the stacks of office floors all look the same because they all fulfil the same function, while ground-floor shop windows and top-floor promenade take different forms because they have different functions. And Sullivan takes the plant as his model, so the building is visually 'rooted' firmly to the ground and ornament swirls in inventive organic manner, while the top of the building, set above ranks of repetitive 'Chicago windows' (typically wide with large central areas of plate glass flanked by narrow opening sashes) blossoms like a flower on its stem.*

A couple of blocks west of State Street, on the corner of West Adams Street and South La Salle Street, is the Rookery of 1886 – Burnham and Root's first significant surviving high-rise building, rational in form but immensely rich in eclectic ornamental detail, with a splendid top-lit internal light court redecorated in 1906 by Frank Lloyd Wright. Immediately south of the Rookery – on West Van Buren Street that runs back to State Street – is the astonishing Monadnock Building. Designed by John Root just before he died in January 1891, the Monadnock is wide, deep, seventeen storeys high and utterly sublime with virtually no external ornament.

---

* For Sullivan's earliest surviving Chicago building with Dankmar Adler see the Jewellers' Building at 15–19 Wabash Avenue, just round the corner from the Reliance. Built in 1881–2 the building is exquisite, with stylized floral decoration that reveals how Sullivan was already exploring plants as the analogy for architecture. Information thanks to Tim Samuelson of the Chicago Cultural Center.

OVERLEAF
The Auditorium Theater Building, designed in 1887 by Sullivan & Adler, has a massive and elemental urban quality. When completed it was the largest single building in the United States and the tallest building in Chicago.

It is a *tour de force* of minimal, abstract architecture – mostly imposed by a very cost conscious client – and is way before its time. Just to the south of the Monadnock, on Dearborn Street, is the nineteen-storey terracotta-clad Fisher Building – designed in 1893 for Lucius Fisher by Charles Atwood while he was working on the Reliance. The Fisher Building, not completed until 1896 and after Atwood's sudden and premature death, makes a fascinating companion to the Reliance; clearly they are both from the same stable, but the Fisher has less glazing, more historicizing ornament and seems to represent a slight retreat from the avant-garde threshold marked out by the Reliance.

This journey into Chicago's extraordinary architectural history now reaches its climax. Next to the Fisher Building is the sixteen-storey Manhattan Building, designed by William Le Baron Jenney in 1888 and the city's first fully steel-framed skyscraper. But, despite this epic and pioneering role in the birth of the sleek modern high-rise, the Manhattan Building still has masonry concealing its steel frame and sports jovial history-inspired ornament, including a series of grimacing demonic faces worthy of a Renaissance Mannerist palazzo. Then back onto State Street, where the huge bulk of the Leiter II Building looms up. Designed in 1889 as a department store by Jenney for Levi Leiter after he split from Marshall Field, the building is not a high-rise but it expands across an entire city block. It's fascinating to see the direction Jenney took straight after the Manhattan Building. The Leiter Building still sports traditional ornament – notably giant Doric pilasters that articulate its elevation – and the steel frame is once again masonry clad, but all is far simpler and more rational. It is plain to see that here is a functional building about to emerge from the cocoon of history. And then, finally, we reach one of the most significant buildings in Chicago and in late-nineteenth-century America. State Street runs across Congress Parkway and there, just to the east, is the Auditorium Theater. Designed in

1887 by Louis Sullivan and Dankmar Adler for a consortium of Chicago businessmen the building, which incorporates a 4,300-seat auditorium, was designed to put the city on the cultural map and to rival New York's Metropolitan Opera House that had opened in 1883 on Broadway. The consortium was headed by Ferdinand Peck, a real estate millionaire and philanthropist, and included Martin A. Ryerson, a lawyer and businessman who in 1892, at the age of thirty-six, was the richest man in Chicago and one of the city's leading art collectors; George Pullman, an engineer and industrialist who developed the luxurious 'Pullman' sleeping car for the nation's railroads; and department store owner Marshall Field. When completed in 1889 the Auditorium was the largest building in the United States and, with its eighteen-storey tower, the tallest in Chicago.

These people and the buildings they created did much to determine the architectural and urban world we now inhabit. Once you know the tale they have to tell you will never see the modern city in quite the same way again.

John Wellborn Root: Atlanta, Liverpool and New York

The siege of Atlanta, Georgia started in the summer of 1864. It was not as long, bloody or brutal as the sieges of the Confederate cities of Vicksburg or Petersburg, but it was bad. And among the besieged were Sidney and Mary Root and their family, including their fourteen-year-old son John Wellborn Root.

Atlanta was a prime target for the Union army on its march through Georgia, which had commenced in May. Major General William Tecumseh Sherman's 62,000 men set out to destroy the material means and the will of the Confederate people to persevere in their war of independence from the Union. It was a huge punitive raid with physical destruction and terror among its principal aims.

Sherman explained his chilling objectives in a letter dated 31 January 1864. It was addressed to Major R. M. Sawyer, the assistant adjutant general of his army, but written for publication and circulation among the Union's foes. Sherman wrote that his commanders, when they conquered and occupied Confederate districts, should 'assemble the inhabitants and… tell them that it is now for them to say whether they and their children shall inherit the beautiful land which by the accident of nature had fallen to their share.' To retain their inheritance rebels had to do no more than renounce their cause and rejoin the Union. But, threatened Sherman, 'if they want eternal war, well and good; we accept the issue, and will dispossess them and put our friends in their places.'

Reflecting on the last three years of ever-escalating war, and the series of Union entreaties that the Confederacy had consistently ignored, Sherman continued that

last year rebels [if they had recanted] could have saved
their slaves, but now it is too late. All the powers on earth
cannot return to them their slaves, any more than their dead
grandfathers. Next year their lands will be taken; for in war
we can take them, and rightfully, too, and in another year they
may beg in vain for their lives. A people who will persevere in
war beyond a certain limit ought to know the consequences.
Many other peoples with less pertinacity have been wiped out of
national existence... To the petulant and persistent secessionist,
why, death is mercy, and the quicker he or she is disposed of the
better...[1]

The subjugation of the city of Atlanta, with a population in 1860
of just over 9,500, was essential to the Union cause because the
city was the linchpin of the Confederate system of railways and
thus a vital centre of communications. Atlanta was the meeting
point of the Western & Atlantic Railroad from the north, the
Macon Railroad to the south, the Georgia Railroad to the east
and the Atlanta & Western Railroad to the southwest. Its role
as a railway interchange had been one of the key reasons for
Atlanta's pre-war importance and now, as its citizens well knew,
gave it great military significance and made it a place worth
attacking, and defending, with utmost vigour. As the *Atlanta
Daily Constitutionalist* stated on 1 May 1864: 'Atlanta is the great
strategic point... The approaches to the Gate City – every one of
them – must be made a second Thermopylae.'[2]

This importance as a hub by which troops and materiel
could be directed and moved at speed through the whole Lower
South made Atlanta a legitimate military target that could,
by the conventions of war, be destroyed by the enemy without
compunction. It was obvious to most in the spring of 1864 that
this small but thriving city was a potential battlefield and that
its streets and surrounding fields could become a bloody killing
ground.

When the Union army commenced its deliberate, destructive and seemingly unstoppable march towards Atlanta, its inhabitants, as they fortified their city, had much to trouble their minds. Sidney Root must have been more troubled than most. As a merchant with stock and investments and an urgent need to trade, he had much to lose to a hostile invading force and to the uncertainties of war. Also, as a born Northerner he could expect harsh treatment from the Union authorities. The legalities of the situation were subtle but to Sherman's soldiers Root's Southern-born neighbours were merely rebels, while he – arguably – was a traitor.

The Roots were relatively new arrivals in the city. In the 1840s Sidney Root had moved south from New England and had opened a dry-goods store in Lumpkin, Georgia. Here he married Mary Clarke, the daughter of Judge James Clarke (sometimes spelled Clark), a reserved and taciturn but able jurist, and Permelia Wellborn. Both these families had been long established in Georgia. On 10 January 1850 John was born at the family home in Lumpkin.

Business prospered and Sidney Root's ambitions grew too large for this small town in the cotton belt, surrounded by plantations worked by thousands of slaves; in 1857 the Root family moved to Atlanta, which was then expanding due largely to its increasing importance as a railway interchange. At the same time the Clarke family also appears to have moved to Atlanta from Lumpkin. Sidney Root did well in his new home and seems to have made his son's education a priority. As Harriet Monroe explains in her 1896 biography of John Root – which is a most revealing and intimate affair because she was John's doting sister-in-law and privy to much family history – Sidney Root had longed to be an architect and loved the arts. But he was prevented by his father from indulging these interests and so determined, predictably, to realize them through his son. So, while his son was still very young Sidney ensured that John was made familiar with – and if possible able in – the arts. Music, poetry, painting and architecture became the focus of his early education. And, as evidence suggests, Sidney was not disappointed in his son because John quickly displayed not just interest in these subjects but real talent, particularly in painting and poetry.

But by June 1861 this idyll was at an end. Georgia, along with ten other states, had seceded from the Union and the Civil War had begun. According to Monroe, Sidney Root soon 'became active in the service of the Southern Confederacy and invested his capital in blockade runners, swift steamers built in the Clyde to elude the Federal guard at Confederate ports and bring merchandise to the beleaguered States.'[3]

As well as craft being built on the Clyde in Scotland others were commissioned from shipyards in Liverpool and Birkenhead, with Liverpool – to all intents and purposes – becoming the centre of the Confederate navy, and indeed of the secessionist cause, in Europe. Not only were ships built in and around Liverpool – which was a key port for the South's cotton industry – but crews were recruited to man the blockade runners and goods purchased for export to the Confederacy. This, of course, led to bitter complaint from the Federal government, insisting that Britain as a neutral nation must not in any way aid or abet the Confederacy or allow British industries to do so. This led to restrictions being imposed on Liverpool merchants and industrialists by the British authorities, so that the construction of ships for the Confederacy was illegal and could be undertaken only in secret. These controls and restrictions made the life of investors like Root financially risky. But there were still greater risks. As Monroe notes, 'one third of the cruisers fell to the enemy, and such losses could spell ruin for investors. But this high rate of attrition could also make fortunes because it vastly increased the value of the cargoes that did get through.' Monroe suggests that Sidney Root was among the lucky few who made a 'large fortune… before the close of the war.' He was also, states Monroe, 'in the confidence' of the Confederate government in Richmond and 'intrusted by President Davis with special missions to one or two foreign courts'.[4] Monroe writes little about John at this time, besides suggesting that he was big for his age and precocious because, when he was thirteen, his father took the precaution of furnishing his son with 'a sworn statement of his age.' John was instructed to carry this document at all times to prevent him being 'drafted by conscription officers, who thought him three years older'.[5]

Sidney Root's long absences abroad were probably noted with some suspicion by his fellow citizens. Certainly his partner John N. Beach came under critical scrutiny. As might be expected, some wondered why men such as Beach chose to leave Atlanta as the city approached its hour of need. Were these absentees shirking their duty or were they something worse – traitors? As historian Thomas G. Dyer explains, the standing of John N. Beach 'as a Southern man' was publicly questioned in Atlanta. Why, it was asked, did this rich merchant spend so much time in Europe? Finally the highly respected pro-Confederate Atlanta physician Joseph P. Logan came to Beach's aid and seems to have saved his reputation, and perhaps his life. Logan put his own reputation on the line by insisting that Beach was indeed abroad for the 'honourable' purpose of forging – or at least attempting to forge – Confederate trade links with Europe and was not merely using the war as an opportunity for personal profiteering from a comfortable berth out of harm's way.[6] The nature of Logan's relationship with Beach – and presumably the basis of his faith in Beach's activities and intentions – is revealed by the records of Atlanta's Central Presbyterian Church, founded in 1858. These tell us that Dr J. P. Logan was one of its founding Elders while its trustees included John N. Beach.[7] Such, it seems, was the way reputations were made and protected, in the God-fearing Confederate States of America.

Presumably Sidney Root was susceptible to the same criticism of absenteeism or profiteering as his partner. However, there is no record of popular discontent with his conduct during the summer of 1864 even though his father-in-law Judge Clarke must have enraged many Southern patriots because he was, according to Monroe, 'the only prominent man in Atlanta who persistently opposed the war, and predicted the ultimate triumph of the North.'[8] So it is possible that Root felt uncomfortable in Atlanta, especially since he was a Northern man by birth and upbringing, and life could have been difficult for his family. If Root's family was in some distress then things could only have got worse when the Union forces finally closed in on Atlanta in late July because, as Monroe explains, Sidney Root was then 'absent on one of the embassies'.[9] So, at this critical moment, the Root family found itself exposed. The South was a paternalistic society, so Sidney Root's absence would have been significant, particularly since he was the maker and protector of the family's fortunes as well as being, as far as we can now tell, his son John's guiding light.

By the time the Union forces arrived Atlanta was defended by a ring of formidable fortifications that stretched about one and a quarter miles in diameter and formed a perimeter of ten miles around the city. But the new commander of the army of defence, Lieutenant General John B. Hood, was well aware of the old military maxim that the best defence is attack. Hood also knew that his predecessor – Joseph E. Johnston – had been sacked because he had allowed himself during the previous couple of months to be repeatedly outflanked by Sherman's forces and compelled to retreat ever further south through Georgia to the outskirts of Atlanta. For these reasons Hood did not want to play a passive role and allow himself to be encircled and trapped within the city's defences. So on 20 July, with the admirable desire to grab the initiative and defeat the attackers in open battle in a war of manoeuvre, Hood launched his 'First Sortie'.

When Sherman heard that Hood had replaced Johnston he was happy because Hood had a reputation for recklessness, a reputation supported by the fact that this young but ferociously bearded Southern general now had only one leg and one operable arm. Even Hood's old friend, Major General William H. T. Walker, was sceptical. When he heard of Hood's sudden promotion to the command of the army he observed that while Hood had 'gone up like a rocket', he feared that he could well 'come down like the stick'.[10] Both these men were to prove justified in their happiness and in their fear. Hood's sortie was not well planned or executed and the Confederacy suffered nearly 25 per cent casualties among the attacking force of 20,000 men, for no tangible gain. The Union force they attacked was of similar size and its casualties were less than half those of their opponents. Undaunted, Hood determined on a yet more ambitious extensive manoeuvre in an attempt to catch the Union forces unawares and wrong-foot them. Hood split his command and sent one portion on a fifteen-mile night march to the southeast of the city, while the remaining troops retired within Atlanta's defences. As this manoeuvre was going on Union forces attacked and grabbed critical hilltop positions of the city's perimeter defence. By evening the successful Union troops were able to look out over the entire city, spread helplessly at their feet.

The following day – 22 July – Hood attempted his 'Second Sortie'. The fighting was fierce and once again the Confederates lost – in dead, wounded and captured – a quarter of their force, more than 50 per cent more than the total Union losses. Among the Confederate dead was General William H. T. Walker, whose fear that his friend lacked the ability to launch, sustain and develop a successful defensive operation was confirmed in the most painful manner possible.

Looking north along Peachtree Street in central Atlanta in late 1865.
In the foreground is the ruined Atlanta Bank and billiard saloon.

After this reverse Hood crept back into the city's defences. By 27 July the Union forces had more or less encircled the city as the preliminary to a formal siege. But Hood remained willing to gamble with the blood of others and on 28 July attempted his 'Third Sortie' by sending out a large body of troops with no more coherent purpose than launching opportunistic attacks on Union troops, who were then tightening the ring around the city. The result, for the Confederates, was disastrous. They found themselves assaulting well-armed Union troops in already prepared positions. By nightfall, when they retreated back to the city, the Confederates had suffered around 5,000 casualties in comparison with Union losses of about 600 men. Hood's attempt to defeat the attackers through a war of manoeuvre was at an end. The battle now settled into a regular siege in which Union heavy guns almost casually lobbed large shells into the city, wreaking death and injury in a most arbitrary manner, while the cavalry of both sides skirmished indecisively outside the city and conducted inconclusive raids on each other's lines of communication.

Monroe hints at fourteen-year-old John Root's life within the fortifications of the besieged Atlanta. War, when it had started back in April 1861, might have seemed exciting and romantic to boys such as John, a thing of martial beauty, glorious uniforms and poetic splendour. But by mid-1864, during such a desperate siege, war had been 'robbed of its glamour for Southern children', with the Confederate soldier now being a 'very bedraggled person' and hardly likely to inspire emulation or enthusiasm. Children were, she notes, 'kept in cellars, for shells fell too often and too near'.

But John seems to have been bold and inquisitive. One day he 'pried open one of these destructive demons and found it stuffed with harmless sawdust instead of powder and scrap.'[11] This odd story, which evidently entered the family annals, suggests that the Union munitions industry was either incompetent or – more likely – that it was being sabotaged by Confederate sympathizers among its workforce. Such a discovery, suggesting support in an unexpected quarter, must have given much-needed encouragement to the embattled citizens of the city.

But such tiny fragments of hope were transient. On 25 August, after nearly a month of siege, Sherman initiated a push to take the city by assault. The attack was slow, methodical – and ultimately successful. By 31 August the Confederate forces had been thrust back, outmanoeuvred and compelled to undertake costly counter-attacks, notably during an ad hoc sortie rather grandly named the Battle of Jonesboro that did little more than distract and pin down defending troops to the south of the city. By the end of the day's fighting the Confederate casualties of 1,725 were ten times those of the Union attackers.

Effectively, the siege of Atlanta was over. On 1 September, as the fighting around Jonesboro spluttered on in a futile manner, Union forces entered the city and Sherman was able to write that evening that 'Atlanta is ours & fairly won.'[12]

Hood, with what was left of his army, was allowed to slip away, and as they did so they followed a 'scorched earth' policy. Railway repair and manufacturing facilities were destroyed to prevent them falling into Union hands, while Hood's ammunition train was set ablaze. This was a militarily wise move no doubt, but like most of Hood's decisions it was disastrous for Atlanta. The train cars exploded with a mighty roar and started a fire that eventually engulfed whole districts of the city.

The siege, bombardment and fighting had inflicted severe damage on those parts of the city spared by the fire. The scene was described by Major General John W. Geary in a letter dated 3 September: 'The city is a very pretty place… and contained about 15,000 inhabitants [but] there is scarcely a house that does [not] exhibit in some degree the effects of the battle which so fearfully raged around it. Many of the best are utterly ruined, and many of the ornamental trees are cut down by our shells.'[13] Union forces set about adding to the ruin of the city by destroying buildings that were deemed to be of military importance. But this was a casual, rapid and very inexact process. As historian David J. Eicher observes, 'Sherman did not care if the destroyed property offered military value for the opposing army [or not]'. Indeed, Sherman made his attitude clear by his actions and his words. He ordered the immediate evacuation of civilians from the city, which was to become no more than a huge military camp with its surviving best houses occupied by his officers and administrative staff, and he wrote that 'If the people raise a howl against my barbarity & cruelty, I will answer that War is War & and not popularity seeking… If they want Peace, they and their relations must stop War.'[14] He made it clear that 'the only way the people of Atlanta can hope once more to live in peace and quiet at home' was to admit that the war was 'began in error and is perpetuated in pride'.[15]

Sherman's conduct was no more than an expression of his established military policy – indeed philosophy: 'War is Hell' – as he was later to say – and the best and most speedy way to end the Civil War was, for Sherman, to make its further prosecution as painful as possible for the enemy, civilians as well as soldiers. As he wrote: 'War is cruelty… the crueller it is, the sooner it will be over.'

The Root family had first-hand experience of this cruelty. 'All non-combatants were ordered to leave the city within twenty-four hours [so] the little wife of Sidney Root valiantly gathered her children and a handful of valuables together and departed into the wilderness' as the residences of the Clarkes and the Roots were surrendered to Federal generals, who within them 'sheltered... in unwonted comfort'.[16]

Mary Root led her family to one of the Clarke plantations, where they stayed for several weeks until Northern troops departed from Atlanta and it was possible to return home. The family would, on its return, have been confronted by a scene of devastation, but we know that at least one of the family homes in Atlanta survived because it survives still. In 1859 Mary Root's father had built a large, brick house, now numbered 325, on the northwest corner of Washington Street and Jones Street (now Woodward Avenue). It is possible that the Root family established itself here if its own house was too damaged to occupy.[17]

If John did live in the Clarke house on Washington Street it was not for long because in October he set out on a great adventure. As Monroe explains: 'As John could do little studying in these turbulent times, Mr. Robert T. Wilson, an old friend and business associate of Sidney Root, offered to take the boy with him to England, whither he was about to sail on one of the blockade-runners, which he partly owned'.[18] Although fraught with danger, this might well have appeared the safest course at the time. The war could drag on for years and John would be eligible for military service in little over a year, perhaps even sooner if things got more desperate for the South. The Roots were no doubt patriotic but for them, as for many families, the life of their son came first. If John could make it safely to England all could yet be well. He could be 'received into the household of the English partner of Sidney Root',[19] where he could continue his education and – far more important – could escape the horrors and dangers of combat. There is no record of John's attitude to this proposal to flee the Confederacy. All that is known is that he, along with Wilson and another boy, stole out of Atlanta and that the group, dodging Union and Confederate patrols (who might have either imprisoned them or conscripted them), succeeded in making its way to the port of Wilmington, North Carolina. This was the South's major port in the last year of the war and, despite being attacked and blockaded, was able to defend itself and dispatch cruisers and receive goods until February 1865, when its fall hastened the end of the war.

John was accommodated aboard a vessel that, shrouded by fog, slipped out of the harbour and past waiting Union vessels. They fired on the swift blockade-running craft but failed to stop her, so John, and in all probability a cargo of cotton, made their escape. On 17 November 1864 John sent a letter to his sister, describing his precarious but successful journey: 'I am here in Liverpool at last, after being on the ocean 18 days. We came through the blockade without having but three shots fired at us, and arrived in Bermuda after 2½ days passage.'

Bermuda, a British possession, was a favoured port of call for Confederate ships that were able, in tightly controlled circumstances, to use the facilities offered by the island without blatantly compromising Britain's neutrality. Supplies could be bought, basic repairs undertaken, goods could be sold and if prisoners had been seized by commerce raiders like the Birkenhead-built CSS *Alabama* they would be offloaded into British hands.

John's letter reveals an awareness of beauty. At this stage – he was still little more than a child – this might have been no more than a reflection of his father's tutelage. But there are some observations that have the ring of an authentic regard for form, colour and visual poetry. In conventional manner he commended the picturesque setting of the port to his sister: 'How you would have relished and appreciated the beautiful bay, crowded by stately ships and graceful steamers, and above all the beautiful village of St. George, almost buried in the lap of the bright green hills, whose fortress-capped summits bristled with heavy cannon.'

More telling is his critical and reflective observation about the people he saw, particularly the brightly garbed British soldiers or marines. There were, he informed his sister, 'very many soldiers with bright scarlet coats and black pants who strutted through the streets, and looked as neat and prim as Confederate soldiers are dirty and ragged.'[20] Among other things, this comment appears to confirm a boyish sorrow that the siege of Atlanta had lacked the beauty, the pageantry and the glory of war that the fourteen-year-old had hoped for. Even the victors were dowdy. In later years John recalled the entry into Atlanta of 'Old Tecumseh' – the 'ruthless conqueror about whose head' he had dreaded – or hoped – to see a 'lurid halo of horror'. But to his disappointment, 'neither the glory nor the terror of war lodged in this grim, battered warrior, unwashed, unshaven, shabbily clad from soft hat to dusty top boots'.[21] The visual aspect of war was, for the young Root, far from poetic and something of a disappointment.

In his letter John also told his sister a little about the vessel that carried him to England. It was, he wrote, a 'steamship called the Mileta, a large boat over 250 feet long and about 30 feet broad.' No ship called the *Mileta* is recorded in the records of the Confederate navy, nor among the privateers that the Southern cause encouraged to operate as little more than buccaneers. She could have been British or foreign-registered, and it seems unlikely that she had anything to do with Robert Wilson. They failed to reach Wilmington in time to catch the ship they were actually booked for, and that Wilson partly owned, and so were obliged to take another vessel. This, as it turned out, was a stroke of luck because Wilson's ship was seized by the Union force blockading the port.

The young Root reached Liverpool safely after a fifteen-day journey from Bermuda. He described his first impression of the city to his sister and revealed, once again, a keen and telling eye for aesthetic detail – and architecture: 'From the place where we anchored we could see the long line of shipping (over 7 miles in length) and the almost numberless ships that steamed or sailed through the bay [he means the Mersey Estuary]. Some were being dragged through the water by curious-looking little boats called "Tuggs".'

Of the architecture and life of the docks and the city of Liverpool, Root observed that 'the wharfs are built of solid granite and surrounded by tall warehouses… the streets are lined with handsome buildings and thronged with people' – there were 400,000 inhabitants, he noted – and 'cabs and drays rattle along the street'. But, John observed regretfully, 'the sun does not shine as brightly, and the climate is not as fine as that of the south, but the atmosphere is smoky and damp.' Intriguingly. John wrote a little about his place of reception in Liverpool – 'Mr Beach lives in a large house, and it is elegantly furnished.'[22] This, presumably, refers to John N. Beach of Atlanta, Sidney Root's partner in Georgia, but is he synonymous with Root's 'English partner', into whose large and elegant Liverpool household John was about to enter? If so, it would seem that the suspicion in Atlanta about Beach's commitment to the Southern cause was not without foundation. While his city succumbed and the Confederacy collapsed in a welter of blood and destruction, Beach lived profitably and comfortably in Liverpool.

In her biography Harriet Monroe records that John 'was put to school in Claremont, near Liverpool, where the bent of his mind towards architecture and music was fostered by special courses',[23] and he soon wrote home that '"in drawing and singing

I have been as successful as my most flattering hopes would have foretold." Now, as always, beauty was the chief thing in the world for him; his heart thrilled to the appeal of the arts.'[24] A little more information about John's Liverpool schooling is added by Donald Hoffmann in his 1973 biography of Root. The 'Clare Mount School' – as Hoffmann terms it – was in Wallasey, the headmaster was the Rev. W. C. Greene and John did indeed flourish because in mid-1866 he passed the entrance exam for a place at the University of Oxford, being placed in the second division of the pass list.[25]

From this record we can see that Root's school progress was good, but how was his character developing and how deeply rooted was his apparent love of the arts? An answer of a kind is offered by the boy's letters home to his family. These letters, which eventually came into Monroe's hands for inclusion in her biography, are peculiar – certainly to modern eyes – because they appear strangely self-assured and assertive for a fifteen- or sixteen-year-old and wonderfully self-conscious. The boy wrote home to one or other of his relatives to tell them that 'few persons exist, and but few deserve to exist, who have not in their souls that which echoes each strain of Nature's music, and thrills with delight in the perusal of each line of Nature's poetry, poetry written on every leaf, and on every enchanting landscape.'[26]

These statements echo some of the big ideas of the age. The scientific discoveries of geologists such as Charles Lyell (explained in his *Principles of Geology* of 1830 and 1833) and of naturalist Charles Darwin, whose *On the Origin of Species* was published in 1859, rattled the conventional, Christian perception of Divine Creation. Science revealed that the world appeared to have evolved in an experimental and inexplicable manner over millions of years and not to a consistent or evolving divine plan over a mere 5,800 years, as many Christians still believed. (See Bishop James Ussher's authoritative *Annales Veteris Testamentis* of 1650, which dated creation to 4004 BC.) This revelation shocked many, but rapidly a new Christian vision emerged, one that sought to reconcile objective scientific truth with the time-honoured mysteries of the Christian faith. The Bible offered, it was argued after the Darwinian revolution, not a literal but a symbolic account of the origin of the earth. God's Creation, it was argued, was not challenged by the new scientific discoveries but confirmed by the stunning wonders and the inventive diversity of nature that these discoveries revealed. There was indeed a divine plan at work, but one vastly more complex than originally imagined and generally beyond human comprehension. Professor Sir Henry W. Acland, the inspirational instigator in 1850 of the Oxford University Museum of Natural History, expressed the spirit of the age and the significance of the natural world by referring to the insights of the pioneering seventeenth-century polymath Sir Thomas Browne, who seemed to have anticipated the mid-nineteenth-century crisis of faith. When explaining the objectives of the 'promoters' of the new museum, Acland quoted Browne: 'There are two bookes from whence I collect my Divinity; besides that written one of God [the Bible], another of his servant, Nature, that universal and publik Manuscript that lies expans'd unto the eyes of all.' The 'Book of Nature', for Acland, revealed God's 'natural works' and by so doing explained and confirmed 'His wonder'.[27]

For architects and engineers in the latter part of the nineteenth century – including of course John Root – the new appreciation of nature, spurred by scientific discovery, was to have a profound influence. Combined with the potential offered by new materials – notably the structural use of wrought iron and then steel – this new vision stimulated the development of structural systems that were pioneering in their bold scale and engineered form. For example the design of the steel-fabricated Forth railway bridge, begun in 1882 to the design of John Fowler and Benjamin Baker, was inspired by cantilever principles expressed in the skeletons of large mammals. This awareness of the creative potential of nature also led to a new approach to surface decoration. Louis Sullivan in the United States (see page 150), Otto Wagner in Austria and Charles Rennie Macintosh in Scotland all examined the possibilities offered by natural forms, and evolved idiosyncratic and characterful decorative vocabularies that went well beyond the convention of merely copying and interpreting historic styles.

The writings of the young Root suggest that he was not a mere juvenile romantic, swept along by the new notions of the age and the beguiling artistic possibilities offered by nature. He also seems to have been a practical-minded realist who saw a love of beauty – as personified by the divine creation of Nature – not as a distraction from the hard grind for material success but as the potential root of that success. In the letter to his family, that Monroe quotes, Root also observed that 'he who would win the great human race must devote himself with unflinching determination to his task... must quaff deeply of the cup which gives

new life, and read each page of the great folio in which Nature has written her majestic poetry.' The path seemed obvious to the young Root: learn the lessons latent in Nature and apply them in your creative work – music or architecture – and success must follow. Follow nature, appreciate 'the revelations she makes to us, and our life cannot fail to be in itself an unwritten poem, with passages as sublime as any Homer wrote.'[28] Many men in previous generations – such as the architect Andrea Palladio in mid-sixteenth-century Italy – had seemingly believed much the same.

What else did Root see and experience while in Liverpool? His letter of 17 November to his sister makes it clear that he had an eye for architecture and in Liverpool in the mid-1860s there was

The sublime engineered commercial architecture of Liverpool –
such as the Albert Dock – must have had a profound influence on
the young John Root when he arrived in the city in November 1864.

much heroic, visually stirring and groundbreaking architecture to see. There were the vast warehouses of the docks that Root touched on in his letter. The most visible and dramatic of these when Root arrived were around the Albert Dock, which lay beside the Mersey and near the centre of the city. The warehouses were – and remain – sublime in their vast scale and functional yet monumental simplicity. Constructed of brick and granite load-bearing walls incorporating cast-iron columns, they were given 'fire-proof' interiors of iron and masonry and iron-framed and iron-clad roofs. An unusual and striking feature of the buildings is that they make absolutely no structural use of timber. The engineers responsible for this remarkable creation, completed in 1846, were Jesse Hartley and Philip Hardwick. No one who saw the Albert Dock in the 1860s could fail to be impressed, and someone as architecturally aware as the young Root would surely have been overwhelmed.

But Liverpool had many other large and architecturally or structurally novel buildings. As Donald Hoffmann explains, in 1864 Liverpool 'could claim the prototypes of the most characteristic structures of the nineteenth century.' These included 'the Brunswick Buildings of 1843 as the earliest office block apart from factory or warehouse', and 'the earliest train shed', which dated from 1830 and was part of George Stephenson's Crown Street Station. This station, the Liverpool terminus of the Liverpool and Manchester Railroad, opened on the same day as the company's Liverpool Road Terminus in Manchester, making them the world's first intercity passenger stations. In 1836 this station, located on the edge of the city centre and deemed inadequate, was replaced by Lime Street Station. This was a heroic affair, that Root must have known. In 1864 it possessed a wide span and majestic shed formed of wrought-iron ribs that had been completed in 1849 to the designs of ironmaster Richard Turner, who had pioneered the large-scale, structural use of wrought iron in 1844 for the Palm

Oriel Chambers in Liverpool is a commercial building of pioneering design and construction. The young Root must have seen this building and been amazed. Its oriel windows form the prototype for the 'Chicago Window' that Root did much to evolve.

House in Kew Gardens in London. Walking the streets of central Liverpool, Root would have seen office blocks incorporating internal courts and utilizing novel materials and means of construction. Among the most notable were Oriel Chambers in Water Street, completed in the year Root arrived in Liverpool, and 16 Cook Street – 'those strange creatures', as Hoffmann describes them, 'conceived by Peter Ellis, Jr.... constructed of plate glass and iron' that Root 'could hardly have forgotten'.[29] Both of these structures incorporate features that Root was later to use in his work and it seems certain (although it has yet to be proved) that they influenced him. Oriel Chambers is the more significant of the two. It was constructed with a cast-iron frame, yet clad with stone embellished with simple historically inspired details, such as Gothic-inspired dogtooth mouldings of most geometric form and classical cornice details, to help it fit in more easily with its historical city-centre neighbours; it has floors supported on brick arches to make it robust and more fire-proof and makes great use of large panes of plate-glass, then still something of a novelty, set in bays – or oriels – that project beyond the slender stone-clad piers. Within the courtyard the architecture is more radical still, for it incorporates an elevation that is made largely of glass and unadorned with historicist ornament: here was a pioneering triumph of unadorned functionalism and pioneering example of a 'curtain wall', which is to say an elevation that is not integrated with the prime structure of the building and has no structural responsibility beyond supporting its own weight. Completed in 1866, 16 Cook Street also includes a curtain wall rear elevation and – more spectacular – a fully glazed cylindrical staircase tower that is, in its minimalism and absence of ornament, astonishing for its date.

Root remained nearly two years in Liverpool. In June 1866 he was summoned back to the United States. His father did not return to Atlanta after the war – presumably the ravaged city had little to attract him, or perhaps his long absence during the war made him unwelcome – but went to where money was to be made. By 1866 the Root family had established itself in New York and this booming city became John Root's new home. And things moved fast. By September 1866 he was enrolled as a sophomore at the University of the City of New York, studying for the degree of bachelor of science and civil engineering. This was the nearest thing to a degree in architecture then available; in 1866 there was no school of architecture in the United States with the first professor of architecture appointed only in 1865 at the then recently founded Massachusetts Institute of Technology (MIT). The pioneering professor was Henry Van Brunt, who had been a pupil of Richard Morris Hunt. Both these men were to play important roles in Root's later architectural life.

These tumultuous two years must have been an extraordinary experience for the young Root – from besieged Atlanta and the collapse of the Confederacy, to school and university in the great port, manufacturing and commercial cities of Liverpool and New York. Monroe in her biography offers few insights into this period, but she does suggest that Root's position in his new home city might have been far from certain and secure. Sidney Root, she writes, was 'living sumptuously, making unlucky investments, and beginning to lose his large fortune more rapidly than he had won it.' [30]Root had indeed profiteered during the war and now this ill-starred fortune was disappearing within the Yankee economic powerhouse of New York.

But Monroe does tell one curious and revealing story. She claims that with his fellow students in New York John Root 'never discussed' the Civil War. This is not perhaps surprising. Most of his university contemporaries would have been Northern-born and supporters of the Union while, as Monroe puts it, Root's 'sympathy, naturally, had been with his Southern home'. But he might also have been sensitive about his conduct. Despite 'his sympathy' and apparent patriotism Root failed to fight for the Southern cause even though many of his age had. But on one occasion at least, Root seems to have abandoned his reticence about his Southern allegiance or mastered his sense of shame. Monroe was told the tale by Robert W. Haskins, who had been one of Root's classmates: 'one evening, seated at the chapel organ after prayers... his hands passed easily over the keys in search of an old familiar theme. Suddenly it was found, a smile lit his face, and turning to the writer, who stood by his side, he broke into "Dixie", the song of his motherland. We were hushed, touched, thrilled by the soul that rose like a lark from the nest.'

This atmospheric image of Root performing the rebel anthem, evidently with passion, in a Northern bastion only a few years after the end of the war reveals, among other things, that he was most fortunate in his choice of friends. They were moved by the way he 'suffered in the lost cause' and accepted seemingly without censure that Root's only contribution to the defence of his beloved 'motherland' was to take refuge during her final years in the rural retreat of Wallasey.[31]

Root graduated in 1869, ranking fifth in his class, and the same year was taken into the office of New York architects Renwick and Sands as an unpaid apprentice. James Renwick's reputation in 1869 rested largely on two buildings designed, with grace and gusto, within the spirit of the European Gothic Revival – the Smithsonian Institution Building in Washington DC, of 1847–55, that was designed in a castellated medieval manner, and the large, flamboyant and twin-spired Roman Catholic St Patrick's Cathedral on Fifth Avenue, New York that had been started in 1858 and was not complete until 1879. As with all extensive building projects, the whole process of the design and construction of St Patrick's must have formed something of an informal college of building for Renwick's young associates. But Root stayed with Renwick and Sands for only about a year and then joined the office of J. B. Snook, who agreed to pay Root a small salary. Given the increasing financial plight of Sidney Root this was, no doubt, very much needed.[32]

Snook had been born in London in 1815 but had lived in New York for many years. His output was more obscure than that of Renwick and it is doubtful whether Root learned much from him, nor a surprise to read in Monroe's biography that Root's 'New York career was cut short by the Chicago Fire'. That calamity created a great opportunity for architects. Over a third of a wealthy and rapidly expanding city of commerce and trade – notable as a railhead and transportation hub connecting key portions of the United States and its territories – had been destroyed, with nine square kilometres of its central area laid waste.

Two weeks after the fire Root wrote to his friends in Atlanta that 'Chicago wants me'. He sent some sketches to Peter Bonnett Wight – a successful New York architect who had himself just moved to Chicago in the hope of benefiting from the fire. Root probably knew Wight and certainly would have known his work: in 1863 he designed the National Academy of Design, a high-profile building in a Venetian Gothic style inspired by the Doge's Palace in Venice and by the writings of the English architectural historian and critic John Ruskin. Presumably Root admired Wight's work or his role in the Society for the Advancement of Truth in Art that Wight had helped found in 1863.[33] Wight responded by offering Root employment in the architectural and building practice he ran with Asher Carter and William Drake. 'Accordingly he started West, with three hundred dollars and a portfolio of experimental designs as his capital, and in his heart confidence to banish care…'.[34]

Chicago: 1871–1891

When John W. Root arrived in Chicago, probably in early November 1871, Peter Wight put him to work as a draughtsman. In the Carter, Drake and Wight office the following year he met Daniel Hudson Burnham, a few years his senior, who had also found work there as a draughtsman. Burnham later recalled his first impression of Root 'as he stood before a large drawing-board with his sleeves rolled up to his elbows.' Straight away the sight of Root 'pleased' Burnham: 'the strength of his muscles, the babyish whiteness of his skin, his frank smile and manner appealed to me, and we became great cronies.'[1]

In 1873 the pair started their own partnership. The reconstruction of Chicago after the fire included a building boom on the city's fringes and Burnham knew some of the speculators who had 'agreed to push a certain suburb' where a 'new town was to be laid out' complete with a railway station, academy and shops. As Monroe puts it, the speculators 'wished to get out of the rut of base architecture' and so lured the 'youthful talent' of Burnham & Root with the offer of fees of five per cent of the commissions. The pair accepted the challenge and set themselves up in business.[2] The gamble paid off; over the next eighteen years Burnham & Root became not only one of the leading architectural practices in Chicago but also significant on the world stage.

Their success had many ingredients but essentially the pair managed to forge, out of diverse influences and by utilizing emerging technologies, an architecture that reflected the commercial and artistic aspirations of the age, and of Chicago in particular. And this fusion was ultimately founded – as are most successful partnerships – on the creative marriage of two very different yet complementary characters. Root was intuitive and artistic with a powerful romantic streak and a talent for music, poetry and design. As Monroe put it, he possessed 'that happy union of invention and facility' that was to make him 'an original force in his profession'.[3] Burnham possessed other talents. As

John Root (*right*) and Daniel H. Burnham, in their office in The Rookery building in 1890, when at the pinnacle of their partnership.

events were to demonstrate, he was skilled at business, at making the deal, at resolving the pragmatic and complex realities of the design and construction industries and thus provided 'the plasmic influence' that Root required to give shape and purpose to his particular genius.[4] But Burnham's start in his chosen profession was shaky and uncertain and initially it did not seem that his ambition would be met with success. He had been born in Henderson, New York in 1846, and had made his way to Chicago, where he got a job with architect William Le Baron Jenney. This didn't come to much. He tried his hand at other business ventures, but these were failures and so Burnham returned to architecture and by 1872 was in the office of Carter, Drake and Wight.

As with many small architectural practices, in their early days Burnham & Root's commissions were modest and diverse, but evidently this variety permitted the pair to hone their skills and secure invaluable contacts and patrons within the upper echelons of Chicago's society and business community. Early commissions included the Union Stock Yard Gate of 1875 in Exchange Avenue. This formed the ceremonial entrance to Chicago's vast stockyards and meat packing district and was designed by Root in a whimsical Gothic style that included a large and striking portrait above its portal of a prize bull named Sherman. Given Root's traumatic experience in Atlanta during the Civil War at the hands of another Sherman, this choice of subject might seem odd, but was in fact no more than a jolly compliment to John B. Sherman, the superintendent of the Union Stock Yards who had given the young architects the commission. Sherman was a significant power in the city and gaining his patronage was a great prize for the pair. As Erik Larsen explains, Sherman 'ruled an empire of blood that employed 25,000 men, women, and children and each year slaughtered fourteen million animals' and on which one fifth of Chicago's population depended, directly or indirectly, for its economic survival.[5]

In fact the gate was not the first commission from Sherman. In 1874, in a move that was to do much to establish the young practice, Sherman had commissioned them to build him a mansion on Prairie Avenue at Twenty-first Street. The commission was a success – Monroe calls the house 'revolutionary, epoch-making'[6] – and won Burnham more than just a productive relationship with a powerful new client. It also won him a wife. During construction Sherman's daughter Margaret often visited the site, evidently to see Burnham more than her emerging new home. The pair became engaged and eventually married, but not before Burnham had to throw himself upon Sherman's mercy. During the engagement it emerged that Burnham's elder brother had been forging cheques. This could have been a fatal scandal for the newly betrothed pair. Burnham offered to terminate the engagement to spare Sherman embarrassment by association. Sherman said that such a desperate action was not necessary because 'there is a black sheep in every family'.[7] Sherman clearly knew what he was talking about because a few years later he left his wife and family and absconded to Europe with the daughter of a friend.

Burnham met not only his wife through the construction of the Sherman House, but also a man who was to become one of the most inventive architectural forces in late-nineteenth-century America. Louis Sullivan was born in Boston in 1856, trained for a year as a very precocious architectural student at MIT and, like many, was attracted to Chicago while no more than a youth, by the vast building opportunities created by the Great Fire. He initially found work with William Le Baron Jenney. Evidently the men did not meet in the Jenny office, where Burnham had also worked, because in his autobiography, published in 1924, the year of his death, Sullivan remembers their fateful first encounter that took place – when he was just eighteen – in a Chicago suburb. Referring to himself rather portentously in the third person, Sullivan recounts that

> his mind a whorl of ambitious ideas, and at a time somewhat prior to his departure for Paris, he had occasion one day to pass in the neighbourhood of Prairie Avenue and Twenty-first Street, Chicago [where] his eye was attracted by a residence, nearing completion, which seemed far better than the average run of such structures inasmuch as it exhibited a certain allure or style indicating personality. It was the best-designed residence he had seen in Chicago.

When he moved closer to inspect the house Sullivan 'noticed a fine looking young man… standing in the roadway, absorbed in contemplation of the growing work. Louis, without ceremony, introduced himself.' The response was open, and generous. The man said that he had heard of the young Sullivan, was glad to meet him, that his name was Burnham and, evidently with much pride, declared that 'my partner John Root, is a wonder, a great artist'.

Sullivan's account of this first meeting suggests that Burnham was garrulous. He seemingly blurted out that Root and he had 'only started a few years ago', that so far they'd 'done mostly residences' and that the one before them was for his 'prospective father-in-law John Sherman', of whom – 'as a big stockyards man' – Sullivan, no doubt, had heard. 'But', Burnham apparently proclaimed, 'I'm not going to stay satisfied with houses; my idea is to work up a big business, to handle big things, deal with big business men and to build up a big organization.' This rang alarm bells with Sullivan, who regarded himself much more as an artist than as a businessman architect. But he merely noted that, at this first meeting, he 'found Burnham a sentimentalist, a dreamer, a man of fixed determination and strong will… a shade pompous, a mystic.' Thus started the long, competitive and increasingly

Burnham & Root's tradition-inspired domestic architecture: *(left)* the John B. Sherman House, South Prairie Avenue, Chicago, 1874–6 and, *(right)* the Sidney Kent House, South Michigan Avenue, Chicago, 1882–3, designed in a permutation of 'Queen Anne' style.

strained love–hate relationship between Sullivan, Burnham and Root that ultimately had a significant influence on the work produced by all three men.[8]

The Chicago stockyards also provided John Root with his first wife. He designed a house for John Walker, the president of the yards, and soon married his daughter Mary. But whereas Burnham's courtship had been haunted by his brother's fraud, Root's courtship was haunted by death itself. Soon after the pair were engaged Mary developed tuberculosis and went into rapid decline. But the marriage went ahead. Dora, the sister of Root's biographer Harriet Monroe, was the only bridesmaid at the wedding, which took place in the house Root had designed for the family. It was a macabre affair. The bride was pale, thin, weak and it was obvious to all that she was dying. Harriet Monroe, who was present, could not but feel that Mary's attempt at 'gayety… seemed like jewels on a skull.'[9] Within six weeks – 'of joy and suffering' – Mary was dead.[10] Two years later Root married the former bridesmaid Dora. As Eric Larson correctly observes, the marriage must have broken Harriet's heart because it seems 'beyond dispute' that she loved Root. Her fulsome 1896 biography of Root, 'that would have made an angel blush', is one piece of

evidence.[11] Another is what she wrote in her memoir, *A Poet's Life*. Here she explains that Root and her sister's marriage was 'so completely happy that my own dreams of happiness, confirmed by their example, demanded as fortunate a fulfilment, and could accept nothing less.'[12] Harriet never found a man to measure up to Root and consequently never married.

Another of the practice's early projects, dating from 1882 and also designed by Root, is the Kent House, which survives on South Michigan Avenue, Chicago. It was designed in the eclectic classical Queen Anne style influenced by the English Aesthetic Movement that, in its antiquarianism, favoured the homely and relaxed English classical vernacular architecture of the seventeenth century. Root travelled in England and in France, accompanied by his wife and little daughter; they visited London, Chester, Oxford, Canterbury, Paris, Amiens and Rouen – but not until the summer of 1886.[13] So from where in 1882 would he have gleaned his knowledge of contemporary English architecture? From publications, no doubt, and perhaps from conversations with travellers. But there is, potentially, an additional source.

OSCAR WILDE IN NORTH AMERICA

In January 1882 Oscar Wilde landed in New York and during the following six months undertook an astonishingly demanding lecture tour around the United States and Canada. He had a limited series of lectures that he delivered 'upwards of 150' times in the great cities and far-flung regional centres of North America. It really was an extraordinary adventure. Some key facts about this tour, including lecture topics and the press response to them, can be found in a slight but well-designed pamphlet that now lodges in a neat little box in the British Library.

The pamphlet, fragile and ephemeral and presumably produced under Wilde's control, is a piece of promotional 'literature' intended to drum up business for a series of lectures he was to give in Britain after his return from North America. Entitled *Mr Oscar Wilde's Lectures, Season 1883–84*, it was printed and published by O. Norman and Sons of Covent Garden and, in particular, it promotes a talk he was shortly to deliver in Leeds. The pamphlet explains Wilde's position. It declares that from the publication in 1881 of *Poems by Oscar Wilde* – an event that established Wilde as a key figure in the evolving Aesthetic Movement – he had proposed to devote 'his time to public addresses'.

This was obviously an attempt by Wilde to capitalize on his new fame as a provocative and interestingly avant-garde artistic character, and by 1882 this exploitation of his commercial potential was a priority because he had 'almost run through his small patrimony and was in desperate need of funds.'[14]

THE AESTHETIC MOVEMENT

The Aesthetic Movement, of which by 1882 Wilde was acknowledged to be a leading figure, had diverse and complex origins, but was essentially a reaction against what many design reformers saw as the vacuous pomposity, meaningless clutter and myriad sources of historic reference that characterized the mid-nineteenth-century interior of the British house. Among those who inspired the movement were the art critic and theorist John Ruskin, Henry Cole – a key founder of what is now the Victoria and Albert Museum – the Prince Consort himself, and Owen Jones. His *Grammar of Ornament*, published in 1856, was a repository of historically correct decorative motif and intended to inspire contemporary British designers in their quest for a distinct national style based on an informed use of history. And of particular significance in the movement was the Oxford academic Walter Pater, whose well-honed art criticisms and historical writings were, from the late 1860s, to prove inspirational.

Under Pater's influence the more radical advocates of the movement preached the theory of art for art's sake (a credo in fact derived from the early-nineteenth-century radical French slogan 'l'art pour l'art', said to have been coined by the philosopher Victor Cousin), which held that beauty was more important than practical or moral concerns, and promoted a minimalism and clarity inspired by Japanese art and an ornamental vocabulary derived from flora and fauna – typically, gilded carved flowers, sunflower motifs, stylized peacock feathers and blue and white china emblazoned with plant motifs.[15]

The movement's seemingly amoral attitude – that art was about passion and sensation and that visual beauty in art and architecture was at least as important as subject or purpose – offended many who believed that all great art ultimately had a moral and uplifting message. Evangelical Christians were

particularly uneasy about the movement's apparent amorality.

Walter Pater, the primary source of the movement's epicureanism, seems to have lost his Christian faith – and certainly to have abandoned the guiding principles of Christianity – while an undergraduate at Oxford. The absence of conventional Christian certainties and dogmas in his writings and his apparent promotion of hedonism – notable in his *Studies in the History of the Renaissance* of 1873 – provoked condemnation from even the agnostic Mary Anne Evans (better known as George Eliot and notorious at the time as a married woman living so openly with a man married to another woman that she seemed to be practising polygamy), who called Pater's book 'quite poisonous in its false principles... and false conceptions of life.'[16]

Association with Pater did much to gain the Aesthetic Movement a reputation for sensuality, even decadence – or at least moral ambivalence – and ensured that it got noticed, to the delight of course of Oscar Wilde, who by the end of the 1880s had secured his position as the personification of the more lurid aspects of the movement. In his essay 'The Critic as Artist' Wilde, in his most succinct and exotic manner, put the aesthete's point of view: 'Aesthetics are higher than ethics. They belong to a more spiritual sphere. To discern the beauty of a thing is the finest point to which we can arrive. Even a colour sense is more important, in the development of an individual, than a sense of right and wrong.' This essay was both inspired by Pater and, upon publication, praised by him.[17]

For Wilde the North American tour was primarily a commercial, self-promotional exercise. It was a way to make money through fees and a glorious opportunity to display himself before a vast new audience of potential readers and patrons. And it offered the chance to meet North America's rich, influential and mostly Anglophile artistic society. For some of his audience at least, Wilde's witty talk, posturing and presence proved inspiring. He kicked off his tour on 9 January 1882 in New York with a lecture on 'The Renaissance in English Art'. This 'address', the promotional pamphlet explains, 'was in effect a history of the Aesthetic Movement in England' illustrating 'the influences of this new artistic spirit upon modern poetry, architecture, criticism, culture and drama, and upon the ordinary life of the English people.'

Oscar Wilde commissioned a highly calculated series of portraits of himself from Napoleon Sarony in January 1882, soon after arriving in New York. Dressed in outlandish garb, Wilde used these to promote himself and the English Aesthetic Movement.

The declared object of this series of lectures was ambitious indeed. As the pamphlet somewhat earnestly reminds its readers, they were intended 'to awaken a spirit of inquiry... to stimulate artistic feeling and culture, and to cause attention to be directed to the true artistic decoration of the homes of the people.'[18] The pamphlet, which was almost certainly penned by Wilde himself some time in early 1883, also announces that this opening 'address' to the upper echelons of New York's artistically orientated society was 'widely quoted and commented upon by the American press, in some cases with sarcasm, in others with eulogy.'

The pamphlet also includes a few press comments, presumably selected by Wilde. The one for the New York talk suggests that the event realized Wilde's wildest dreams: 'Everybody known in New York society seemed to be there. Mr Wilde was vigorously applauded and recalled to bow his acknowledgements at the close of his lecture.'[19] But the remarks of the critics – whether positive or negative – failed to draw Wilde into a debate. The character he had created for his North American performance had to remain aloof. The pamphlet tells us that 'Mr Wilde' displayed 'a spirit of absolute indifference to all criticism'. Thus did Wilde attempt to disarm, wrong-foot and, of course, infuriate his detractors by apparently putting himself and his works above their criticism.

In fact the wide publicity enjoyed by Wilde's performances caused an unexpected problem. Because the lectures were so fully reported in the press, new audiences could find out in advance what was coming by reading detailed accounts of previous lectures. The lack of surprise and novelty, Wilde realized, would lead to tedium and dwindling attendance. Something had to be done – and the obvious solution was to write additional lectures. This he did during a week's break in Chicago,[20] probably after his first lecture in the city. This was delivered on 13 February 1882 at the Central Music Hall (long demolished, but it had been designed in 1879 by Dankmar Adler and was a building of great distinction. It stood very near the site on which the Reliance Building was soon to rise) and was on the by then familiar topic of the 'Decorative Arts'.

Wilde then composed two new lectures – one on 'House Decoration' and the other on 'The Value and Character of the Handicrafts'. Wilde was probably able to do this on the hoof, with only limited research material to hand, because his friendships and conversations with the London-based painter James McNeill Whistler and the avant-garde architect E. W. Godwin would have given him many ideas and insights about new styles of decoration. For example, in 1877 Godwin had designed the White House in Tite Street, Chelsea for Whistler in a manner so simple that it became the talk of the town and caused offence to the freeholders of the site. In 1884 Godwin was to decorate Wilde's own home in Tite Street in a startlingly original manner inspired largely by Japanese design.

Wilde borrowed more directly and extensively for this pair of new lectures from the writings of the English art theorist John Ruskin and from the designer, novelist, socialist and architectural campaigner William Morris. The result can be seen as little more than an act of plagiarism on Wilde's part because it is uncertain – indeed unlikely – that he fully acknowledged the sources of the ideas he laid before the American public. But, be this as it may, it was surely through Wilde's lectures that many Americans were first introduced to some of Ruskin and Morris's more provocative ideas on the arts and crafts and on methods of production. As Gere and Hoskins observe, there is in the handicrafts lecture composed by Wilde in Chicago 'more than a hint of Morris's forthright talk on *The Lesser Arts*, first composed in 1877 and already in print in 1882.' They point out that among 'the most patent plagiarisms Wilde said: "Have nothing in your house that has not given pleasure to the man who made it and is not a pleasure to those who use it. Have nothing in your house that is

not useful or beautiful," [which combines] echoes of Morris's…
"Have nothing in your houses that you do not know to be useful,
or believe to be beautiful (*Hopes and Fears for Art*, 1882), with a
Ruskinian belief in the dignity of labour.'[21]

When Wilde spoke next in Chicago – on 11 March, again at the
Central Music Hall[22]– he delivered one of his new lectures. But
by now the title of the talk had changed slightly but significantly
from 'House Decoration' to 'The House Beautiful'. This change
of title is interesting and revealing. Gere and Hoskins explain:
'The title of Wilde's lecture on interior decoration varied between
House Decoration… and the House Beautiful, the later cleverly
reflecting a successful instruction manual on the subject of the
interior written by the American art critic Clarence Cook.'[23]
Evidently Wilde was constantly obliged to live on his wits as he
gave his lecture tour, rapidly absorbing new information and
influences, changing and adapting his performances to prevent
tedium among his audiences and to keep up-to-the-minute with
evolving fashions. His bold and confident – if often patronizing
and condescending – delivery papered over the cracks and
obscured Wilde's sometimes shaky grasp of his subjects.

This facility is hardly surprising. Wilde was himself a self-
consciously wrought work of art so, predictably, his lectures were
performances offered in the authentic manner of the Aesthetic
Movement: style and presentation were far more important
than solid fact or genuine knowledge about the subjects under
review. As Gere and Hoskins observe, the practical advice offered
during the lectures 'was delivered with an assurance that Wilde's
views, hastily recycled from the works of Ruskin and Morris,
hardly merited [since] he was still without the slightest practical
experience of home decorating.'[24]

The publication that provided information and a title for
Wilde's lecture has, itself, a curious and derivative history.
Clarence Cook's *The House Beautiful: Essays on Beds and Tables,*

Stools and Candlesticks was published in 1878 and was little more than a collection of articles by Cook that had been published in *Scribner's Monthly* since 1875. Cook was a disciple of Ruskin and in 1863 was a co-founder of the Society for the Advancement of Truth, essentially an American version of the English Pre-Raphaelite Brotherhood, which itself had been founded in 1848 by painters and poets, including Dante Gabriel Rossetti under the influence of the writings of Ruskin. The book sought simply to introduce some of the key principles of the Aesthetic Movement into American homes. This, of course, was very much Wilde's game. He must have been a little disturbed before the start of his tour by this native publication that might steal his show by anticipating much of what he would say. But on the other hand, perhaps he had not heard of the book when he left England or, if he had, perhaps he held it in some contempt as a mere 'provincial' attempt to appropriate the English Aesthetic Movement.

Even the title of the book might have offended Wilde. The 'House Beautiful' was a phrase associated with Walter Pater, and the model for the structure of Cook's book appears to have been Charles Eastlake's *Hints on Household Taste in Furniture, Upholstery, and other details*, published in 1869 in Britain and in 1872 in the United States. Eastlake was a learned and highly influential promoter of the Gothic Revival in Britain and its Empire but he was almost of the generation before Wilde. Consequently in 1882 Wilde might have felt – perhaps without thinking about it too hard – that an enterprise inspired so directly by Eastlake was bound to be a little old hat. But if this was the case, by March Wilde had evidently changed his mind and seemingly thought enough of Cook and his Eastlake-inspired book to appropriate its title for one of his new talks. What Cook thought of this state of affairs is not known.

What Wilde's lecture tour reveals is his opportunism and gift for purloining the opinions – even the words – of others and giving them the appearance of freshness courtesy of his ready wit and self-proclaimed genius and originality. James McNeill Whistler is said to have told Wilde 'you will, Oscar, you will', after Wilde declared that he wished he had made some witty comment that Whistler had just uttered. If this is true then Whistler clearly knew his man.

The content of Wilde's lecture on 'The House Beautiful' is summarized in the 1883 pamphlet, which makes the performance sound – at least in part – much like Wilde's 'The Renaissance in English Art' lecture. We learn that 'for the most part' the 'House Beautiful' lecture 'was an exposition of the application of the principles of true artistic decoration to the exterior and interior of the homes of the people', in which Wilde took up 'in detail each one of the elements that enter into the complete artistic furnishing of a room', gave an 'elaborate schemes of colour and art decoration which properly supplement each other' and offered 'some observations upon style and dress for the house and in the street; on the influence of artistic surroundings upon children; and on the value of handicrafts as the basis of education.'[25] This description – seemingly confirming the influences of Cook, Eastlake and Morris – makes one wonder to what extent Wilde's lectures overlapped in their content and intentions.

Partly plagiarized, almost certainly derivative, this lecture as delivered by Wilde in theatrical, charismatic style seems to have given an impression of great presence and power. On 29 May Wilde gave the talk again – in Woodstock, Ontario – and this time a member of the audience, Mary Ann Tillson, was so taken by his ideas – or perhaps Eastlake's, Morris's and Cook's ideas as freshened up, given focus and represented by Wilde as his own – that she immediately decorated the interior of her newly built house in the Aesthetic Movement style that Wilde promoted. The house – now called the Annandale Historic Site, in Tillsonburg, Ontario – is one of Canada's most prized and best-loved examples of nineteenth-century domestic architecture.[26] Evidently Wilde's words could inspire and move some of his audience to flights of artistic excellence. Perhaps a similar thing happened in Chicago. There is no record that Root or Burnham attended Wilde's lecture on 11 March but it is possible – even probable – that one or other of them did. The press comment on one or other of Wilde's Chicago lectures, from the *Chicago News* and included in the pamphlet, states that the audience that greeted Wilde was 'dignified… appreciative [and] vast'. If Root was present then perhaps it was Wilde's performance in Chicago that influenced some of Root's subsequent work or that – at the very least – confirmed him in his conviction that nature held the key to architectural beauty and structural solidity.

There is another possibility, of course. During his week or so in Chicago Wilde could have met Root and Burnham. A meeting would have been likely, if circumstances allowed, but no record of such a meeting exists. And if Wilde did meet them, what of their work could he have seen and in what manner could they have influenced his ideas? Burnham and Root's significant buildings lay in the future with, in early 1882, just a clutch of private houses, such as the Queen Anne-style Kent House, completed or on the drawing board. It is possible that the pair's first high-rise commercial building, the Montauk Block, was being designed when Wilde was in Chicago but this austere brute of an office building – as pioneering and fascinating as it was – would hardly have interested Wilde or informed his ponderings on the 'House Beautiful'.

While Wilde's lecture tour had a significant influence on members of his North American audience, it also had a profound influence on him. Indeed it was the single most important event in Wilde's life up to that point and did much to define his identity – and appearance – for years to come. This is made clear by a series of portraits Wilde commissioned in New York in early January 1882 and taken in the Union Square studio of photographer Napoleon Sarony. These photographs were highly studied, remorselessly posed and calculated to proclaim Wilde's striking individualism as the globetrotting prophet of the Aesthetic Movement. In this sense they worked brilliantly and created an enduring, visually distinctive and memorable image of Wilde. They were, in short, superlative self-advertisement and fundamental to the creation of what would in modern times be known as the Oscar Wilde 'brand'.

They also, arguably and more interestingly, epitomized Wilde's lifelong determination to challenge whatever he thought to be an expression of unthinking convention. In the Sarony series he sports long hair with a centre parting, an enormous fur-trimmed overcoat (that had been made especially for the North American jaunt and that highly amused Whistler, who begged Wilde to return it to the theatrical costumier from whom he had surely borrowed it), a large soft hat and long cape.

Wilde's repertoire of dress for this series of photographs also reveals the origin of his North American lecture tour and one of its key purposes. Included among the garb in which he posed for Sarony is the 'poet's' costume made famous by the Gilbert and Sullivan comic opera *Patience* – velvet jacket and waistcoat, breeches, hose and pumps as worn by the character Bunthorne. First staged in London in April 1881, *Patience* was a satire on the Aesthetic Movement, mocking its superficiality and pretentious-ness, with Bunthorne – a preposterous and self-regarding poet – seemingly being an amalgamation in his verse and dress of the Aesthetic Movement stalwarts and dandies Algernon Charles Swinburne, Dante Gabriel Rossetti, James McNeill Whistler and, of course, Wilde himself – dandies and aesthetes all.

The quick-witted and opportunistic Wilde – in search of fame as an artist but happy to settle for notoriety – was delighted to capitalize on the publicity offered by *Patience*. Richard D'Oyly Carte, the theatrical impresario behind the opera, thought it a good idea for Wilde to go to America to drum up interest in the production and familiarize potential audiences with the nuances of the English Aesthetic Movement and let them know who and what to laugh at. Wilde, who was the butt of some of the humour in the opera, was, far from being offended, only too ready to agree and so in late December 1881 set out on his North American tour, during which he was happy to live up to the caricature offered by *Patience* (as Sarony's photographs confirm) and present a parody of a parody of himself. Or perhaps it is more accurate to state that Wilde was happy to imitate an imitation of himself; for it seems likely that Bunthorne's poetic costume was in fact inspired by the clothes Wilde had occasionally – but no doubt very publicly – worn while an undergraduate at Oxford. As Gere and Hoskins point out breeches and velvet jacket were actually the uniform of the Apollo Masonic lodge in Oxford into which Wilde was accepted in February 1875.[27] Decoding Wilde's dress is indeed a complex business.

Wilde no doubt hoped that his often calculatedly brazen behaviour – such as telling a customs official when he arrived in New York that he had nothing to declare but his genius – and his bizarre dress, combined with his natural ability to produce snappy and witty, if often absurd, one-liners for the consumption of the press, would get him noticed and ingratiate him with North America's leading figures in the arts. So Sarony's photographs are in a sense advertising in the literal manner, little more than publicity stills for both the opera and for Wilde.

In April 1883 Wilde had a second series of photographs made by Sarony and these seem to confirm that his 1882 tour was essentially a self-promotional publicity stunt, undertaken in fancy dress. In this second series, taken when Wilde returned to New York to oversee the production of his play *Vera; or, the Nihilists*,* his hair is short, although bobbed in a curious manner, and instead of cloak and breeches he wears an extravagant cravat, velvet blazer, flannels and a straw boater and carries a cane. But, if less extreme in appearance, Wilde still contrived to look extraordinary, certainly individual, and once again is dressed to make a point and to provoke. For Wilde, with his Aesthetic Movement-inspired belief that style and presentation were at least as important as content, dress was an issue, a shock weapon in his war against the common, the vulgar, the ugly and the banal. When Wilde had landed in America in early January 1882 'the first thing' that struck him, he later wrote, 'was that if the Americans are not the most well-dressed people in the world, they are the most comfortably dressed.' In his world this was not a compliment. For Wilde it was elegance and beauty that mattered, not comfort, and he relished the fact that his brand of aesthetic individualism could startle, hopefully even offend, the self-righteous, the priggish and the dull.[28]

RISE OF THE CHICAGO 'SKYSCRAPER'

At the same time as Wilde was sowing the seeds of his ideas in North America, Root was fighting his own battle against the common, the predictable and the banal. While he was dabbling in the ornamental intricacies and eccentricities of the delicate Queen Anne Revival style and the Aesthetic Movement, he and Burnham were also designing the Montauk Building or Block. Commissioned in 1881 for a city-centre site on Monroe

---

* It was an embarrassing failure that rather undermined Wilde's posture as an exquisite if self-proclaimed artistic genius.

The Montauk Block, Monroe Street, Chicago, commissioned in 1881 from Burnham & Root. Ten storeys high and utilitarian in design, this is said to be the first building in the world to be termed a 'skyscraper'.

Street, Chicago, the building, in stark contrast with the architect's charming Queen Anne Revival houses, sought to tackle the exorbitant demands of the modern commercial world. It was an office block that rose ten storeys and according to Erik Larson was the first building in the world to be termed a 'skyscraper'.[29]

Chicago became the breeding ground in the 1880s for this new type of building because of a combination of circumstances. The city's economy was booming and its downtown commercial area needed to expand but its physical area was constrained by the Chicago River to the north and west, Lake Michigan to the east and the rail yards to the south. So 'the only way to go was up' and the consequence was Chicago's 'premier role in the development of the high-rise skyscraper'.[30]

In simple terms the pioneering Chicago skyscrapers were multi-storey buildings with interiors and elevations supported primarily by fire-proofed metal frames. The principles underpinning this form of construction had been developed in Europe

for mills, factories and warehouses during the late-eighteenth-century Industrial Revolution and, combined with 'jack-arch' brick floors the technique was intended to produce structures that were strong and relatively fire resistant. An early example of the type is Marshall, Benyon and Bage's flax mill in Ditherington, Shrewsbury of 1796, which incorporates a cast-iron frame within brick-built external walls. Root would have been intimately familiar with slightly later examples of this type of construction from his years in Liverpool, notably the Albert Dock warehouses of 1846 (see page 45). In contrast to traditional construction – and indeed in contrast to earlier metal-framed buildings – the only load-bearing role of the external 'skins' of the early skyscrapers was to bear their own weight, and usually to be no more than masonry façades attached to but structurally independent of, the load-bearing metal frame. Relieved of a primary structural role, external walls could be pierced by large windows, allowing light to flood in and external prospects to be enjoyed.

The Montauk Building was, as with many an early high-rise, something of a hybrid structure. It was of metal-frame construction, but with the frame set within load-bearing masonry walls. The building was demolished in 1902 so the precise nature of its structural frame is now impossible to establish but it was probably made of steel used in combination with some small amounts of wrought and cast iron. As well as utilizing a structural system rooted in the functional industrial tradition, the Montauk Building also possessed façades of most austere design with all windows – except those on the ground and first floors – of remorselessly similar form and scale. Ornament was limited to a simple crowning cornice and an arched two-storey entrance. This was in large part due to the puritanical strictures of the building's developer Peter Chardon Brooks III, a young Massachusetts investor whose family fortune was based on the shipping-insurance business. Building for maximum profit in 1880s

The interior of Marshall, Benyon and Bage's flax mill in Ditherington, Shrewsbury, England. Built in 1796, it pioneered the use of a structural frame, here formed with cast iron stanchions and beams set within load-bearing brick external walls.

Chicago meant building offices high and – for Brooks at least – it meant frugality and architectural simplicity with the only real test of design being whether it functioned or not. For him buildings were to be lean and fit for purpose and nothing more. As Larson explains, Brooks 'issued instructions that anticipated by many years Louis Sullivan's famous admonition that form must follow function (see page 21), "the building throughout is to be for use and not for ornament … its beauty will be in its all-adaptation to its use".[31] Such stern demands, perhaps sensible in themselves, only frustrated Brooks's architects and led them to believe that their creative aspirations were being unduly muzzled.

The manner in which Burnham and Root met Brooks is indicative of the character of the post-fire Chicago business community. In 1879 Root went to a party and met a well-educated and well-travelled young lawyer named Owen F. Aldis, who came from a Vermont legal family and, like Brooks, Burnham and Root, had been drawn to Chicago by the calamity of the 1871 fire. The pair chatted until the small hours and Aldis later recalled that 'no other man ever impressed me so quickly and so deeply'.[32]

One of Aldis's most important professional tasks was to recommend promising architects to wealthy clients and developers and – seemingly an investor himself in commercial property – made it his business to promote skyscrapers. And he did this not just because the physical constraints of Chicago were pushing commercial buildings skywards. As Donald L. Miller explains, Aldis was able to convince fellow speculators that building tall could bring tall profits because the skyscraper 'made it far easier to do business in Chicago than in London, where much time was wasted in going from firm to firm all over the sprawling city and climbing the steep stairs of run-down buildings to small, poorly lit offices that were dusty and foul-smelling'.[33] So for Aldis skyscrapers had inherent commercial advantages because they could – in efficient manner – bring many businesses together in

The Home Insurance Building, Chicago. Built in 1885 to the designs of
William Le Baron Jenney this was, arguably, the first fully metal-framed
building ever constructed.

the same building and in a wholesale atmosphere conducive to productive enterprise.

The day after he met Root Aldis brought him, and Burnham, a commission. It was from Amos Grannis and produced the Grannis Block, a seven-storey office building on Dearborn Street. This was the beginning of big things for the practice. As Burnham later wrote, 'here our originality began to show... it was a wonder. Everybody went to see it, and the town was proud of it.'[34] In fact the building, with a brick and terracotta elevation, cast-iron interior columns and much joinery, was fairly traditional in its construction, which was largely the reason for its destruction by fire in February 1885.[35] Then, in 1881, Brooks, following an introduction from Aldis, gave them the Montauk Block to design.

The block, when completed in 1883, contained over 150 separate offices, 300 office workers toiling in strictly uniform

The Elevation of *(above)* and decorative demonic detail from *(right)*, the Manhattan Building on South Dearborn Street, Chicago, completed in 1888 by William Le Baron Jenney, now the world's oldest extant fully steel-framed high-rise.

spaces and transported around the building by a pair of elevators. These were critical to the block's functional success because the elevator was among the key technical innovations that made high-rise life possible. The idea of elevators, lifts, 'ascending rooms' or 'flying chairs' is as old as Archimedes and Greece but it was only in 1852 that the elevator became a practicable proposition when New York-based Elisha Otis invented the 'safety elevator', which incorporated a 'governor' preventing the fall of the cab if the cable broke. Thus made safe, and with steam and hydraulic power systems improved, the Otis elevator – demonstrated to great acclaim at the New York's 'Exhibition of the Industry of All Nations', a World's Fair held in 1853 – became an increasingly familiar component of contemporary construction, with the first Otis passenger elevator being installed in 1857 at the five-story, iron-fronted E. V. Haughwout Building, a china and glass emporium, at 488 Broadway, New York.

With its functional form, minimum ornament and modern technology the Montauk Block was truly an up-to-the-minute well-honed machine for clerk-fuelled capitalism and the precise physical expression of an economic system that was turning the commercial quarter of Chicago into a vast counting house.

Due to the height of the Montauk Block, the repetitive and practical nature of its design, and it being the first building in

Chicago to utilize a structural frame that was largely made of steel, Thomas Tallmadge – a Chicago architect who worked for Burnham in the early twentieth century – proclaimed that 'what Chartres was to the Gothic cathedral, the Montauk Block was to the high commercial building.'[36] One of the odder pioneering aspects of the Montauk Block was its foundations. Harriet Monroe states that Aldis, whom she describes as one of the owners of the building, objected that the conventional system of foundations as initially proposed would have needed stone piers of immense size seriously obstructing the basement and the ground floors and leaving little room for dynamos.[37] Larson claims this reservation was made by Brooks, the building's client, who feared that the established system of foundations for Chicago – the creation of a series of pyramids of stone to spread the load, with the apex of each pyramid supporting a load-bearing column – would for a tall building lead to pyramids of huge size with the basement 'transformed into a Giza of stone.'[38]

Aldis's reservations, and perhaps Brooks's own, led Root, who according to his brother Walter 'personally calculated the footings' of the Montauk Block , to rethink the construction of its foundations and basement from first principles.[39] Root came up with the idea of fabricating piles from old steel rails coated in concrete to prevent rust. These, he argued, would be strong, result in more slender structural piers and be cheaper and quicker to construct than conventional driven foundations. Root's calculations were approved by engineers and this novel system was utilized, and so successful did it prove that it formed the basis of the 'grillage' foundation system that Burnham & Root used for later large projects in Chicago.

The Montauk Block, now almost mythic since its life as the embodiment of the coming age of skyscrapers was cut brutally short, seems to have crystallized and divided opinion from the start. A most revealing story is told by Harriet Monroe. Shortly before he died Root had an interview with a prospective client. 'Well then, Mr. Root,' the evidently troubled man said, 'I like most of your buildings immensely, but I do not like the Montauk Block.' The man had made it clear what he did not want from the architect but was fearful that he had caused offence. But Root was evidently used to such criticism. He 'put his hand on his critic's shoulder and shocked him black and blue by exclaiming, "My dear Mr. X, who in H--- does?"'[40]

THE CHICAGO SCHOOL OF ARCHITECTURE

But loathe it or love it, the Montauk Block was undoubtedly a harbinger of things to come and a crucial and pioneering building in what became known as the Chicago School of architecture. This school consisted of a body of architecture created by a group of Chicago-based architects from the early 1880s and into the early twentieth century. Their buildings were almost invariably commercial in use – an alternative and early name for the movement was indeed the Commercial School – and they were high-rise, of iron and steel frame and masonry shell construction (often utilizing fire-proof terracotta as well as brick and stone), typically of relatively austere design and functional in form and organization. The steel frames not only allowed for the creation of open-plan and flexible interiors suited to the commercial function of the buildings but also, by relieving the outer walls of much of their load-bearing role, allowed for the creation of large windows. For these a characteristic window design evolved – the 'Chicago Window' – which was functional, incorporated a large area of fixed plate-glass flanked by narrow sliding sashes and that could be manufactured flat or in oriel form. These generously glazed tripartite windows, permitting light to flood in and offering stunning prospects from the interiors – pioneered the generously glazed 'curtain wall' that became a key characteristic of twentieth-century Modernism.

These key features not only made Chicago School buildings significant precursors of functionalist twentieth-century Modernism but also in a most intriguing manner suggest the influence of Liverpool's commercial architecture of the 1860s, notably Peter Ellis's Oriel Chambers. Given Root's crucial role in the development of the Chicago School, and his direct experience of Liverpool in the late 1860s, this connection is not surprising (see pages 46–8).

THE ROOKERY

In 1886 Burnham and Root created a building that made another major – if idiosyncratic – contribution to the development of the Chicago School and which was arguably the masterpiece of their years of collaboration. The Rookery, as the building was called, was built on South La Salle Street to serve as offices. It's an extraordinary creation, once again designed largely by Root. It is ruthlessly functional and proto-modern – and so very much in the essence of the Chicago School – in its plan and spatial organization, while Romantic, almost expressionistic in its form, with decorative details that are steeped in history. The building is a deeply considered fusion of the inspiration of the past and the potential of the modern.

The Rookery is eleven storeys high and once again combines steel-frame construction with masonry load-bearing outer walls in which much use is made of large areas of plate-glass. But by the time the Rookery was being built Chicago had acquired another

The main elevation of The Rookery, designed by Burnham & Root and completed in 1886. Structurally and functionally a most progressive building, but with elevations that are an eclectic mix of ornamental historic styles.

groundbreaking building that was an inevitable influence on newer structures. In 1885 William Le Baron Jenney, for whom Burnham had worked briefly in the late 1860s, completed the ten-storey-high (extended to twelve in 1890 and demolished in 1931) Home Insurance Building on the corner of La Salle and Adams Streets. This was, in a sense, the first fully metal-framed building ever constructed. While earlier high-rise constructions – including the Montauk – had combined a metal frame with masonry outer walls, the Home Insurance Building possessed what was essentially a full-skeletal frame of wrought-iron and steel construction. The exterior stonework was generally no more than an ornamental veneer, but the building's epoch-making status is compromised – or at least confused – by the fact that the load-bearing role of its metal frame was substantially supplemented by the structural use of a number of brick and granite piers.

But a few years later, in 1888, Jenney resolved this structural ambiguity with his sixteen-storey Manhattan Building, South Dearborn Street, Chicago. Its primary structure was a steel

Detail of the main entrance of Burnham & Root's Rookery, showing the mix of stone and terracotta ornament.

frame, although this was still clad with a bulky masonry skin ornamented with historicist details. This was characteristic of the moment and is typical of the strange phenomenon that when new technology arrives it is often concealed – even denied – and apes the appearance of the technology it has superseded. As Harboe explains, architects like Jenney, and Burnham and Root, were 'initially hesitant to express the inherent slenderness and grid-like nature of the steel frame, fearing it would make their buildings look "flimsy" or monotonous', so 'many early skyscrapers were clad in heavily detailed masonry skins which reflected the previous grammar of load bearing wall construction'.[41]

Despite this visual ambiguity the Manhattan Building survives as the world's oldest extant fully steel-framed high-rise. Arguably the earliest building in which the metal frame was honestly expressed – and which made its novel materials and means of construction its primary ornament – was the thirteen-storey Tacoma Building, Chicago, of 1886 to 1889 (demolished 1929) by Holabird and Roche, in which the slender steel and iron frame (for the first time fixed together with rivets) was clearly implied – being clad in only minimal manner with a facing of brick and terracotta – with the potential for large windows boldly exploited. Although load-bearing walls supported the interior, the main elevations were true curtain walls that had no load-bearing role beyond supporting their own weight. .

This group of buildings offered a world of potential possibilities. Eric Larson observes that Jenney was the first to design skyscrapers 'in which the burden of supporting the structure was shifted from the exterior walls to a skeleton of iron and steel' and that 'Burnham and Root realized that Jenney's innovation freed builders from the last physical constraints on altitude'.[42] Quite simply, the inherent strength of wrought-iron and steel-frame construction meant that from the mid-1880s buildings could, in theory at least, 'be carried to a seemingly

infinite height, and opened to a maximum of window area'.[43]

When Burnham & Root started work on the Rookery the full extent of Jenney's pioneering thinking was not evident – indeed was not fully evolved – and it wasn't until the construction of their ten-storey-high Rand McNally Building of 1889–90, on Adams Street, Chicago (demolished in 1911), that Burnham & Root designed a high-rise that had a full steel-frame construction, supplemented by the novel use of fire-proof terracotta as a cladding material.

But although some key innovations lay a few years in the future the Rookery does offer examples of Root's love of novelty and forward thinking. The foundations, which are another engineering achievement utilizing steel rails to form piers, as in the Montauk Block, are combined with cross-beams to create a concrete-encased 'floating' foundation. This 'grillage' system – essentially forming a steel-reinforced concrete slab supported by steel-reinforced concrete piers – was well calculated for the construction of heavy high-rise buildings on Chicago's notoriously swampy soil.

While the foundations are innovative, the Rookery's elevations are an almost bizarre and eclectic confection of history-based decoration. In his quest for an original language of ornament Root combined the influence of Moorish, Byzantine, Venetian and Romanesque sources and disposed all of them within a composition possessing, on its front elevation, a strict symmetry worthy of Roman classicism. The result is indeed original, and with its rich detailing as much a work of art as of architecture, but too odd and too whimsical to provide a workable prototype. The mixing of architectural styles in a single building was one of the great taboos of mid- to late-nineteenth-century design. It was the obvious way to attempt novelty – and the gentle mixing of related styles, such as Grecian and Italianate classicism, could work – but few tried it and virtually none with great critical

The Tacoma Building, on North La Salle Street, Chicago, was built between 1886 and 1889 to the designs of Holabird & Roche and demonstrated the potential of large windows and minimal cladding.

success when contrasting styles, such as Gothic and Classical, were brought together. So, in the authentic spirit of eclecticism, the Rookery has windows grouped below semicircular arches of early Renaissance or Romanesque feel, and the centre bay of the main elevation contains a low and massive stone arched entry that features stylized leaf decoration and massive Roman-inspired stone rustication. The storeys above the arch, in the centre of the main elevation, are a riot of weird, wildly mixed decorative motifs. At lower levels there are generously glazed shallow bays, then, above a bold cornice, are pinnacles that seem inspired by sixteenth-century mosque architecture.

Aspects of the Rookery's peculiar architecture had been pioneered by the Louisiana-born Henry Hobson Richardson, who evolved a very powerful and personal interpretation of the early-medieval European Romanesque style, in which rich detailing, round arches and axial symmetry were combined. An early and much-published example of Richardson's work that Root must have known is Trinity Church, Boston, completed in 1877. Also no doubt inspirational were Richardson's contributions to the New York State Capitol at Albany, started in 1867 and still under construction in 1886, and the Albany City Hall, New York, which was completed in 1883 and in which generally strict symmetry was softened with a touch of Gothic asymmetry by the addition of a massive campanile at one corner of the building.

But closer to home for Root was Richardson's astonishingly rugged, massive and strictly symmetrical seven-storey-high wholesale store for Marshall Field & Company that occupied a whole city block in central Chicago and was built between 1885 and 1887 in a manner that fused Romanesque with Renaissance palazzo models. This masterpiece of commercial architecture was demolished in 1930, but it must not only have inspired Root in some of its details and forms but also, as it neared completion in 1886, spurred him to surpass it. The Rookery in its rich variety of

Wholesale Store for Marshall Field & Company in North State Street, Chicago. Built 1883–87 to the designs of H. H. Richardson, it was the supreme – and highly influential – example of a palazzo of commerce.

detail can be seen as a child of, but also a spirited riposte to, the almost austere Romanesque Renaissance repetition of Marshall Field's Wholesale Store.

Arguably the Rookery was intended to make a statement about the direction in which modern architecture could go, suggesting that new technology could be fully embraced yet fused with history to ensure that pioneering structures retained the cultural pedigree of the past. This meshes with one of the great architectural debates of the time – how to forge an authentic architecture for the late nineteenth century that possessed some of the creative power and originality of earlier architecture that seemed to define the spirit of the age in which it was made – whether the Gothic architecture of the Middle Ages or the classical architecture of the Italian Renaissance. Root seems to have been fully aware that the creation of a vibrant modern architecture based on history was a significant intellectual and artistic challenge. What worked in the past and possessed an unselfconscious and creative power can, when repeated centuries later, demonstrate nothing but the dead hand of imitation. The question was how to bring history to life and imbue past styles of architecture with a contemporary meaning.

Harriet Monroe quotes a telling lecture that, she says,

Root delivered to an audience of architectural connoisseurs. He observed that '"Periods" and "styles" are all well enough', but pointed out that when there was a period or style worth imitating, 'its inner spirit was so closely fitted to the age wherein it flourished, that the style could not be fully preserved' in modern copies.[44] Root was right, of course, but for him and his generation the answer was not to give up the challenge but, almost like alchemists seeking the 'philosopher's stone' to try various compilations and fusions in an attempt to bring the past to life and make it relevant to the modern age. The Rookery is, among other things, such an experiment, and presumably its architects felt that the experiment was a success because they moved their offices into the building's eleventh floor and used its architecture as a showcase for their talents.

The Rookery also touched upon a separate, yet closely related, issue that greatly exercised the minds of eighteenth- and nineteenth-century architectural theorists – what is architecture and what is mere building? Clearly the natures of the two overlapped – to provide firm and secure shelter and to function as structures – but there were also intriguing differences. Architecture clearly strove to express a poetic purpose – a beauty, a symbolism – beyond simple function, while buildings might be little more than practical shelters. Over 2,000 years ago the

Roman architect Vitruvius put the case pretty clearly. Buildings, to qualify as architecture, had to possess not only 'firmness' and 'commodity' – that is be well built and functional – but also 'delight', in other words poetic beauty.*

The increasing application of emerging technologies and the drive for functionalism represented by the Chicago School tended to blur the distinction between architecture and building, making resolution of this question more urgent. With the Rookery Root makes his position clear – a structure might be little more than a modern technical marvel, but apply ornament to the structure and the building also gains beauty and meaning. And if the ornament is well chosen, and applied with reason, then the beauty could be great indeed.

Augustus W. N. Pugin offered a clue as to how this should be done when he observed in 1841 that in Gothic architecture – for him the exemplary style – 'all ornament should consist of enrichment of the essential construction of the building' and that in 'pure' architecture the 'smallest detail should have a meaning and serve a purpose'.[45] Root, of course, would have taken inspiration from these words as, no doubt, he did from the definition of architecture offered by John Ruskin in the chapter entitled 'The Lamp of Sacrifice' in his *Seven Lamps of Architecture* of 1849. For Ruskin 'architecture proposes an effect on the human mind not merely a service to the human frame', and is the 'art which... adorns the edifices raised by man and makes a building agreeable to the eye... or honourable by the addition of certain useless characters'. To make his point clear Ruskin referred to the example of a functional fortification: 'no one would call the laws architectural which determine the height of a breastwork or the position of a bastion. But if to the stone facing of the

---

* 'Firmitas, utilitas, and venustas' as Marcus Vitruvius Pollo expressed it in his *De Architectura*, or *Ten Books of Architecture* of c.30 BC.

The 'Light Court' in the Rookery was created by Burnham & Root and redecorated by Frank Lloyd Wright in 1906.

bastion be added an unnecessary feature, as a cable moulding, that is architecture.'[46] So, putting it brutally simply, for Ruskin and his disciples – such as Root – architecture lay in the addition to essential structure of practically 'useless' and functionally 'unnecessary' ornament – perhaps rich in historic associations and artistic skill – that raised mere vulgar building to the status of architecture, and bestowed upon structures both beauty and meaning. It is essential to understand this thinking if any sense is to be made of the seemingly contradictory nature of the Rookery, with its boldly revealed, almost industrial structure and its excess of history-based ornamentation.

The most dramatic expression of the Rookery's strange and conflictive nature lies at its heart where Root created a wide open well to allow as much natural light as possible to penetrate the building's deep plan. The two lower storeys of the well are topped by a metal and glass roof to create the spectacular 'Light Court', in which the structure was exposed in an honest manner and galleries and sculptural snaking staircases were handled in a very ornamental style. Other elements in the Rookery included a glazed, curving staircase that seems inspired by the staircase Peter Ellis designed in the mid-1860s for an office in Cook Street,

Liverpool. Originally the court was decorated with rich detail and dark in hue but by 1906 Root's colours and details – already seen as dated – were changed or obscured by Frank Lloyd Wright.

Employing Wright to revamp the court was a radical move. He had been employed by Adler & Sullivan in the late 1880s and knew the Chicago building world well, but by 1906 he had started to leave historicist architecture behind and was involved with the evolution of the Prairie School, which, although rooted in the Arts and Crafts Movement, favoured ever-increasing simplicity and bold geometrical forms. It was in this spirit that Wright approached the Rookery's Light Court, which he made brighter and lighter, with a white and gold paint scheme and with ornament visually simplified. Another possible reason for Wright's radical handling of the Root 'Light Court' is that there had long been no love lost between his old firm Adler & Sullivan and Burnham & Root, and his rough handling of Burnham & Root's work was perhaps a belated act of revenge.

SULLIVAN VERSUS BURNHAM

The antipathy that darkened the relationship between Sullivan and Burnham & Root seems to have come to a head in 1887 when Adler & Sullivan beat Burnham & Root to win the commission to build the vast Auditorium Building in Chicago, the largest building in the United States when work was completed in 1889, containing a rich mix of uses, including an opera hall, a concert theatre and a hotel. Wright was an apprentice in the architects' office and had worked on the interior detailing. The disappointment of losing the prestigious commission clearly rankled, and when Root saw early designs for the Auditorium Building he merely noted somewhat meanly that it appeared

The beautiful, curving and generously glazed staircase in the Rookery.

Sullivan was about to 'smear another façade with ornament'.[47]

But the ill-will between the practices – and particularly between Sullivan and Burnham – had been smouldering for years. Louis Sullivan wrote his somewhat dyspeptic autobiography in his final years, which were characterized by professional decline and too much drink, and when it appeared that Burnham had won the long competition between them for a defining role in American architecture. So Sullivan's autobiography must be treated with some caution as a historic document. He was, after all, a deeply disappointed man, but his observations about Burnham and Root surely contain at least some truth and they do offer a welcome antidote to Harriet Monroe's generally uncritical and saccharine account of the pair. Sullivan tends to coat his venom with a veneer of praise so his essential opinions are sometimes hard to determine, but what is clear is that he had a lot more time for Root than he did for Burnham.

After meeting Burnham by chance in 1874, Sullivan did not meet Root until 'probably... the early eighties' and then 'grew to know him well'. Like Monroe, Sullivan was charmed by Root's obvious qualities. He was instantly 'attracted by Root's magnetic personality', by his 'alert... mind that sparkled', his 'keen sense of humour' and his generally 'debonair' manner as 'a man of quick-witted all-round culture which he carried easily and jauntily'. But there was a sting. Sullivan also observed that Root was not only 'quick to grasp ideas, and quicker to appropriate them' but also 'vain to the limits of the skies'. Root was, notes Sullivan in a sardonic twist, 'a man of the world, of the flesh, and considerably of the devil', whose 'immediate ambition was... to be the center of admiration', and who displayed a 'mania... to be the first to do this or that or the other' so that he 'grasped at novelties like a child with new toys'. These traits, Sullivan explains, made Root 'pitifully susceptible to flattery'.

Yet 'beneath all this superficial nonsense' Sullivan 'saw the man of power... had faith in him and took joy in him as a prospective and real stimulant in rivalry', and admitted that Root's sudden death left him with a 'deep sense of vacancy and loss' because 'Root had it in him to be great'. On the other hand, all Burnham had in him – as far as Sullivan could see – was 'to be big', and his 'megalomania concerning the largest, the tallest, the most costly and sensational, moved on its sure orbit, as he painfully learned to use the jargon of big business.' Burnham was, observed Sullivan in his most cutting manner, 'elephantine, tactless, and blurting'. Flattery was, noted Sullivan, one of Burnham's key weapons. At first, when seeing this weapon being wielded on selected targets, Sullivan 'was amazed at Burnham's effrontery, only to be more amazingly amazed at the drooling of the recipient. The method was crude but it worked.'

Sullivan attempted to summarize the essential conflict between himself and Burnham and put it in broad architectural, human and political context. 'There came,' he wrote, 'into prominence in the architectural world of Chicago two firms. Burnham & Root and Adler & Sullivan... Burnham was obsessed by the feudal idea of power. Louis Sullivan was equally obsessed by the beneficent idea of Democratic power. Daniel chose the easier way, Louis the harder [and] he watched through the years the growing of Daniel Hudson Burnham into a colossal merchandiser.' As for Root, Sullivan feared he was 'so self-indulgent that there was risk he might never draw upon his underlying power', even if sudden death had not put a premature end to his efforts.

When Sullivan wrote this damning assessment, Burnham had been dead a dozen years and so could not defend himself. But more important – and more galling for Sullivan – at the time of Burnham's death in 1912 he was regarded as the pre-eminent architect in America and D. H. Burnham and Company had become the largest private architectural practice in the world. By comparison, Adler & Sullivan had been dissolved in 1894 due to severe financial difficulties and lack of commissions and during the following twenty years Sullivan's career had dwindled to virtual non-existence. Burnham's business-orientated, can-do – even amoral – attitude to architecture, characterized by his famed quote – 'Make no little plans; they have no magic to stir men's blood'[48] – had prevailed, at least in the short term.

Burnham & Root's failure to win the commission to design the Auditorium Building was followed by the collapse during construction of a hotel the firm had designed for Kansas City. One man was killed and several injured. A coroner's inquest was convened and Burnham was obliged to attend because the building's design was examined as a possible contributory cause of the tragedy. As Larson observes, 'for the first time in his career Burnham found himself facing public attack.'[49] Burnham was far from happy but, true to his sturdy nature, he remained stoical. He wrote to his wife that 'there will no doubt be censure… which we will shoulder in a simple, straightforward, manly way…'[50] Such was the code of the late-nineteenth-century gentleman. It didn't much matter what happened to a man, but what did matter was how he behaved. The practice was not damaged by this questioning of its competence; or at least it quickly recovered, and soon undertook what remains in some ways one of its most astonishing architectural creations.

THE MONADNOCK BUILDING

The next, and next to last, major building with which Root was involved was the Monadnock Building, on West Jackson Boulevard, Chicago. His role was cut painfully short by his sudden death in January 1891 but it seems that he was still able to steer the design in a direction that was to culminate, when the building was completed in 1891, with one of the most surprising and sublime designs ever realized in the United States. The building – comprising shops and offices – was to rise seventeen storeys or 60 metres high, a composite structure comprising a steel frame supporting the floors set within load-bearing brick walls. The height, as with the Montauk Block, was the result of real estate economics in late-nineteenth-century Chicago that pushed for ever greater height, tempered by the rule of thumb calculations that affirmed it was 'demonstrable' that 'ultimates' – as ultra high buildings were then termed – were limited to 'sixteen stories or 200 feet... so long as present building materials are used.'[51]

What makes the Monadnock distinct is that this drive to build as high as possible was combined with a ruthless desire to maximize profits by creating a building that was architecturally simple and, in consequence, as cheap as possible to construct. The architects were familiar with this approach from their experience with the Montauk, and could hardly have been surprised since the Brooks family with Owen F. Aldis once again formed the development team. But this time Brooks and Aldis wanted functionally superfluous ornament not just pared back but omitted entirely. This, in the 1890s for a city centre site, was a shocking proposition.

The Monadnock was on the drawing board in the architects' office perhaps as early as 1885 but certainly by 1889 and Root was – once again – the lead designer. The height of the proposed building and its bulk provoked Root to name it 'Jumbo'. This was evidently going to be an urban giant but Root wanted to make sure it didn't also become an urban monster. His major problem, at least initially, was Aldis. According to Harriet Monroe, Aldis 'controlled the investment' and 'kept urging upon his architects extreme simplicity, rejecting one or two of Root's sketches as too ornate.' It was probably Aldis who insisted that the shell of the building be constructed of load-bearing brick because this was the cheapest option, despite the labour costs of raising thick brick walls to a height of 60 metres, for a relatively long and thin building that was to occupy a large portion of an urban block. The client's insistence on brick is perhaps another reason why Root nicknamed the proposed building 'Jumbo'; the bricks likely to be used were reddish grey in colour.

A break occurred in the battle between Root and Aldis over the use of more or less ornament when the architect took a fortnight's holiday. This absence offered Burnham, ever the pragmatist, the opportunity to break the deadlock and speed the project onwards. In an attempt to humour the client – necessary for most business-minded and ambitious architects – Burnham 'ordered from one of [his] draughtsmen a design of a straight-up-and-down, uncompromising, unornamented façade' for 'Jumbo'. Needless to say Root, when he returned to the office, was 'indignant' and claimed the design was nothing more than a huge brick box. But if not a pragmatist of Burnham's stamp, Root was a realist and – what's more – liked a challenge. So instead of going into a deep artistic sulk he rose to the architectural challenge put before him, which was – essentially – how to turn a functional brick box into a piece of poetic and culturally nuanced architecture.

History, of course, held the answer. The load-bearing nature of the building's brick skin meant the portion of wall nearer the ground needed to be thicker than the higher courses because it had more weight to bear. The honest expression of this increased thickness meant that the profile of the elevation was 'battered', in other words its lower areas sloped out slightly. This allowed Root to take advantage of the problem in a most creative manner. He told Aldis that 'the heavy sloping lines of an Egyptian pylon had gotten into his mind as the basis of this design, and that he thought he would "throw the thing up without a single ornament".[52] And this is just what happened. Monroe states that

An initial design, perhaps as early as 1885, by John Root for the Monadnock Building. Note the restrained neo-Egyptian details and the slightly flared top – an idea that was to be developed in the final design of c. 1889.

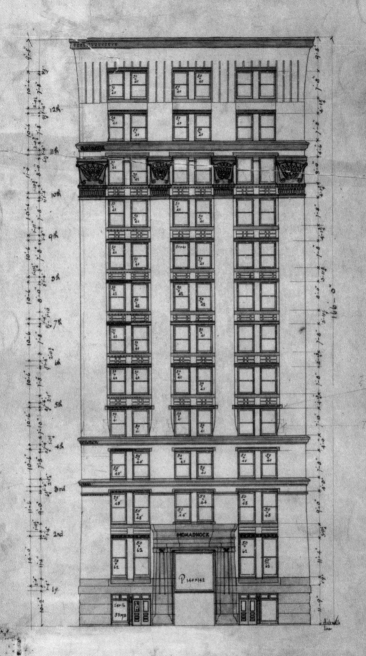

Jackson St. Elevation
Monadnock Block

Scale 1/8 inch = 1 foot

Burnham & Root, Archts.

Root handed the foreman of the office a design that he was to turn into working drawings. It was – according to the foreman – 'shaped something like a capital I – a perfect plain building, curving outwards at base and cornice.' This, writes Monroe, was 'the germ of the final design', which, she records a few years after the building was completed, left critics divided 'as to the value of [its] design.' Some – shocked by the absence of conventional ennobling external surface decoration – declared that it was 'not architecture at all,' while others – entering into the pioneering spirit of the thing – pronounced it 'the best of all tall office buildings'.[53]

Those who now visit the Monadnock Building, and who penetrate its well and authentically restored interior, might be surprised by its reputation as an unornamented building. The exterior is indeed simple, sculptural and sublime – and now famous for load-bearing brick walls that are the tallest ever constructed. But the interior corridors, a trifle gloomy because of the long narrow plan and general absence of direct daylight, are very atmospheric and relatively rich in detail. The corridors are lit by low-powered electric light in ornate fittings, as was originally the case and the first example of this technology in Chicago; ceilings are very simply coffered and the staircases are delicate, highly decorated and very sculptural as they sweep up through the building and are thought to be the earliest examples of the structural use of aluminium in architecture.

When it was completed in 1891, the Monadnock helped to change the nature of Chicago. At about the same time the Burnham & Root-designed Masonic Temple Building on the corner of Randolph and State Streets had been finished, with parts of it rising as high as twenty-one storeys. It was, at the time, heralded as the tallest building in the world. The audacious heights of these two buildings – putting some no doubt in mind of the Biblical Tower of Babel that, as an example of human

The Monadnock building – sublime in its simplicity – completed in 1891 to the designs of Burnham & Root. The ancient Egyptian inspiration is implied by pylon form rather than, as earlier, by Egyptian ornament.

ambition, seems to have alarmed even God – prompted the city to impose height regulations that ensured that no skyscrapers were constructed in Chicago taller than this overweening pair until well into the twentieth century.

The Reliance Building – the initial phase of which was John Wellborn Root's final design – was no doubt being worked on as the Masonic Temple and Monadnock were being finalized, and was arguably and ultimately a victim of their excess. The Reliance rises only sixteen storeys (including mezzanine and attic), that might well have been a reaction to gathering political and popular opinion ranged against the prospect of skyscrapers dominating Downtown Chicago. But this matters little because the aspirations of the designers of the Reliance Building, which were ultimately to make it of great international significance, were never to do primarily with its height.

Soon after the Monadnock Building was completed it was enlarged by a second phase – generally similar in design but significantly more ornate, and executed not by Burnham's office but by the Chicago architects Holabird & Roche.* When this second phase was completed in 1893, the Monadnock was the largest office building in the world.

But by 1893 Burnham had other things on his mind. In 1890 he had become the impresario of the greatest show on earth and by 1893 was one of the great men of American architecture, masterminding an enterprise that offered many a glittering prize but which, if it all went wrong, could mean the end of his career.

---

* After 1914 the practice changed its name to Holabird & Root when John Wellborn Root's son – also named John – joined it as a partner.

The Masonic Temple, Chicago, built between 1891–2 to the designs of Burnham & Root but demolished in 1939. A strange hybrid mix of historic forms and repetitive modern construction, it contained offices and upper level halls for Masonic use.

The 'White City'

The construction of the Reliance Building, which turned out to be one of the most heroic pieces of architecture created in nineteenth-century America, started in 1890 in extremely unusual circumstances. The man behind the project was William E. Hale, a leading member of the band of entrepreneurs and developers that helped rebuild Chicago after the fire of 1871. In December 1882 he acquired the site on which the Reliance was to rise and the existing building (one of the few in the district to survive the fire), which was a five-storey, masonry-built bank constructed in 1868. By the beginning of 1890 Hale had initiated his scheme to build a fifteen- to sixteen-storey commercial tower on the site. This was ambitious. At the time it was generally accepted that, on Chicago's notoriously swampy soil, sixteen storeys or 200 feet (60.9 metres) was just about the maximum height that could be reached in the city (see page 97), so Hale was aiming as high as possible. But he had a potential problem. The leases of some of the tenants of the existing 1868, masonry-built five-storey building still had four years to run. However for an inventive and ambitious man like Hale, ever keen to get on with making money, this was not to prove a serious obstacle to immediate action.

An article in the 2 March 1890 edition of the *Chicago Inter Ocean* newspaper announced that Hale was about to 'improve' his existing building 'in a novel manner'.[1] The 'novel manner' entailed starting the construction of the new building while tenants were still occupying most of the old one. This opportunity was presented by the fortunate fact that the ground floor and basement had fallen vacant. This allowed Hale to start the rebuilding project by supporting and raising the upper floor of the building on jackscrews while he removed and rebuilt the existing foundations, basement and ground floor on which the new building would eventually rise. This tricky exercise was carried out successfully, with the tenants of the upper floors continuing to conduct business as usual during the works. The architect in charge was John Wellborn Root, working in conjunction with his partner Daniel Burnham. At some point in early 1890 Root designed the scheme of foundations, basement and ground floors for Hale's new building. He also probably produced a design for the entire building but – if so – this design is now lost.

By the time the Reliance was completed in March 1895, having been extended upwards by means of a steel frame to reach its envisioned height, the world of American architecture had changed for ever. The change had taken place on two fronts during the prolonged construction of the Reliance Building. In the mid-1890s it would appear that the most obvious – and seemingly most important – change had been brought about by the World's Columbian Exposition, held in Chicago in 1893 and masterminded and partly realized by the main protagonists in the Reliance project. The second change – more subtle, yet more profound and enduring – was brought about by the Reliance Building itself, which had been completed by Charles B. Atwood, who was appointed by Daniel Burnham following Root's sudden death in January 1891. Although not the world's first multi-storey, metal-framed commercial 'skyscraper' – this title can be claimed by William Le Baron Jenney's Home Insurance Building of 1885 and his Manhattan Building of 1888 (see page 84) – the Reliance was the most architecturally consistent, functionally excellent, visually restrained, structurally rational and technologically innovative high-rise then built and it was – in the aesthetic expression of its techniques of construction – the key prototype for high-rise architecture of the coming century. As the eminent architectural historian Carl Condit put it: 'the building is the triumph of the structuralist and functionalist approach of the Chicago School. In its grace and airiness, in the purity and exactitude of its proportions and details, in the brilliant perfection of its transparent elevations [the Reliance Building] anticipated the future.'[2]

THE WORLD'S COLUMBIAN EXPOSITION

The World's Columbian Exposition, which opened on 1 May 1893, was a national celebration of the European 'discovery' of America 400 years earlier by Christopher Columbus. Although the design of the Exposition was in theory no more than a means to an end – the aim was to reveal the technological, commercial and cultural achievements of the United States and the forty-six participating nations – the Exposition's fourteen 'Great Buildings' stole the show. Set within an idyllic landscape with its vast water features – notably a huge, lake-like, 'Grand Basin', canals and lagoons – these buildings looked sensational and did much to establish earnest and large-scale Roman-Renaissance classicism as America's national style for decades to come, particularly for public and institutional buildings.

This architectural success was in many ways extraordinary. It had been calculated – even connived at – by the majority of the architects involved, who worked in close collaboration when designing the Exposition's 'Great Buildings'. The grandiose style, seemingly reflecting national aspirations and character and

bestowing upon the new nation of the United States the trappings and pedigree of ancient European civilizations, was a triumphal success even though most of the Exposition's vast classical palaces were temporary structures, destined to be cleared away within the year. Only one survives – the Palace of Fine Arts designed by Charles Atwood, which had to be more substantial and 'fire-proof' than its fellows to make it suitable to house valuable works of art. Somewhat altered, it now serves as Chicago's Museum of Science and Industry.

Another of the curious, even paradoxical, aspects of the Exposition is that the conservative classical style it launched was at odds with the high-rise technology-driven urban architecture being pioneered simultaneously in city-centre Chicago by some of the key men behind the design of the Exposition's installations. As history soon revealed, it was the high-rise model of the Reliance Building that would define American architecture – and to a significant extent world architecture – in the twentieth century, not the overblown classicism promoted by the Exposition.

To more fully understand the context in which the Reliance Building was created, and the way in which it was seemingly up-staged by a resurgence of classicism, it is necessary to explore how the World's Columbian Exposition was conceived and realized and to place this epic event in the setting of 1890s America.

'AMERICAN EXCEPTIONALISM'

The decision to hold an Exposition celebrating Columbus's arrival in the 'New World' was taken by the United States Congress in 1888. The key question was where should it be staged? New York, Washington DC and St Louis were among the favoured contenders but in early 1890 Congress approved

The Palace of Fine Arts (now the Museum of Science and Industry), in Chicago's Jackson Park and the only major World's Columbian Exposition building to survive.

Chicago as host for the Exposition. The city had lobbied hard and done its utmost to demonstrate that it had the means and the will to give a show that would honour the nation and that the world would remember. Not only was the Exposition to showcase new technology and proclaim America's cultural sophistication, it was evidently intended to also demonstrate, without being explicit about it, the then popular notion of 'American Exceptionalism'. The argument was that the United States, due to its revolutionary and visionary origin as a land of liberty, democracy and equality, was an unprecedented nation in world history. The attractive conceit had been current from at least the 1830s when the French political scientist and historian Alexis de Tocqueville observed in *Democracy in America*[3] that 'the position of the Americans is… quite exceptional, and it may be believed that no other democratic people will ever be placed in a similar one.'[4]

It was this belief in the exceptional nature of America, what Abraham Lincoln in his Gettysburg Address of November 1863 called 'a new nation, conceived in Liberty, and dedicated to the proposition that all men are created equal', that ultimately was used to justify the bloody suffering of the Civil War. The war had not been undertaken to extend liberty and equality for all in the United States or to end slavery but to preserve the Union. Lincoln had made this clear in his inaugural address of 4 March 1861 and in his letter of 22 August 1862 to *New York Tribune* editor Horace Greeley, in which he stated that his 'paramount object' was to 'save the Union' and that if this aim could be achieved 'without freeing *any* slaves I would do it; and if I could save it by freeing *all* the slaves I would do it; and if I could save it be freeing some and leaving others alone I would also do that.' But in January 1863 Lincoln shifted his position and recast the war in terms in American Exceptionalism by issuing his militarily risky although politically astute Emancipation Proclamation by which slaves in rebel states were in theory if not in fact freed. As Lincoln put it, when concluding the Gettysburg Address, the war was by then being fought to ensure that the great and enlightened experiment of 'government of the people, by the people, for the people, shall not perish from the earth' and that America – with its missionary role in world history – would, with a Union victory, become in fact what in theory its 1776 Declaration of Independence intended – an exemplary and inspirational free and democratic nation.

By the 1880s American Exceptionalism was expressed, in the popular imagination at least, by the nation's ability to think big, by the opportunities and rewards offered to individual enterprise galvanized by laissez-faire economics and by Americans' generally optimistic 'can do' attitude. To many at the time this image of the nation was supported by the evidence offered by its rapid growth and generally phenomenal rise in little more than a hundred years from backwater colony to veritable world power. And Chicago seemed the ideal choice for this self-congratulatory Exposition because to many the city – in its wealth, in its miraculous recovery from the Great Fire of 1871 and in its cultural aspiration (or at least pretentions) – was the embodiment of 'American Exceptionalism'.

What is now strange, of course, is that few Americans in the 1880s seemed greatly concerned that the noble principles on which their visionary and exceptional nation had been founded remained largely illusionary. Not only had a large portion of the fledgling nation's economic success been founded on the institution of slavery but even in the 1880s liberty and equality were still limited to sections of the white population. Despite Lincoln's 1863 prediction that a Union victory in the Civil War would ensure a 'new birth of freedom' for America, the growth and success of the nation since the end of the war had, in part at least, been achieved by a disparate band of European immigrants who believed it was their 'manifest destiny'* to rule and ruthlessly exploit the land at the expense of its early inhabitants.

It was, of course, the superficial expression of some aspects of this 'Exceptionalism' that caught Oscar Wilde's eye during his North American lecture tour of 1882, the year in which the Columbian Exposition was first being discussed (see page 61).[5] In his sardonic way, Wilde noted the American obsession with newfangled technology and science – 'the application' of which, he wrote, 'is there the shortest road to wealth'. 'There is no country in the world,' he wrote with heavy irony, 'where machinery is so lovely as in America… it was not until I had seen the water-works at Chicago that I realized the wonders of machinery: the rise and fall of steel rods, the symmetrical motion of the great wheels…'[6]

He also could not resist satirizing American's obsession with gigantism. As he observed: 'one is impressed in America, but not favourably impressed, by the inordinate size of everything. The country seems to try to bully one into a belief in its power by its impressive bigness.' He was also amused by Americans' predilection for what he regarded as often uncouth and dangerous individualism that, paradoxically, could carry with it a requirement to conform. The individualism that Wilde noted can be seen as synonymous with an American yearning to make its 'Exceptionalism' tangible. When he planned to go to Leadville, high in the Rocky Mountains in Colorado – 'the richest city in the world' and also 'the roughest [where] every man carries a revolver' – Wilde claimed that he was warned that 'they would be sure to shoot me or my travelling manager'. The point Wilde was labouring to impress upon his readers was that his brand of individualism was thought to be too provocative, too exquisite for American individualists. Wilde claims that his response was to

---

* A phrase credited to newspaper editor John O'Sullivan in 1845 to present the westward expansion of America's white population as justified and inevitable.

declare that 'nothing that they could do to my travelling manager would intimidate me' and off he went to Leadville to lecture the 'miners'. According to his account, the talk he gave – on the 'Ethics of Art' – was such a success that he was subsequently treated by his appreciative audience to a subterranean supper where the 'first course was whisky, the second whisky and the third whisky.'[7]

THE EXPOSITION GETS UNDERWAY

It was on 24 February 1890† that Congress passed the Act approving the City of Chicago as host for the 1893 Exposition. This was largely due to the fact that the city's leading businesses and Exposition sponsors – including Marshall Field and Philip Armour – had pledged $15 million to underwrite the Exposition and because banker Lyman Gage raised several million extra dollars in a matter of hours to see off New York's best final offer. The decision by Congress set in motion the process to select the precise site and to choose the artists, architects, landscape designers and engineers who would make the dream a reality and – hopefully – give it world-class quality. The process proved incredibly complex and fraught – time, if not money, became a major issue – and subtly but significantly differing versions of events entered competing accounts of what was, as most soon agreed, a truly defining moment in the history of the young nation.

Initially the realization of the Exposition was vested in a

---

† According to Harriet Monroe; April 1890 according to Banister Fletcher and finally confirmed in December by a Presidential Proclamation after the funding had been checked and approved.

national Commission that consisted of two Commissioners from each of the nation's states and eight special members. The duties of the Commission were 'to approve of the site, the buildings and general arrangements, to make allotments of space, to classify exhibits, to appoint juries, to confirm awards and to make all arrangements with foreign exhibitors.'[8]

One of the Commission's first acts was to involve John W. Root in strategic discussions about the precise location and general organization of the Exposition. According to his biographer Harriet Monroe, from the start 'Root took the high ground in regard to the fair'. Root viewed it as the occasion for a grand flourish of American Exceptionalism. Monroe states that initially 'few hoped' that Chicago would rival the hugely successful Paris World's Fair of 1889 that – among many other things – had given the city the Eiffel Tower. But Root's attitude was that 'we have more space, more money… and we have the lake (so) why should we not surpass Paris?'[9]

Apparently the site Root initially suggested for the Exposition was the 'strip of public land east of Michigan Avenue' and fronting on to the lake. This site was approved on 9 May by the first meeting of the Grounds and Buildings Committee[10] but numerous problems arose and on 15 May they were seeking another site.

Now things get confusing – indeed contradictory. Monroe states that initially the 'forlorn waste of sand and bogs' that was Jackson Park was offered by the South Park Commissioners and 'on the 10th August Mr. Frederick Law Olmsted, the distinguished landscape architect, came to Chicago at the invitation of the Committee.' Burnham and Root 'offered him the hospitality of their large offices', and she states 'that from this time he and Root, renewing an old acquaintance, were continually in conference.'[11] Other accounts and unassailable facts suggest a significantly different sequence of events. The crucial factor is the role of Jackson Park. Soon after the South Park Commission was created in 1869, by state legislature, it commissioned Olmsted and Calvert Vaux to lay out the 1,055 acre (4.27 square km) park, which included Midway Plaisance and Washington Park. By the mid-1870s Olmsted had devised a scheme and had made it clear that 'Jackson Park should be water orientated, with a yacht harbour, winding walkways around the lagoons, small bridges, bathing pavilions, and plenty of space for boating.'[12]

Olmsted's initial scheme remained unexecuted in 1890 but water features of the sort he had suggested, fed by Lake Michigan, were among the key characteristics of the Exposition as eventually created and it would appear that these were based on Olmsted's earlier vision for the site. But Monroe, in her hagiography of Root, created a very different impression. She tells two stories to suggest that Root – fascinated by the 'alluring problem' of giving form to 'the great show' – had conceived the basic plan with its water features, perhaps even before the Exposition was formally awarded to Chicago.[13] The evidence she offers for this most important claim is little more than hearsay. Monroe merely states that in early 1890 Root made a quick sketch showing large water features for 'an Eastern girl who was visiting the family', and who later passed the story to Monroe. When the girl asked Root where he would get the water for the lagoons and waterways in the plan he had apparently said: 'Lake Michigan is large enough to furnish it.' And to cap the impromptu presentation Root indicated 'a pivotal point in the plan' and stated that 'the principal building – the building for offices – will stand here', referring, apparently, to the future site of the Administration Building, which was eventually designed by Richard M. Hunt and ultimately the architectural highlight of the Exposition.[14]

According to Monroe, Root repeated the exercise, in greater detail, for Captain Horace G. H. Tarr, a Civil War veteran who served with the infantry of the Union army, who later recalled that Root 'sketched a plan of the buildings, inlets, and grounds… and

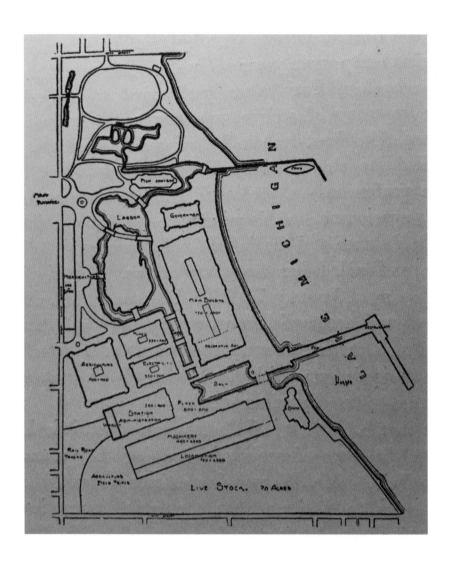

(*above*) John Root's sketch plan for the Chicago World's Columbian Exposition, published in the *New York Tribune* in December 1890; (*right*) the Exposition as realized in 1893, under the control of Daniel Burnham and Frederick Law Olmsted and his office. The broad similarities between the two plans are striking.

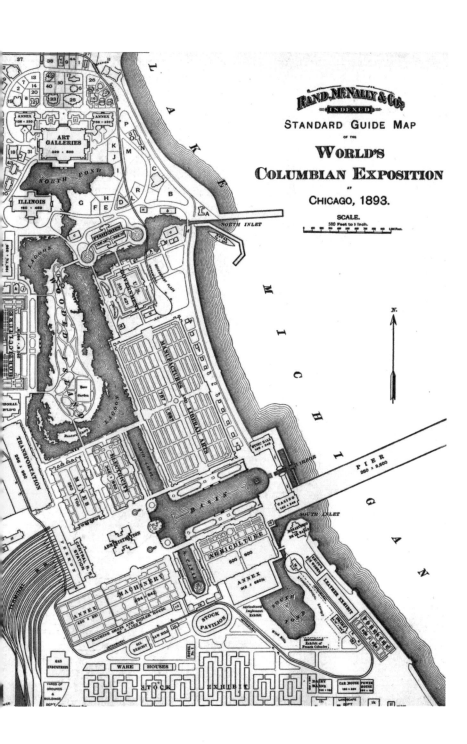

I saw… a vision of beauty and grandeur which was not surpassed over three years later when I stood in the (Exposition) thinking of his hope and witnessing its fulfilment.'[15] In addition Monroe states that as soon as he was appointed 'consulting architect' Root summoned his 'friend and employee' Jules Wegman and they started work on the Exposition design. Monroe quotes Wegman as saying Root 'mapped out the lagoons, the island, the principal buildings, etc., essentially on the lines finally laid down.'[16] Root's sketch, or a version of it, was published in the *New York Tribune* of 21 December 1890 and is reproduced on page 226 of Monroe's book, alongside the 'Final Ground-plan of the Columbian Exposition'. The resemblances are indeed striking.

So, by Monroe's account of events, and based on her assemblage of evidence, the creation of the dramatic water features and the placement of the main buildings was Root's personal vision. But, in a somewhat baffling manner, she also concedes that 'lagoons were inevitable in Jackson Park' because 'as early as 1870' Olmsted had conceived the site as 'Lagoon Park'.[17]

What appears uncontested, and is included in Monroe's account, is that on 20 August 1890 the Grounds and Building Committee appointed Messrs. F. L. Olmsted and Co. consulting landscape architects and the next day confirmed John Root as consulting architect, 'an appointment amended on September 4th, at Root's request, so as to include his partner [Daniel Burnham].' On the day of Olmsted's appointment Root, according to Monroe, told the Committee that 'there is no more eminent architect living than Mr. Olmsted… a genius…' whose 'appointment means much for the Fair [and] is an omen of highest promise.' On the same day as his appointment Root made his initial presentation to the Committee, explaining 'his ideas for the great show'.[18] The water features no doubt figured prominently in the presentation.

The alternative account of the authorship of the Exposition's watery landscape is recorded by Erik Mattie, in *World's Fairs*.[19]

He states unequivocally that it was Olmsted – not Root – who recommended the Jackson Park site for the Exposition, and who – naturally – put forward ideas – including lagoons – from his 1870 proposal for the site. But perhaps these competing claims of authorship can be reconciled.

Root's admiration for Olmsted and his willingness to adhere to his earlier design for the site – even to appropriate it – is easy to understand. Indeed the easy and guiltless absorption of things that he thought were good was perhaps part of Root's nature as an artist. After all as Louis Sullivan, who played a significant role in the Exposition, observed Root was 'quick to grasp ideas, and quicker to appropriate them'.[20] The grounds for admiration are obvious. Olmsted had been highly acclaimed for years for his landscape designs for many cities in North America – notably Central Park in New York, created between 1858 and 1873 – and he was nearly thirty years older than Root and so was a most suitable mentor.

But there is something else. Both Olmsted and Root had spent time in Liverpool and this might have formed a special bond. It seems highly probable that Root's architecture was inspired by what he'd seen in Liverpool (see page 45) but, with Olmsted, we can be more certain of the Liverpool's inspirational role. In 1850 – over a decade before Root arrived in the city – Olmsted visited Birkenhead Park, which had been opened in 1847. Designed by Joseph Paxton, it was arguably the first publicly funded park in the world and was a model of how to successfully integrate a new park within an urban setting. Its picturesque lake and garden buildings, flower beds, walks and cunningly manipulated landscape that reduced the visual dominance of the park's urban setting and increased its sense of space made so great an impression on Olmsted that he used many of its features years later when laying out Central Park.

However it happened and whoever was responsible the

choice of Jackson Park for the Exposition was brave. It was seven miles south of the centre of Chicago and as one visitor to the Exposition later wrote, it 'consists for the most part of a level trackless plain and marshy wilderness, placed on the edge, as it were, of the boundless prairie, and on the shore of an inland sea, which stretches for a space of 360 miles x 60 miles in front of it.' To 'most people' it seemed 'an impossible site for an exposition'.[21] The visitor who made this remark was a twenty-seven-year-old English architect named Banister Fletcher, who was ultimately to win fame not for his architecture but for the writing and publication from 1896 of the magisterial and authoritative *History of Architecture on the comparative method.** In 1893 Fletcher won the Godwin Bursary, a competitive prize founded in 1881 by George Godwin, editor of the London-based *Builder* magazine, which was intended to encourage young British architects to travel abroad to study modern construction techniques. The prize money allowed Fletcher to visit Chicago during the Exposition. He travelled first to New York, arriving on 24 May 1893 and subsequently spent five weeks in Chicago, returning to England in the middle of August. His report is a perceptive and very well-informed 'eyewitness' account that includes information about the process by which the Exposition was created and incorporates an invaluable collection of photographs and drawings.[22]

Banister Fletcher records that on 25 July 1890 (not 20 August as Monroe states) Olmsted had been commissioned as landscape architect for the Exposition. Fletcher also confirms that the initial decision to split the site into four quadrants, each with a distinct architectural and landscape character reflecting its function within the Exposition, was agreed by all involved in the design.

---

* Banister Fletcher wrote the book with his father, rewrote it in 1921 and left funds with the Royal Institute of British Architects and the University of London to ensure regular revision and reprints. The centennial twentieth edition was published in 1996.

Fletcher states that the consulting architects, Burnham & Root, 'acted in conjunction with the landscape architects in preparing a general scheme for the occupation of the site,' with 'the leading motive being to plan such a disposition of the greater buildings as should make the best and most effective use of the natural conditions of the site.' [23] In practical terms this meant that the Exposition's main buildings were to be arranged around a vast, symmetrical 'Grand Basin' of water. This could be seen as a symbol of the ocean that Columbus had to navigate to discover the 'New World'. But the fact that the 'Grand Basin' was at the heart of the so-called 'Court of Honor' is most revealing.

This is a planning arrangement, associated with French classical architecture of the seventeenth century, in which the main block of a chateau looks onto a formally designed *cour d'honneur* partly framed by ranges of subsidiary buildings. So it is clear, from the moment the Grand Basin and the buildings that were to flank it became known as the Court of Honor, that the core architectural and cultural inspiration for the main portion of the Exposition was to be French classicism of the formal kind, which was then being promoted and made fashionable by the teaching and influence of the highly esteemed and influential *École des Beaux-Arts* in Paris. Henry Sergeant Codman – the extremely able partner whom Olmsted put in charge of the Exposition project – is said, by Monroe, to have come up with the idea of 'formalizing the great central court'.[24] Significantly, Codman had studied landscape design in France under Édouard François André, who in 1868 had won the competition to design Sefton Park in Liverpool. This park, a stupendous exercise with lakes and carriage walks, was one of Britain's first great public parks, intended to increase the health and pleasure of the city's people, and was highly admired and influential. This park also, of course, provides another Liverpool connection in the curious story of the Chicago Exposition.

In addition to the formal arrangement of the Court of Honor and its flanking buildings the Exposition was also to have a more asymmetrical and picturesque portion within which the international pavilions were to be located, a scenic lagoon and a fairground area, slightly removed to the Midway Plaisance.[25]

Once the process was agreed by which the landscape of the Exposition was to be designed and work set in motion, the question of building 'procurement' arose. It was evident that, since the landscape design was to have a Beaux-Arts aspect, many key buildings would be permutations of the classical tradition. But who was to design them? Or rather who was to choose the architects who were to design them?

What is known for certain is that on 8 November 1890 all prior appointments were suspended by the directors of the Exposition – including the appointments of Olmsted and Co. as landscape architect and of Root. From this date Burnham was designated 'chief of construction' and put in charge, with all others reappointed to supervisory or consultant roles. Root's biographer Donald Hoffmann concluded that this 'manoeuvring' was necessary to 'sanction' the 'pre-eminence' that Burnham had managed to achieve.[26] Burnham, having been brought in by Root, was now first among equals. Exactly what Root felt about this state of affairs is not recorded. Nor is it clear to what extent the decisions Burnham made after 8 November were in fact based on the strategy that he and Root had already agreed. What seems pretty clear is that Burnham was prepared to delegate powers and decisions that, one might assume, were the prerogative of the chief of construction – and this seems to have included, to a degree, the responsibility for awarding commissions. In his autobiography Louis Sullivan records a conversation he witnessed in the late 1880s between Root and Burnham in which Burnham gave it as his opinion that 'the only way to handle big business is to *delegate, delegate, delegate*.' This led Sullivan to conclude that Burnham was not an 'artist' like Root and himself, but just a 'colossal merchandiser'.[27] So, since the Exposition was the biggest business with which Burnham had ever been involved, his willingness to delegate can come as no very great surprise.

Banister Fletcher sheds a little more light on the process by which buildings were commissioned. In his report he suggests firmly that Root had been involved in the key decision about the principle by which architects were to be selected for the design of the fourteen 'Great Buildings' to be located around the watery Court of Honor. Resolving this principle was, he writes, a 'most delicate and difficult problem'. A report was drawn up, 'when the grounds were in a sufficiently advanced state, by Messrs. Burnham, Root & Olmsted to the effect that four ways lay open to the committee for procuring designs.' These were 'i. The selection of one architect to design the entire work. ii. Competition with the whole profession. iii. Competition among a selected few. iv. Direct selection.' Fletcher states that for several reasons, including 'time limitations' and the fear that 'more prominent architects would not compete', direct selection was chosen. The 'advantages' of this method were, he writes, that an architect could be chosen for projects that, by their nature, allowed him to produce work that 'would be most nearly parallel to his best achievement'; that it would allow time to produce and compare preliminary studies so as to 'bring the scheme into one harmonious whole, and permit a "Council of Architects"' to be convened 'who should work together for the benefit of the whole scheme.'[28] This direct method of selection also gave the selecting architects strong stylistic control over the designs produced and executed. The proposal, signed by Burnham, Root, Olmsted and A. Gottlieb, the chief engineer, was accepted by the Exposition's Grounds and Buildings Committee, and thus the scene was set for the architecturally most significant – and ultimately most controversial and puzzling – aspect of the Exposition.

Evidently Burnham came under some considerable pressure. Chicago had won the bid to host the Exposition but this did not mean that men from the competing cities were to be excluded. According to his biographer, Charles Moore, Burnham, 'on the request of the committee… selected five men or firms, and the committee promptly confirmed the selection' so that on 12 December 1890 – with the full support of the Board of Directors of the World's Columbian Exposition – they invited the selected team to accept commissions to design 'the main group of buildings in Jackson Park'.[29] This was the defining moment in the evolution of the architecture of the Exposition because, as Erik Mattie explains, the 'prized commissions for the buildings on the Court of Honor… were awarded… to a group of highly distinguished architects largely from the East Coast'[30] and these were almost exclusively Beaux-Arts-trained architects from New York. This ensured that the classical preference implied by designating the 'Grand Basin' and its buildings the Court of Honor was to be realized with a vengeance.

The list comprised Richard M. Hunt of New York; McKim, Mead and White of New York; George B. Post of New York; Peabody and Stearns of Boston and Van Brunt and Howe of Kansas City, the Midwestern-based exception to the inner circle but with very strong East Coast connections. The terms of the commission are most interesting – and revealing. It was, on Burnham's part, to be the greatest of his acts of delegation, no doubt intended to save time by reducing debate, toing and froing and committee time but which also granted the architects considerable creative freedom. The five practices were told that, as to the 'artistic aspects' of the proposed buildings, the intention was to 'place the problem entirely in your hands… and you may determine among yourselves whether to make a joint design of the whole as one, or each to take up separate parts to be modified to meet such views as shall be expressed in your conferences from time to time.'[31] The architects were also told that John Root, 'our Consulting Architect', would act as 'your interpreter when you are absent' but 'without imparting into the work any of his own feelings'.[32]

Given such creative leeway, the prestigious nature of the commission and the honour and precedent-setting potential of being the first practices chosen, it might be expected that these architects leapt at the offer. But according to Burnham's biographer, this was not so. On 22 December Burnham met a number of them for dinner in New York. The Eastern architects were, apparently, 'lukewarm, Chicago was a long way from home, they were sceptical as to funds' and 'it took all of Burnham's power of persuasion to win them over'.[33] But win them over he did; however, by this process of courtship Burnham evidently made the architects feel heady with power. At about this time they held a meeting in the New York office of McKim, Mead & White with the clear intention of exploiting to the full the design liberties implied in the commission and, by so doing, deciding the architectural expression of the Exposition.

Significantly – and it now seems most strangely – Burnham was not present; Richard Morris Hunt assumed the chair as the senior architect present. Hunt, a New Englander, was in 1890 not just the nation's most eminent architect and co-founder in 1857 of the influential American Institute of Architects, but was also a committed Beaux-Arts-educated classicist. This was highly significant. The meeting decided to go for visual harmony, coherence and 'orderly arrangement', which meant that in the varied buildings designed by this group 'the classic motive should be used' and all were to be united by a 'common height of cornice' – which implied that all were to be relatively low-rise. Years later William Mead told Charles Moore that he could not remember who first suggested that all the buildings designed by the 'Eastern Architects' should be classical but he had the 'distinct impression' that it was their 'unanimous opinion'.[34] It was also agreed that the buildings and decorations would largely be constructed of timber and 'staff', a bright white plaster and Portland cement mixture that was quick and cheap to use.

Soon after his New York meeting of 22 December Burnham was 'authorized' to select five Chicago architects to design the 'five other great structures of the Exposition'. He named Burling & Whitehouse; Jenney & Mundie; Henry Ives Cobb; Solon S. Beman (who was New York-born but Chicago-based for over a decade) and Adler and Sullivan. All accepted. But there was trouble in store. The East Coast architects, being selected first, had instantly formed a cabal, grabbed the initiative and, using the loose terms of their commission had determined the classical look – and even height – of the 'Great Buildings'. At this point a 'Council of Architects' involved with key Exposition structures – as earlier proposed by Burnham, Root and Olmsted – came into being. Hunt, given the Eastern architects' head start, almost inevitably became its chairman and so the Council pushed the New York line. The late-coming Chicago architects had either to conform or refuse the commission, the latter being an almost impossible option since it would mean that the look of Chicago's great Exposition would be surrendered entirely to East Coast architects. Honour would not allow this – but could honour be kept by the unconditional acceptance of the classical style? In the 1890s things were done very differently in Chicago and New York. Chicago architects had, after all, formed their own loose but essentially lean and functionalist Chicago School and were not given to high-flown classical rhetoric. Charles Moore asserts that the 'classical motive' chosen by the East Coast architects for the Exposition buildings 'was absolutely new to Chicago, no architect in that city having used it up to the time of the Fair'.[35] This sounds like something of an exaggeration – most Chicago architects had, during the 1880s, incorporated classical motifs in their designs. But Moore is correct that none had chosen to adopt the thoroughgoing Beaux-Arts, neoclassical style found in New York and East Coast cities.

Christmas 1890 must have been tough for Chicago's avant-garde architectural fraternity as it pondered how to deal with the problem before them and wondered how one of their own, Daniel Burnham, had got them into this pickle.

The awarding of these commissions – and indeed the order in which they had been awarded – was, to put it mildly, complex and highly sensitive. Many issues came into play, regional and political aspirations as well as artistic allegiances. Even the legacy of the Civil War was an issue. As Erik Mattie explains: 'Burnham's position was nothing if not delicate.' He had been:

> obligated to choose from the New York-based architectural establishment (he had to answer to a national committee nervous about Chicago's supposed provincialism); the architects he chose had to represent the various regions of a united nation (the Civil War still weighed on the American conscience); and he wanted architects capable of a stylistically unified architectural statement that would eclipse any European precedent. Regardless of its effect on the future of American architecture… Burnham's choice of École des Beaux-Arts-trained architects from the east (and one from St Louis) satisfied these obligations.[36]

This analysis is supported by the English architect Banister Fletcher who, when writing in 1893 about the Exposition, was positive about the architectural harmony that the Council of Architects had imposed. 'It was perhaps a fortunate thing,' he wrote, 'that at the head of the Council of Architects, by mutual consent, was Mr. Richard M. Hunt who is looked up to as the Nestor of the architectural profession in the States & who exercised a controlling influence on the members.' Fletcher also reveals the intimate connections that bound the 'Eastern

OVERLEAF
What appears to be an exploratory design, titled 'canal portal', made by John Root in 1890 for the World's Columbian Exposition. It is very different to the Beaux-Arts classicism that was adopted after Root's death for the Exposition's 'Great Buildings'.

Architects' so closely together and which allowed them to operate with such powerful singleness of purpose. It was 'more fortunate still' for the cause of harmony, he observes, that

> the architects of the buildings surrounding the great court were all pupils or direct followers of Mr. Hunt. Mr. Post and Mr. Van Brunt were pupils, while Messrs Howe, Peabody & Stearns had been pupils of Mr. Van Brunt and Mr. McKim was, by education at the Ecole des Beaux-Arts in Paris, of the same school of thought & design. Under the controlling influence of Mr. Hunt as their natural head harmony was assured.[37]

Two accounts of early meetings of the Council of Architects give a flavour of the strange times, and suggest what some Chicago architects thought about Burnham and his decision to favour their colleagues from the East. One is heroic, the other bleak and tragic. The heroic version appears in Charles Moore's biography of Burnham. It records that on 'January 10 1891 the first meeting of the architects took place in the office of Burnham & Root, with Mr. Hunt in the chair', and with Louis Sullivan – one of the Chicago appointees – 'acting as secretary'. Root arrived late, having just returned from a trip to Georgia. It seems he was already taking something of a back seat in the realization of the Exposition, and was not challenging Burnham's role as chief of construction. The biographer explains that in the afternoon Burnham took the delegation to Jackson Park, while Root stayed in the office. The prospect that confronted the group was daunting. As Burnham remembered, 'it was a cold winter day... the sky was overcast... The Lake was covered with foam,' and one delegate – Robert Swain Peabody of Boston – asked Burnham 'Do you mean to say that you really propose opening a Fair here by '93? – it can't be done.' Burnham was undeterred, his will unshaken. 'Yes – we intend to... that point is settled,' he replied.[38]

The competing – almost despairing – view of the way in

which Burnham operated as chief of construction was offered by secretary Louis Sullivan, and appeared years after the event in his 1924 autobiography. When describing a subsequent meeting of the architects, at some point in February 1891, Sullivan makes it very clear that he was not to be moved by the elemental challenge of the Jackson Park site or by the romance of rising to a seemingly impossible task. He merely recalled that 'after an examination of the site, which by this time was dreary enough in its state of raw upheaval, the company retired for active conference,' with 'Richard Hunt, acknowledged dean of his profession, in the chair.' There had long been personal and professional tension between Sullivan and Burnham (see pages 58–9) but even so, his account of the meeting is surprisingly brutal. Burnham, we are told, 'was not facile on his feet' and 'it soon became noticeable that he was progressively and grossly apologizing to the Eastern men for the presence of their benighted brethren of the West.' Hunt apparently told Burnham to snap out of it: 'Hell, we haven't come out here on a missionary expedition. Let's get to work.' Everyone agreed and Burnham, who 'learned slowly but surely, within the limits of his understanding… came out of his somnambulistic vagary and joined in.'[39]

THE DEATH OF JOHN W. ROOT

A shattering event separated these two meetings and no doubt explains, in part, Sullivan's negative view. A few days after the meeting on 10 January John Root sickened and died. This was a completely unexpected event that shocked and profoundly unsettled all involved with the Exposition. Despite Burnham's rise in the hierarchy of the Exposition Root remained – for many – its visionary presence, the man able to guarantee architectural excellence. And suddenly he was dead, at a critical moment. 'Who would now take up the foils he had dropped,' wondered Sullivan? There was, he feared, 'none!'[40]

The circumstances of Root's death are dramatic and were described by contemporaries with the morbid sentimentality typical of the age. On 11 January Root once again failed to join the Council of Architects for their morning meeting, but his surprising absence was explained by Mrs Root, who called Burnham to explain that her husband had a bad cold and hoped to join them in the afternoon. But in the afternoon she called again to tell Burnham that Root had pneumonia. Burnham went quickly to see Root and in his biography states that 'during the next three days I remained with him nearly all the time, day and night'.[41] But work had to continue, and when Burnham returned to Root after a meeting with Harry Codman he found Root breathing rapidly. 'You won't leave me again,' pleaded Root and Burnham promised he would not. Root was large, robust, aged only forty-one and a few days earlier had appeared in the prime of health, but now it was obvious to all that he was dying, and there was nothing anyone could do. Harriet Monroe described Root's last hours, when 'sweet illusions assailed his brain, and he talked of them… "Do you see that… isn't it beautiful – all white and gold!" As the early night came on, he whispered huskily, "Do you hear that music?"… his fingers played the celestial air… "That's what I call music – grand." And so, into color and music, his soul passed out from earth… he was dead.'[42]

Burnham was with Root just before he died. Concerned about Root's wife, who herself was ill, he had left the bedside of the dying man for a moment to talk to her. While he was with the distraught woman her Aunt Nettie entered the room and told them Root had just died. Burnham's immediate reaction was witnessed by Aunt Nettie, who subsequently reported it to her niece Harriet Monroe. The man was shocked – but also disappointed and no doubt horrified by the prospect of the mighty project before him. Burnham was the gifted organizer, the delegator, the pragmatist – or the 'colossal merchandiser', as Sullivan would have it. Root was the architectural genius, the artist, the man of integrity. Each man had known that the other was needed, and that their collaboration had to function superbly, if they were to make a success of the Exposition. Now Burnham had to tackle the daunting task alone. Aunt Nettie recorded that Burnham paced the floor, distracted and clearly a very worried man: 'I have worked,' he muttered to himself, 'I have schemed and dreamed to make us the greatest architects in the world – I have made him see it and kept him at it – and now he dies – damn! damn! damn!'[43]

John Root's sudden death, combined with Burnham's busy routine and his predilection for delegation, left Richard Hunt – the 'Dean' of American architects[44] and chairman of the Council of Architects – effectively if unofficially in charge of the Exposition's architecture. Thus, with Root dead and Burnham distracted, Hunt and his East Coast colleagues were free to ensure that the Exposition's 'Great Buildings' were to be in reality what had already been agreed in principle – a harmoniously designed group of neo-classical palaces, united by a common main cornice height of around sixty feet and realized in white faux marble. It is true to say that this is not the architecture Root hoped for or intended. Harriet Monroe said as much in her biography (see page 165) and even Burnham, in Moore's biography, admits that, although he did not believe that the architecture of the Exposition 'would have been better' had Root lived, 'it certainly would have been modified and stamped with something of his great individuality.'[45] It seems clear that if Root had lived the process of designing and building the Exposition would have been more complex, more debated – and probably more time-consuming. If this was the case then there must have been some who were relieved by his removal from the scene.

Given the consensus that Root's sudden death changed the architecture of the Exposition significantly and that much of his power passed to Hunt, it is important – to do Hunt justice – to realize that he did not simply impose his own architectural prejudices on the Exposition and make it a vehicle for his architectural convictions. Despite his Beaux-Arts training and tastes Hunt had explored other architectural directions, for example, in the mid-1870s he designed the progressive, nine-storey *New York Tribune* building, on Printing House Square, which was served by elevators and although of load-bearing masonry construction with historically derived ornament it was a pioneering commercial skyscraper.* And so it would seem that Hunt's preference for a unifying and ennobling classicism was a simple consequence of his belief that this was the right 'house-style' for the Exposition's major buildings.

Having appointed the architects and practices that were to design the Exposition's major buildings, the next step was to agree finally what these buildings should be, how they were to relate to the site and to each other and – the big question – who was to design what. Burnham's biography states that 'discussions of the architects extended through the week after the death of Mr. Root' and no doubt these were of a most urgent and dramatic nature. And they included a discussion about Burnham's future. His biographer claimed that Burnham, shocked and uncertain how to continue, considered surrendering his position at the Exposition and quotes him as declaring that he 'remained with the Exposition only in deference to the judgement and wishes of my friends among the directors.' [46]

This uncertainty could only have strengthened Hunt's position. All Burnham's biography reveals about the progress of work during these tumultuous days is that the 'plan was modified

<hr>

* In 1903 the building was raised to eighteen storeys by D'Oenche & Co., but it was demolished in 1968.

by important changes' and that at the end of the week Burnham, surely acting under the powerful influence of Hunt, 'apportioned the work'. In the circumstances it is not perhaps surprising, even if it is a trifle brazen, that Hunt was awarded the prime commission. He took what was essentially the focal building of the Exposition – the Administrative Building (what Root had called the 'office' building) that was to dominate one side of the Court of Honor. Ultimately Hunt produced a heroically scaled and domed classical structure that did much to win him in 1893 the Royal Institute of British Architects' highly prestigious Royal Gold Medal. Charles McKim – of McKim, Mead & White – was commissioned to design the Agricultural Building, which assumed a Roman grandeur expressed through its central dome and 250-metre-long frontage; George B. Post got the Manufactures and Liberal Arts Building – a vast structure covering an area of 130,000 square metres with its main entry taking the form of a triumphal arch; Henry van Brunt (Boston born and a former New York colleague of Hunt but since 1887 based in Kansas City) and Frank Maynard Howe got the Electricity Building and Boston-based Robert Swain Peabody of Peabody & Stearns got the Machinery Hall.

This appropriation by East Coast classicists of the commissions for many of the Exposition's larger and higher-profile buildings caused 'much bitterness' within the Chicago architectural community[47] – a bitterness that, it must be assumed, was compounded by the obligation to produce classical designs as a prerequisite to gaining a commission for a larger building from Burnham and the Council of Architects. Most of the Chicago architects would have favoured a more function-driven architectural approach. What the five East Coast practices generally got – in contrast with the five Eastern practices – were the lesser commissions, often for locations in the more informal portions of the Exposition site. For example, Burling & Whitehouse were commissioned to design the 'Venetian village'

– a project so inessential that it was soon abandoned.

But, having said this, Chicago-born or -based architects did – ultimately – design half of the 'Great Buildings', even if generally not the biggest or most important. But this was not the case with the Transportation Building. It was a major Exposition building and its design was handed to Adler & Sullivan. This is a most interesting commission, given Burnham and Sullivan's long-running and deep-rooted personal and architectural differences (see pages 58–9). If the commission was fully in Burnham's gift then it was perhaps an attempt to put matters right – as far as it was possible – and to help an architectural practice that he probably knew was in trouble. The design produced by Adler & Sullivan was an exception to the rule established by other buildings around the Court of Honor because it was the one main structure that was not a predictable permutation of Beaux-Arts classicism. Instead it expressed some of the innovative functionalist principles of

A John Root design of 1890 for the 'Art Building Project' at the World's Columbian Exposition, inspired by the 'Chicago School'. This presumably became the Palace of Fine Arts, completed in high classical manner after Root's death by Charles Atwood.

the 'Chicago School' of architecture and was polychromatic and designed in an abstracted Romanesque variant of the Classical style that reflected a more pronounced desire for architectural form to be a direct response to function. But this design was, it must be admitted, structurally and artistically conservative when compared with much of Adler & Sullivan's other work – notably the ten-storey-high, proto-modern, brick-clad Wainwright Building in St. Louis, erected in 1891, that Frank Lloyd Wright – a one-time employee of the firm – was to call 'the very first human expression of a tall steel office-building in architecture.'[48] Evidently the constraints of the Council of Architects imposed could even compromise Sullivan.

The other 'Great Buildings' located around the Court of Honor, on the lagoon, that were designed by Chicago architects included the Mines and Mining Building by Solon S. Beman, who came up with a solid classical design; the Fisheries Building – the smallest of the 'Great Buildings' – by Henry Ives Cobb in a more conventional and more classical Romanesque style than Adler & Sullivan's building, and the Horticultural Building by William Le Baron Jenney and William Bryce Mundie. Jenney's

Main arched entrance to the Transportation Building designed by Adler & Sullivan.
The only one of the 'Great Buildings' that was polychromatic and not in a Beaux-Arts
classical style. This deviation was perhaps tolerated because the building did not front
onto the Court of Honor, but partly towards the adjoining Lagoon to the north.

role is particularly fascinating and confusing. He had designed the Home Insurance Building for a site in Chicago that, when completed in 1885, was arguably the world's first metal-framed skyscraper, but he had acquired part of his architectural and engineering education at the *École Centrale Paris* and the Horticultural Building was conceived as a huge pavilion of Beaux-arts classical design with a large almost transparent metal-wrought dome dominating its exterior and interior.

CHARLES B. ATWOOD ARRIVES

The designs of three of the other buildings around the Court of Honor were, in a sense, taken in-house by Burnham, who commissioned Charles B. Atwood, a new and talented member of his staff, to design the highly prestigious Palace of Fine Arts (the only major building on the site built to last); the Forestry Building and the Anthropology Building.[49] All were vigorously classical, with the Forestry Building being timber-built and conceived in witty manner as a vast 'primitive hut' incorporating tree-trunk columns. Atwood is a fascinating character. His sudden appointment by Burnham as chief designer for Burnham & Root was a direct result of the death of John Root, the lead designer in the office who, as the consulting architect to the Exposition, had been expected to ensure design quality. So Atwood's career, perhaps languishing somewhat because he was a year older than Root, suddenly took off after Root's death. He acquired responsibility for completing the Reliance Building and, through Burnham's patronage, the lion's share of design work for the Exposition, ultimately acquiring responsibility for sixty structures of one kind or another including, on the Court of Honor, the visually vital Peristyle – with its symbolic forty-eight columns, symbolizing the nation's states and territories. This theatrical gesture had been suggested by Augustus Saint-Gaudens, the Irish-born monumental sculptor then famed for his Civil War memorials who had been appointed by Burnham to 'give general advice and… select sculptors' to be used in the Exposition.[50] When Burnham first saw Atwood's design for the Peristyle it was, he told his biographer, 'as if someone had flung open the Golden Gates before me'.[51]

There is little doubt that Atwood rose to the challenges placed before him and, to judge by numerous contemporary reactions, his work at its best possessed qualities that seemed to reflect the high-flown cultural aspirations of the Exposition. The Palace of Fine Arts, the design of which Root had toyed with before his death and which Atwood completed, was regarded by many as superlative. As Donald Hoffmann explains, Atwood's building 'pleased Burnham beyond reason: he thought it chastely beautiful, the most beautiful building he had ever seen; and he told his biographer that Atwood stood "on the page of history as the greatest architect of our times". Saint-Gaudens was similarly enthusiastic and told Burnham that, in his judgement, 'Atwood's Palace of Fine Arts was the best thing done since the Parthenon'.[52]

Atwood's work, pleasing to the practical and pragmatic Burnham and to Beaux-Arts stalwarts, can be seen as a fusion of the Chicago and the East Coast schools of architecture that had, in a sense, been set in competition by the Exposition. In 1893 Atwood was very much a Chicago-based architect, but he had been born on the East Coast, educated at Harvard and gained his architectural training in the Boston office of Ware & Van Brunt (Ware left the practice in 1881 to be replaced by Frank M. Howe), and had worked for Richard M. Hunt on the Vanderbilt houses in New York. So, more than almost any other architect with building projects in the Exposition, Atwood had a foot in both camps.

A single female architect was also appointed with the task of designing the Woman's Building. This was intended to be a progressive move, but this rather crude piece of positive discrimination backfired and was generally deemed to be patronizing towards women, who were just then starting to enter the construction industry. The argument was that women should not be segregated and given special 'female' commissions but should be encouraged to compete openly with, and be treated as the equals of, male architects. The architect chosen, by means of a limited competition, was twenty-five-year-old Sophia Hayden, who lived in Boston, where she had attended the Massachusetts Institute of Technology (MIT) and was the first female to graduate from its four-year architecture programme. Like her male colleagues, Hayden also produced a large pavilion of Beaux-Arts classical design.

Evidently all the architects designing the Exposition's showpiece buildings set around the Court of Honor and lagoon had to broadly accept the design guidelines imposed by Hunt and his Council of Architects – including the adoption of a main cornice height of 60 feet to create an element of visual unity – to ensure that their designs were approved and built. Even Adler & Sullivan had to obey, though their polychromatic Romanesque design slightly challenged the classical orthodoxy of its pale neighbours. So architectural ideology, or at least the quest for architectural harmony and visual cohesion, trumped any notion of individual artistic expression, and even potentially compromised architectural integrity.

At some point in late 1890 a decision was taken that was to cast a spell upon the Exposition and give it the name by which it became known soon after it opened. The plaster and Portland cement mixture called 'staff', with which the vast majority of the buildings were by and large constructed, dries an off-white colour. The initial idea was to paint the 'staff' and Burnham appointed Root's friend William Prettyman 'Director of Color'. After some experimentation Prettyman concluded that ivory was the colour to use. Beman's Mines and Mining Building was painted and Burnham and the architects convened to inspect it. The colour was not thought a success, discussion ensued and, as Burnham told his biographer, 'I don't recall who made the suggestion' but 'finally the thought came "Let us make it all perfectly white"... the decision was mine... I had Beman's building made cream white.' Prettyman had been in the East when the site meeting took place and when he returned he was 'outraged'. He accused Burnham of interfering. Burnham said he 'saw it differently'. Prettyman then threatened that 'he would get out' and no one tried to stop him. Another link with Root was gone.

In place of Prettyman the less flighty Frank Millet was put in charge of what was, more or less, the 'white-washing gang' that developed mass-production painting techniques later adopted by the motor industry.[53] The decision to go for white had been taken for practical reasons – painting all the buildings the same simple, uniform colour would save a lot of time – but it was also artistically inspired. It granted the buildings an ethereal quality, made them appear as if they were wrought of white marble and confirmed the dreamlike quality of the assemblage of large and bold classical palaces. It also ensured that the Exposition, when it opened, became quickly and memorably known as the 'White City'.[54]

As detailed designs were produced for presentation to, discussion with and approval by various committees, a heady – increasingly euphoric – atmosphere appears to have emerged, at least according to Burnham's biographer: 'The winter afternoon was drawing to an end. The room was as still as death, save for the low voice of the speaker commenting on his design...

Finally, when the last drawing had been shown, Mr. Gage drew a long breath. Standing against a window and shutting his eyes, he exclaimed, "Oh, gentlemen, this is a dream." Then, opening his eyes, he smilingly continued, "You have my good wishes, I hope the dream can be realized." Lyman Gage, the banker who had raised funds to help secure the Exposition for Chicago, was president of the Board of Directors. At this same fateful meeting Saint-Gaudens, seemingly in a state of quiet ecstasy, told Burnham: 'Look here, old fellow, do you realize that this is the greatest meeting of artists since the fifteenth century!' In this self-congratulatory mood the 'whole work' was approved 'by all the authorities' in late February 1891 and construction commenced.[55]

A TOUR OF THE EXPOSITION

Banister Fletcher's description of the Exposition offers a fine vignette of this epoch-making event from an objective point of view. Not only was he a perceptive eyewitness able to give a very direct and immediate impression of the buildings and the grounds, and well placed to offer a response to their design, but he also met and talked to some of the Exposition's key men. For example, he had an 'interview' with Olmsted 'at his country house at Brookline, near Boston' where Fletcher 'gleaned many important points that influenced him in this important undertaking.'[56] Fletcher also confirms that it was Olmsted who 'saw the adaptability of the Jackson Park site and strongly advised its selection, especially making excellent use of the lake water for purposes of transit and effect in the grounds.' Fletcher was evidently – and most reasonably – impressed by Olmsted's acumen. 'There is,' he recoded, 'no doubt that [the] sheet of water [gives] the grounds that finish which is so essential to a work of art.'[57]

OVERLEAF
Looking west across the Basin and Court of Honour in 1893. The gigantic figure in the Basin is the twenty-metre-high, partly gilded 'Statue of the Republic' made by Daniel Chester French. It was destroyed by fire in 1896.

Fletcher also criticized aspects of the Exposition, presumably reflecting the consensus of contemporary opinion. He arrived at the Exposition site – as did most visitors – by train. At the 'main entrance to the Exhibition where all the railway lines centralize,' there was a 'great waiting hall'. This had been designed by Charles B. Atwood and was, for Fletcher, 'a most imposing structure' inspired by 'the Baths of Caracalla at Rome'. But this 'great terminus' was not the formal entry. Adjoining it was the 'grand entrance dome of the Exhibition', that Fletcher thought 'a fitting Hall of Honour from which to start on a visit to the buildings'. This hall offered a fine vista along the 'main canal of the waters of Lake Michigan',[58] which must have been a fine piece of architectural theatre in the French Baroque tradition beloved by nineteenth-century Beaux-Arts designers. Fletcher admired the 'two canals' and the 'main basin' cut by Olmsted and 'joining Lake Michigan, around which the principal buildings are grouped… in a stately & formal manner' and with 'matching cornice heights'.[59]

To the north of this 'impressive stateliness' the site possessed a 'more romantic and picturesque' quality that offered, in Fletcher's view, 'a necessary relief in an undertaking of such dimensions'.[60] But despite the creation of visual variety and contrast the vast scale of the Exposition bothered Fletcher. He noted the 'intra-mural elevated railroad' that ran from Atwood's terminus in a five-mile circuit around the ground, and the 'steam launches on the main basin & lagoons', but argued that 'one thing is painfully apparent… the Exhibition is too big'. There were, he wrote, numerous 'cases of fainting from over exhaustion', and he pointed out that 'omnibuses were necessary to transport people from one building to another'.[61]

Clearly the Exposition, because of the vast size of the ground, was physically taxing and inconvenient to visit. In fact it was more difficult than Fletcher suggests because he was writing only about the main Exposition site with its halls, pavilions and various buildings. The public amusements were at the adjoining fairground on Midway Plaisance. A month or two after the Exposition opened these were to include the world's first Ferris wheel. It stood 80 feet high and had 36 cars each able to carry sixty people, with one car reserved for a band that played as the wheel went round. The wheel was the invention of George Ferris and, with its huge scale, eye-catching potential and entertainment value, was intended to rival the Eiffel Tower from the 1889 Paris exhibition.

Fletcher was impressed by the architectural power and harmonious presence of the Exposition, but also slightly doubtful about the architectural message it carried and about the influence it might have. It was, he argued, 'certainly unparalleled in the history of Exhibitions [and] the more satisfactory to architects because it has led to what is practically an Exhibition of architecture.' In previous Expositions and World's Fairs 'excepting Paris', suggested Fletcher, 'we have been accustomed to look at the exhibits, but here the importance of the architecture of the buildings themselves forces itself upon us by the scholarly treatment of the designs.' This statement might now seem strange, with the hindsight of over a hundred years. There is no doubt that the architecture of the Exposition was regarded as deeply significant at the time and much discussed, but for long-lasting architectural importance Chicago is now seen as less important than the Paris *Exposition Universelle* of 1889 or London's Great Exhibition of 1851, which featured the pioneering and utilitarian Crystal Palace, composed of mass-produced cast-iron components assembled on site and incorporating large amounts of glass; one of the most influential structures ever built. It anticipated – and indeed inspired – many aspects of twentieth-century architectural Modernism (see page 263).

Perhaps this changing perspective is simply to do with evolving theories of significance in architecture. The importance of Chicago was seen at the time to lie in the persuasive pressure exerted by the erudite classical design of its 'Great Buildings'. The fact that they were structurally and materially gimcrack seemed, to many at the time, of little importance. Eiffel's tower in Paris and Joseph Paxton's Crystal Palace in London were also meant to be temporary structures but, in addition, were engineering marvels, in which the choice and use of materials and the expression of structure were all-important. And these are qualities we still admire and find of interest. To judge by Fletcher's notes and sketches on the Chicago buildings, he was also – essentially – a modern man. What he explored in detail, and what he drew and collected information about, was not the classical language of design expressed by the elevations of the 'Great Buildings' but their rich array of large-scale and ingenious metal roof structures. As a rule the Exposition required wide-span, open interiors for the display of large machinery or objects and this was usually achieved by a variety of boldly engineered solutions. In this respect the buildings on display in the Exposition had more in common with pioneering engineered structures of the age – such as the Reliance Building – than is immediately apparent. Indeed, in the case of the Reliance Building, the Exposition probably had a very direct and dramatic influence. It has been argued that the decision in 1894 to clad the Reliance Building in glazed white terracotta – and the general lack of colour in the building's exterior – was the direct result of the aesthetic success of the White City by the lake.[62]

Fletcher was understandably puzzled by the Exposition's wholehearted embrace of high-flown European classicism and its promotion as America's national style. For him this struck a false note. 'It is true', he wrote, 'that the expression of American life in architecture is not to be found at the Exposition.' But Fletcher, himself partly educated at the Beaux-Arts in Paris, was determined to be positive, and added that this was forgivable because the Exposition's classicism was capable of teaching great and universal architectural truths and provided 'an object lesson of the accepted canons of architectural art in regard to proportion, and in its union with sculpture & painting.'[63]

But Fletcher could not avoid pointing out the dire consequences if the classical model offered by the Exposition was followed uncritically: 'Let us hope... that the imitative element will not cause these great classic designs to be reproduced for town halls, or museums, or what not, all over the country, but that the American architects, who are already advancing so rapidly along certain new lines of departure, will value the lessons these designs teach without copying the forms which they present.' If the Exposition led to 'a great American classic revival', then in Fletcher's view it would have done 'more to retard the true progress of art in America than if no Exposition had been held at all.'[64]

As events were to reveal, Fletcher's fears were soon realized. The consensus now is that critics like Fletcher were right to be worried about the example offered by the architecture of the Exposition. Erik Mattie confirms that 'classicism, as exemplified by the Columbian Exposition... became the country's de facto national style, as seen in countless governmental buildings and civic works', and 'while skyscrapers of the most advanced design were mushrooming in Chicago the... Exposition was largely closed to the architectural world around it.'[65] Roberto Cavello in *World Fairs*, published in 2000 as part of the TUDelft series on architecture, echoes this now orthodox view: 'Everywhere in America offices and skyscrapers were rising up, built in steel, in their characteristic, unadorned and functional style, and so the historicizing white architecture of the Fair seemed like a step backwards in the development of modern architecture.'[66]

For these reasons, as Mattie concludes, 'the conservatism' of the Exposition's classical architecture 'has long been a subject of criticism'. But this is to simplify what was an apparently contradictory and certainly a complex cultural phenomenon. For one thing, as Mattie points out, the architecture of the Exposition 'struck a positive chord with the American public' – which appears to have been delighted by the evocation of Rome and Venice in the Midwest – and led to valuable cultural initiatives such as the establishment of the American Academy in Rome, which aimed to undertake research into classical architecture and explore its continuing relevance.[67]

Nor is it quite true to state that skyscrapers were rising up 'everywhere' in the States in 1893, or that they were 'unadorned'. Louis Sullivan had written in 1892 that 'it could be greatly for our aesthetic good if we should refrain entirely from the use of ornament' and produce buildings that are 'comely in the nude', relying for effect on 'mass and proportion'.[68] He also later argued, more succinctly and memorably, that 'form ever follows function'.[69] But Sullivan's own architecture was ornamented, although significantly it was an ornament that was inspired by nature and not by one of the conventional historical styles, and it was integrated into the structure of the building and not merely an applied surface decoration.

Nor does the separation of architecture in 1890s America into two camps – the neo-classicists versus the Chicago proto-modern innovators – deal satisfactorily with the apparent paradox that many of the Exposition's classical buildings were designed by Chicago School architects. And there is another serious problem with the condemnation of the Exposition's classical aspirations. The fact is that its immediate architectural consequences were – on occasion – outstanding. Buildings were produced that were far from being pioneers of the coming age of Modernist architecture but nevertheless did, in their boldness, large and generous scale and confidence, capture something of the essence of America. Only two examples need be cited – both built, perhaps predictably, in New York. John Merven Carrère and Thomas Hastings both studied at the École Nationale Supérieure des Beaux-Arts in France, both worked for McKim, Mead & White until the 1880s and in 1897, after they had established their own practice, won the competition to design the New York Public Library. Completed in 1911 in a magnificent and erudite Renaissance style, the library makes gloriously manifest, largely through its grand classical architecture, the civilizing virtues of free public libraries and learning. It soon became – and remains – one of the city's best-loved public buildings.

Even more powerful as a classical composition was Pennsylvania Railway Station that was conceived (like Atwood's railway 'waiting hall' at the Exposition) as a breathtaking essay upon the vast and vaulted Baths of Caracalla in Rome, which the station matched in scale and architectural ambition. It was designed in 1901 by McKim, Mead & White, and instantly became a symbol of New York's importance as a transport hub and a monument to its client and their architects' ability to combine functional excellence with cultural pedigree and architectural beauty. The station was intended to form a sensational point of entry to one of the great cities of the world and succeeded brilliantly. The loss of this sublime station in 1963 remains deeply lamented.

THE 'WHITE CITY'S' INFLUENCE

Classical monuments like the New York Public Library and Pennsylvania Station were a direct, obvious – and surely glorious – architectural consequence of the Exposition. But the Exposition's legacy and the vision of America it represented were expressed in many other ways. Some were direct and benign, others more subtle and troubling. For example, the 'City Beautiful' movement that flourished for the decade after 1893 was inspired by the classical perfection of the White City. Indeed Burnham's 1906 plan for Chicago – a largely visionary rather than realistic affair that sought to order the city's growth – can be seen as an expression of the City Beautiful movement. There was also a hint of the influence of the Garden City, then being promoted in Britain, because Burnham's comprehensive plan for Chicago stated that every resident should be within short walking distance of a park. The plan was sponsored by the Commercial Club of Chicago and Burnham – ever the shrewd businessman – donated his time and in the process gained much good publicity and secured his role as the city's pre-eminent architect. The movement's most prominent supporters, including Richard M. Hunt, argued that harmonious and beautiful architecture and comprehensively controlled and balanced urban growth would lead to social harmony, order and civic virtue. This might seem a harmless notion, if a little naive, but the movement had an arguably more sinister aspect because it was, in many ways, a reaction to the growing tenement districts in the nation's great cities that were home to poor immigrants and perceived by some American elites to be expanding uncontrollably and descending into chaos because of high birth rates and general ignorance of the alien hordes. Viewed in this context the City Beautiful Movement can – like the 1893 Exposition – be seen as yet another expression of American Exceptionalism. Both sought to celebrate and promote the opinion then embraced by people of power and wealth in America. This was, in essence, that the greatness the nation had achieved in little over a hundred years – and the greatness it was yet to achieve – was, and would be, almost exclusively due to the endeavours of Protestant, often Quaker, European settlers and the realization of their social and artistic values and territorial aspirations. It is an extraordinary fact that the Chicago Exposition paid little attention to the indigenous people of America, while non-European cultures and nations were often portrayed in the most patronizing manner. For example, the Midway fairgrounds portion of the Exposition included the display of an 'Esquimaux Village' that provoked outrage among Inuits, who complained of gross misrepresentation and exploitation,[70] a Chinese 'Opium Den' and native Africans who were exhibited as a primitive people alongside exotic 'big game' animals.

AFRICAN-AMERICAN EXCLUSION
FROM THE EXPOSITION

These crude representations were bad enough, but far more significant and now difficult to comprehend was the Exposition's failure to include the story of African-Americans within the upbeat history of the nation. Many had only relatively recently escaped the horror and indignity of hereditary and perpetual slavery and yet the contribution that generations of forced labour had made to the economy and character of the nation went unrecognized. This was an opportunity to start to put things right, to start to identify the creative contribution that African-Americans, despite terrible tribulations, had made to an emerging nation, particularly in the years since the end of the Civil War. But the Exposition failed to rise to the occasion, a failure that inevitably gives the playful title 'White City' a very uncomfortable meaning.

The exclusion of African-Americans from participation in the Exposition was noted at the time and prompted Frederick Douglass – the former slave who became a mighty force for emancipation and African-American human rights during the Civil War – to write the introduction to a pamphlet, published in

1893 towards the end of the Exposition and entitled *The Reason Why the Colored American is not in the World's Columbian Exposition.*

Douglass' text still makes compelling reading. He begins in a conciliatory manner by stating that the

> World's Columbian Exposition, with its splendid display of wealth and power, its triumphs of art and its multitudinous architectural and other attractions, is a fair indication of the elevated and liberal sentiment of the American people, and that to the colored people of America, morally speaking, the World's Fair now in progress, is not a whited sepulcher.

But for 'colored' Americans – even those who desired to join the celebration – the Exposition was indeed an act of grotesque hypocrisy and, like the sepulchre, its superficial sparkling beauty did hide corruption and 'all uncleanness.' (Matthew 23:27). To explain the plight of African-Americans Douglass pointed out that 'we have long had in this country, a system of iniquity which possessed the power of blinding the moral perception, stifling the voice of conscience, blunting all human sensibilities and perverting the plainest teaching of the religion we have here professed, a system... in view of which Thomas Jefferson, himself a slaveholder, said he "trembled for his country" when he reflected "that God is just and that His justice cannot sleep forever." That system was American slavery. Though it is now gone, its asserted spirit remains'with 'coloured' Americans still the victims of 'prejudice, hate and contempt.'

So, when asked 'why we are excluded from the World's Columbian Exposition', Douglass' simple answer was 'Slavery'. Douglass was outraged by the double standards that fatally tarnished the lustre of the White City

America is just now, as never before, posing before the world as a highly liberal and civilized nation, and in many respects she has a right to this reputation. She has brought to her shores and given welcome to a greater variety of mankind than were ever assembled in one place since the day of Pentecost. Japanese, Javanese, Soudanese, Chinese, Cingalese, Syrians, Persians, Tunisians, Algerians, Egyptians, East Indians, Laplanders, Esquimoux

but 'as if to shame the Negro', he was within the Exposition also exhibited as 'a repulsive savage'. The Americans, conceded Douglass, 'are a great and magnanimous people and this great Exposition adds greatly to their honor and renown, but in the pride of their success they have cause for repentance as well as complaisance, and for shame as well as for glory.'

If such writing at the time was thought to be nothing more than the gloomy ponderings of a veteran orator who had become the ever-vociferous moral conscience of the nation then another contributor to the pamphlet made clear that the evil Douglass wrote of was not confined to the years of slavery but was still very much alive. Ida B. Wells noted in her article that as recently as 7 July 1893 – two months after the opening of the Exposition – a black man named C. J. Miller had been lynched, by a frenzied white mob, in Bardwell, Kentucky. Two days earlier two white girls had been found murdered near their home and with no evidence – indeed against actual evidence that had been collected – Miller was seized by the mob, mistreated, and without any form of trial or investigation, and despite his protestations of innocence, was publically lynched. A log-chain around his neck, and hanging from a telegraph pole, Miller's near-naked body was photographed by his executioners and the photograph eventually published in the pamphlet. Nobody was arrested and charged with Miller's murder. Wells, the daughter of a slave and of a white slave owner, was born in Mississippi and through her courage and strong sense of justice became a leading figure in the post-Civil War civil rights movement. During the closing days of the Exposition Wells personally distributed the pamphlet to visitors, letting them know that 235 people had been lynched the previous year, mostly African-Americans and not just in the South. Perhaps many visitors were not as shocked by this as they should have been because the evil was not distant as well as not being ancient. As Donald L. Miller records, in the spring of 1893 a fight broke out, on a Chicago streetcar, between two of the Exposition's construction workers. One was white and the other black, but such was the toxic nature of the onlookers that, as a mob, they rushed the African-American and hanged him by his neck 'from a lamppost in broad daylight in front of hundreds of witnesses, many of them screaming, "Lynch him, lynch the nigger."' As it happens the man did not die because he was speedily rescued by two heroic police officers 'who clubbed their way through the frenzied mob, firing their pistols in the air'. The rescuers and victim were then forced to shelter from the baying mob in a nearby drugstore until the arrival of police reinforcements.[71]

Given these terrible recent events it now seems somewhat odd that, in his introduction to his pamphlet, Douglass observed that 'we shall be censured for the publication of this volume', because its timing 'will be thought to be ill chosen'. A groundless fear, perhaps, since the publication was intended as a riposte to the Exposition and so was all about timing. But no doubt Douglass was right. It's impossible to imagine that the circulation of the pamphlet, with its horrendous photograph, could do other than enrage – and one hopes horrify – the generally ebullient organisers of the White City and its visitors. It was indeed a most sobering document. The pamphlet concluded in sorrow rather than anger. F. L. Barnett merely pointed out that as the 'World's Columbian Exposition draws to a close... that which has been done is without remedy'. The 'failure' of 'the colored people... to be represented is not of our own working and we can only hope that the spirit of freedom and fair play of which some Americans so loudly boast, will so inspire the Nation that in another great National endeavour the Colored American shall not plead for a place in vain.'

THE EXPOSITION
AND FEMALE EMANCIPATION

Perhaps the virtual exclusion of the story of African-Americans from the Exposition did cause shame, and perhaps this shame did ensure that such a thing could never happen again. It is difficult now to say, but if it is the case then the Exposition did, ultimately, make a positive contribution towards the mending and uniting of the nation. The same can, perhaps, be said of the Exposition's contribution to the emancipation of women in the United States. The creation of the Woman's Building – a vast classical pile – provoked debate and dissension. Although it could be presented as a recognition of the role of women within the nation, it was also condemned as little more than a patronizing token gesture. Certainly the Exposition did little or nothing for women in the short term and they continued to live in a man's world – without political power – until 1920 when women, African-American as well as white, won the vote.

But the realization of the Woman's Building also tells another story, essentially about how ambitious and powerful women operated in a male- and merchant-dominated Chicago of the late nineteenth century. The leading protagonist in the evolution of the Woman's Building was the socially ambitious Bertha Palmer. She was married to the successful Chicago businessman Potter Palmer, who had moved from being a merchant in dry goods and French fashions for ladies (he eventually sold his store to a consortium that ultimately transformed it into Marshall Field's) to hotelier and property mogul. As well as business interests Palmer developed – no doubt due to the influence of his wife – an interest in progressive art and from the 1870s into the 1890s the pair were significant collectors. Initially they were advised by Sarah Tyson Hallowell, a Philadelphia aesthete who had introduced them to Parisian art, but by the early 1890s they had become clients of the Paris dealer Paul Durand-Ruel, who almost single-handedly established a reliable and valuable international market in Impressionist art.

Due to Durand-Ruel's influence and persuasive marketing skill the Palmers had, by the time of the Exposition, acquired twenty-nine works by Monet and eleven by Renoir. Hallowell, wanting Chicago to bathe in the glory of possessing what she believed to be the best in contemporary art, persuaded the Palmers to acquire works by Auguste Rodin. The eventual aim was that the Rodin works would be displayed in the Exposition, but this cultural coup almost failed because the explicit nature of his nudes alarmed some of the Exposition committee.*

Given these trade and cultural connections and achievements, it was inevitable that the Palmer family became significant in the planning and realization of the Exposition. The leading role was taken by Bertha. She had the time, she had the inclination – and it seemed she liked the social glitter and the role of cultural leader – and in 1891 she managed to get herself elected as leader of the Exposition's highly influential and prestigious 'Board of Lady Managers'. It was this board that selected Sophia Hayden as architect for the Woman's Building. But soon things started to go wrong. Palmer attempted to influence Hayden's design – it seems

---

* The Palmers' collection now forms the heart of the Art Institute of Chicago's Impressionist collection.

she wanted to turn the commission into an opportunity for very personal patronage, with works incorporated into the building that were owned, collected or created by her female cronies. Quite naturally Hayden objected on principle but Palmer, rather than respecting the young architect's integrity and commitment, had her fired from the project. This seemingly brutal act probably reflects a profound difference of opinion between female social activists in 1890s America. On the one hand there were women like Palmer, well connected, married to rich businessmen who promoted women in the arts, and were happy to do useful charitable work but who accepted the social, political, sexual and racial status quo. It is no doubt significant that when the African-American civil rights activist Ida B. Wells campaigned for African-American women to be represented on the Exposition's 'Board of Lady Managers' Bertha Palmer's response was to appoint a white woman from Kentucky to 'represent the colored people'.[72] On the other hand there were suffragists, often young professional women like Hayden, who wanted significant social change and full civil rights. These two groups, although they had much in common, found it hard to co-exist.[73]

Palmer seems to have pulled strings and in Hayden's place Candace Wheeler was appointed. Aged sixty-six, she was a veteran interior decorator – indeed she virtually introduced the trade as a respectable and remunerative female occupation to the States – and, like Palmer and many of her connections, came from a wealthy and eminently respectable Quaker family. No doubt Palmer found the new appointee far more socially sympathetic. But Wheeler was also a formidable woman with a finely honed social conscience and a well-proven regard for promoting women's rights. Clearly she was not going to be a mere yes-woman. By the early 1890s she had mastered worldwide art fashions, such as the Aesthetic Movement and the Arts and Crafts Movement, and had played a pivotal role in the home-grown Colonial Revival, which, like the English Queen Anne Revival, was an informed if selective evocation of a vigorous vernacular classical style.

In addition – and more interesting than this display of sensibility about changing fashions – Wheeler had in 1877 founded the Society of Decorative Art in New York and in 1878 the New York Exchange for Women's Work. Both offered women the opportunity to work independently and profitably in the art and decorating worlds and both organizations also offered their supporters admirable connections and attractive opportunities for glittering social occasions. Wheeler's associates in these societies included Louis Comfort Tiffany and Elizabeth Custer, the wife of Brevet Major General George Armstrong Custer who had been killed in June 1876 at the Little Big Horn, along with around 268 members of his 7th Cavalry command when he misguidedly attacked a vastly superior number of Lakota/Sioux and Cheyenne.

Libby Custer is the epitome of the redoubtable women who did much to mould late-nineteenth-century America and who played a powerful, if behind-the-scenes, role in the Exposition. Immediately after her husband's profoundly shocking, and nationally humiliating, defeat President Ulysses S. Grant declared that the massacre 'was a sacrifice of troops brought on by Custer himself that was wholly unnecessary.' Grant had an axe to grind – Custer had been involved in publicizing the corruption of Grant's administration, and of the president's brother in particular. But General Sherman and General Sheridan also argued that Custer had been rash and imprudent to attack such a large number of hostiles. By late 1876 it seemed that Custer's reputation was shredded. But Libby fought back and made it her life's work to rebuild and embellish her husband's character. Through books, lectures and lobbying she finally managed, with astonishing if not lasting success, to turn him for a time from tarnished and rash opportunist to mythic hero whose 'last stand' was transformed from a woefully bungled and almost criminally incompetent fiasco into a courageous emblem of American Exceptionalism.

By the time Bertha Palmer ousted Hayden the plan and exterior of the Woman's Building was already resolved and, ultimately, was constructed to the young architect's design. So it was the interior that, under Wheeler's guidance, became the focus for the attention of Palmer and her circle. And a key member of this circle was – predictably – Sarah Tyson Hallowell. The focus of her work was the commission and supervision of two large murals, *The Primitive Woman* by Mary Fairchild MacMonnies and *The Modern Woman* by Mary Cassatt. Unfortunately neither work was particularly memorable, although MacMonnies' *Primitive Women* was generally regarded as the better of the two. Neither artist produced a mural again.

More successful was the mural in the library in the Woman's Building that Wheeler had managed to get commissioned from her daughter Dora Wheeler Keith. A piece of shameless nepotism perhaps, but in fact in 1893 Keith was a famous and interesting enough artist to attract the attention of Oscar Wilde, who, when in New York in 1882, arrived unannounced at Keith's studio on East Twenty-third Street.[74]

As well as producing and collecting work to fill the Woman's Building, Bertha Palmer and her circle of friends and advisers also found time to put pressure on the government to produce a commemorative coin for the Exposition. The result was the silver 'Isabella quarter', named after Queen Isabella I of Castile, who sponsored Columbus's voyages to the New World. The obverse of the coin shows the queen; the reverse shows a woman spinning flax and was intended to symbolize female industry. Like the murals, the coin was not highly regarded as a work of art, with nearly half of the coins being returned to the mint to be melted down.

It is now hard to feel much affection for these highly privileged, socially able, generally affluent and somewhat pushy

OVERLEAF
The Columbus Quadriga and Peristyle, designed by Charles Atwood and emblazoned with the slogan 'Ye shall know the truth and the truth shall make you free' and dedicated 'to the pioneers of civil and religious liberty'.

– or at least opinionated – group of women, who clearly felt a great sense of entitlement. Few of them seem to have been as good or able as they believed themselves to be, and some were evidently capable of virtually destroying those unfortunate souls outside their circle or who had somehow transgressed. It is no doubt horribly revealing that Sophia Hayden never produced another significant building after the Exposition. One can only suppose that her rough handling and dismissal by Palmer fatally disillusioned her.

Another member of the coterie's self-confident women who circled around Bertha Palmer was John Root's sister-in-law and biographer Harriet Monroe. The Monroes were a notable Chicago family and from an early age Harriet was determined to pursue a literary career and fame. As she is quoted as saying, 'I cannot remember when to die without leaving some memorable record did not seem to me a calamity too terrible to be borne.'[75] Poetry was her favoured literary pursuit and by 1893 such was her reputation – or at least such were her Chicago connections – that she managed to get herself commissioned to write the official ode celebrating the opening of the Exposition. The ode is largely a celebration of what Monroe perceived as the enlightened and ennobling notion of American democracy that, characterized by tolerance and liberty, was its gift to the world delivered via the American Revolution and confirmed by the Union victory in the Civil War:

> …For now Democracy doth wake and rise/ From the sweet sloth of youth./By storms made strong, by many dreams made wise./ He clasps the hand of Truth… /The open book of knowledge in his hand. /Food to the starving, to the oppressed release. /And love to all he bears from land to land…[76]

This ode increased Monroe's fame but, unfortunately, not her fortune. However, she had a plan. When the *New York World* published her ode without her consent she sued and eventually was awarded $5,000 compensation. Ultimately she used this, combined with other funds, to set herself up in business as editor of a journal called *Poetry: a magazine of verse*. The magazine, promoting Ezra Pound and later T. S. Eliot, was a long-term success. Monroe, like so many of her Chicago female contemporaries, was determined, highly resourceful and shrewd. Consequently her view of the Exposition is particularly interesting – she was a Chicago insider with great depth of feeling for her brother-in-law. In her biography of Root she not only did her utmost to emphasize his creative contribution to the Exposition as built but she also took it upon herself to tell the world what the Exposition would have looked like if Root had not died so unexpectedly in January 1891. 'If he had lived,' wrote Monroe, 'and his ideas had prevailed, the Columbian Exposition would have been a city of Colour; a queen arrayed in robes not saintly, as for a bridal, but gorgeous, for a festival.'[77]

But Monroe's observations go far deeper than the mere issue of surface colour. They also have to do with the essence and meaning of the classical architecture of the White City.

For Monroe the Exposition was an architectural disappointment and – more to the point – she believed it would also have been a disappointment for Root:

> The fundamental point in Root's creed as an architect was sincerity; a building should frankly express its purpose and its materials. Thus it would have been impossible for him to design, as the chief buildings of the Fair, imitations in staff of marble palaces; these could not express their material; or to adopt a classic motif; this could not express the purpose of a modern American exposition.[78]

Essentially Monroe argued for the proto-functionalist approach of the Chicago School and anticipated the hostility of early-twentieth-century pioneering Modernists to historicist styles of architecture. Instead of the White City passively evoking European greatness and culture, the buildings would, if Root had lived and if he had been able to effectively control the Exposition architects, have been very different. They would more directly and more convincingly have shown America's 'affluence, its sumptuous conquering enthusiasm' and expressed the nation's 'militant democracy' that in 1893 was 'pausing after victory for a song of triumph before taking up its onward march.'[79] But, being a Chicago establishment figure, Monroe was ultimately measured in her criticism, perhaps fearful of offending the rich and powerful who had been behind the creation of the White City. Consequently, she merely assured her readers that the Exposition as built and as she believed Root had envisioned it were 'both worthy of honour'. But whereas one 'embodied in delicate beauty' had come into being and won 'the praises of the world', the other had only ever existed in the imagination and so 'vanished when a great man died.'[80]

Louis Sullivan was more radical. Over a quarter of a century after the Exposition he wrote that the classicism of the Exposition, facilitated and promoted by Burnham, was a 'virus' that, prophesied Sullivan, would 'damage' American architecture 'for half a century from its date, if not longer'. As he saw it,

> after a period of incubation in the architectural profession...
> there came a violent outbreak of the Classic and the Renaissance
> in the East, which slowly spread westwards, contaminating
> all that it touched... Thus Architecture died in the land of the
> free and the home of the brave – in a land declaring its fervid
> democracy, its inventiveness... its unique daring, enterprise and
> progress [and thus] did the virus of a culture, snobbish and alien
> to the land, perform its works of disintegration.[81]

Sullivan also implied that the fashion for Beaux-Arts classicism kindled by the Exposition was at least partly responsible for the troubles that, after 1894, beset his own 'functionalist' architectural practice. After 1893 Adler & Sullivan simply did not get enough commissions to survive the difficult years following the national financial panic of 1893, which – combined with increasing frictions between the two partners – led to their practice being dissolved in 1894. Sullivan struggled on to the end of the decade but after the superb, minimalist twelve-storey Carson, Pirie, Scott department store, constructed in Chicago in 1899, he retired from large-scale design projects.

In his autobiography Sullivan blamed the collapse of his architectural dreams on many factors, including the 'merchandiser' spirit of businessmen architects like Burnham, who in Sullivan's opinion, knew – as Oscar Wilde put it – the 'price of everything and the value of nothing',[82] and on speculators in general. As Sullivan explained, in apocalyptic manner, the financial 'hurricane' of 1893 'swept away the pyramid paper structure of speculation. Its downpour washed away fancied gains; its raindrops, loaded with lethal toxin, fell alike upon the unjust and the just, as in retribution, demanding as atonement in human sacrifices.' One of the sacrifices was, it seems, Adler & Sullivan, who numbered themselves, no doubt, among the 'just'.[83]

DEATH AND THE WHITE CITY

John Root's was not the only sudden death associated with the Exposition. Indeed the enterprise seems to have carried with it a cloud of doom that could, if one were so inclined, make one believe the whole business was cursed. Root's death, because of its timing and because it resulted in the thwarting of his architectural vision for the Exposition, was the most significant. But just as sudden – and far more horrible – were the deaths associated with H. H. Holmes, a Chicago resident in 1893.

The story has been told in admirable and perceptive detail, and placed brilliantly within the context of the Exposition, by Erik Larsen, who in 2003 published *The Devil in the White City*. Subtitled 'Murder, Magic and Madness at the Fair that Changed America', the book tells the stories, in parallel, of Burnham and the Exposition and of Hermann Webster Mudgett, a con man and serial killer. Mudgett became known as Dr H. H. Holmes and built a hotel, which he advertised as a 'World's Fair hotel', in Chicago in anticipation of the crowds that would flock to see the Exposition. But Holmes was not interested in making money from Exposition visitors, or not primarily. What he was interested in was death and terrible torture. As the cover-strap of Larson's book puts it, referring to Burnham and to Holmes, 'one man built a heaven on earth, another built Hell beside it'.

With skill Holmes managed to get a series of different builders to complete his diabolical hotel – located at 601–603 West Sixty-third Street and so big it was known locally as 'The Castle' – so that no one realized what was going on. The hotel contained a labyrinth of rooms with false and one-way doors to confuse and trap guests, bedrooms that were in fact gas chambers and one that was a crematorium. This was used to dispose of the bodies of some of his victims, while others he sold for medical and scientific study. Still other bodies, seemingly those of favoured victims, Holmes carefully reduced to skeletons that were then mounted for display. Nobody knows how many people Holmes killed during that period. Some estimates state over twenty, while others suggest over 200.

The financial crisis of 1893, which hit Chicago hard, drove Holmes into debt and forced him to abandon his 'Castle' and leave the city. He attempted a series of frauds during the following year and was eventually arrested in Boston in November 1894; subsequent investigations gradually revealed the dreadful story of the hotel. Holmes was tried, admitted the murder of twenty-seven people and was eventually hanged in Philadelphia in May 1896. Holmes never made an attempt to explain his actions, but after initially claiming innocence he fell back on the defence that he was possessed by the devil. As for the physical evidence of these horrors, victims' body parts and possessions were found scattered in and around the hotel but the building itself was gutted by fire in August 1895 with its last remnants not being removed until 1938.

While the scene for these terrible events was being set, other deaths continued to interfere with the Exposition. On 13 January 1893 Henry S. Codman – Olmsted's partner and one of the major creative forces behind the layout of the Exposition – died suddenly after an operation to remove his appendix. The obituary that appeared the following day in the *Chicago Tribune* noted Codman's key role in the Exposition and confirmed the by then accepted explanation of the manner in which the site had been chosen. Olmsted and Codman had, it states, 'tramped around sites proposed [for the Exposition] ending their investigation with a recommendation in favour of Jackson Park.' The obituary also confirms that Codman had become 'the active advisor of Chief of Construction Burnham in all matters pertaining to the upbuilding of the Fair', and that 'not one structure was created in the "White City" whose lines of architecture and whose location was not approved by Mr Codman.' Burnham in his biography stated that Codman was 'great in his knowledge and his instinct. He never failed… I loved the man.'[84] The loss, just over three months before the opening of the Exposition, of the man Burnham described as 'one of the strongest men the World's Fair has had',[85] must have been almost crippling.

Then, on 28 October 1893 – just two days before the Exposition closed – Carter Henry Harrison, the mayor of Chicago, who had done much to support the Exposition, was assassinated in his home by a deranged, disgruntled and clearly very disappointed office-seeker. His murder reflected the changing fortunes that overtook Chicago during the life of the Exposition. When it opened in the spring Chicago was full of hope with a belief in rising prosperity, but by the time the Exposition closed in late October Chicago was riven by 'economic crisis and labour upheaval'.[86] There was desperation and madness in the air and Harrison –the city's five-times mayor – became a focus of discontent and the troubled time's most prominent fatality.

Further deaths of leading figures in the Exposition followed fast. On 19 December 1895 Charles B. Atwood died in circumstances that were – and remain – utterly confusing. In 1894 Burnham had made Atwood a partner in D. H. Burnham and Co. in recognition of his outstanding contribution to the Exposition, his design skills in general and predilection for hard work. But over the following year or so – while Atwood was completing the Reliance Building – things started to go wrong. Atwood became ever more frail, mysterious and absent from the office. Burnham, baffled and infuriated, intervened for the good of the company and on 10 December 1895 ordered Atwood to 'retire' from the firm. He was sacked – and died nine days later from what, at the time, was described as 'overwork'. However, Burnham had another view, which he later shared with his biographer, Charles Moore. In his final years, according to Burnham, Atwood had become an opium addict – with results that were in the end fatal. Or, as Moore put it, Atwood finally 'succumbed to his only enemy – himself'.[87]

Donald Hoffmann states that Burnham's office diaries, now in the Burnham Library, record Atwood's fitful attendance at the office during 1895, the decision to force his 'retirement' and Burnham's statement to Moore that Atwood had 'got himself into difficulty and started to use dope. I did not know it, none of us did.'[88]

A few months after Atwood's death Richard Morris Hunt – the man almost single-handedly responsible for the classical-palace look of the White City – also died. But his death was not untimely or unexpected. He was sixty-eight years old and after the White City there was little left for him to achieve beyond giving the Fifth Avenue façade of the Metropolitan Museum of Art in New York a grandiose classical entrance. Clad in white stone and columns and conceived as a Roman triumphal arch, Hunt's creation is, in essence, a permanent memorial to the splendid but ephemeral plaster and Portland cement structures that he had done so much to conjure up in Chicago's fantastical White City.

THE END OF THE SHOW

The Exposition had opened on schedule on 1 May, a great achievement in itself given its size and complexity, although this success was tainted by the fact that it was significantly over budget. It covered 660 acres and contemporary accounts state that it cost £3.75 million to stage. In comparison the Paris *Exposition Universelle* of 1889 covered 173 acres and cost £1.3 million.[89] Success was anticipated even before the official opening. On 25 March a vast celebratory dinner was held in New York. The aim, if undeclared, was to confirm that the rivalry between the cities over the hosting of the Exposition had been healed and to make clear that all America wished Chicago well with the great, upcoming event. Burnham spoke at the dinner, heaping praise upon all involved with the making of the Exposition, including John Root – 'my beloved partner... who fell just when his busy hands had shaped a plan which we have followed ever since.'[90] So, for the history books, Burnham confirmed at this key event that Root was indeed the man who 'shaped' the plan – if not the architecture – of the Exposition.

When the Exposition closed on 30 October it was deemed a great success, despite the economic gloom of the moment, the recent murder of the city's mayor, and the consistent protest from an articulate body of African-Americans at the virtual exclusion of their fellows from the celebration.

One very important reason for its acknowledged success was the fact that the Exposition had been visited by 27.3 million people, suggesting that more than one in three Americans managed to see the show, each paying their much-needed 25 cent entrance fee. But more important, Americans at the time realized that history had been made. Charles Eliot Norton – an art historian and liberal activist who was regarded by many as the most 'cultivated' man in the United States – observed, as the Exposition closed, that it had been the 'United States on show, both in its real aspects and its potentialities'. And, as a symbol of 'all that the county was and could be', the success of the Exposition suggested to many that 'American civilization' had been weighed in the balance and – on the whole - not found wanting.[91]

There were other reasons to deem the Exposition a success, including the fact that it achieved a number of firsts that were, ultimately, to subtly but significantly change the American way of life. There was of course George Ferris's 80-metre-high wheel that established the 'big wheel' as a festive feature and proved so popular that it is credited with helping to balance the Exposition's books. The wheel did not open for business until June but it could – and often did – carry 2,160 people at a time, with tickets costing 50 cents. The Exposition also provided a showcase for the power of electricity; it was illuminated by electric lights, various electric gadgets were on display, including the travelator, and it introduced neon lights to the world.

Numerous branded consumer products that became household names were also premiered in Chicago, including Quaker Oats, Shredded Wheat and Fruit Gums, and the Exposition introduced the hamburger to an eager and susceptible market. More subtle and interesting was the manner in which the Exposition influenced ideas or inspired invention. The array of classical palaces gathered around the Great Basin – looking like buildings in fairyland – was perhaps the model for the Emerald City in L. Frank Baum's *The Wonderful Wizard of Oz*, which was published in 1900 in Chicago. These buildings, along with the Ferris wheel and Exposition fairground, could also have been a seminal influence on Walt Disney's fantasist theme parks. Certainly Disney's father Elias had been a construction worker at the White City, and it could have been familiar to his son – through family conversations – although virtually all the Exposition buildings had been destroyed by the time Walt was born in 1901 in Chicago. In such ways the Exposition – and its imagery and artefacts – informed and inspired the myths, legends and imagination of the nation.

The Reliance
Building

The Reliance Building enshrines several mysteries. It is generally accepted that John Wellborn Root started the project and designed the basement and ground floor just before his death in January 1891. But to what extent did he envisage the design and construction of the upper floors? Did Root establish the direction this pioneering project was to follow or was the upper portion of the building the virtually sole conception of Charles B. Atwood, the architect appointed by Daniel Burnham in July 1893 to complete the building and who oversaw construction between May 1894 and March 1895?[1] The mystery is, to a degree, intensified by the fact that Atwood died in December 1895, just as Root had died on the completion of his portion of the building. It's as if the Reliance wanted to take the secrets of its conception to the grave. And this conception is of significance because the Reliance Building – due to its means and materials of construction and the technology through which it functioned – is a building of the greatest importance in the history of architecture.

Chicago architect T. Gunny Harboe undertook the scholarly repair and restoration of the Reliance Building during the 1990s, after it had suffered decades of decay. He is the current great authority on the building and, as he puts it, 'no other building better presents Chicago's collective achievement in evolving the high-rise metal-framed skyscraper in its most definitive form', with 'every aspect of the building's design' reflecting 'its identity as a metal-framed structure, without reference to previous conventions of solid wall masonry construction', thus confirming its status as 'a pivotal building in the development of Modern architecture'.[2] Quite simply, the Reliance, with the minimalism of its slender steel-frame construction fully expressed, with ornament kept to a minimum and glass its dominant external material, is arguably the first fully realized skyscraper of the modern age.

Clues to the Reliance Building's origins and authorship can be found in contemporary documents and observations and are

The Reliance Building, on the corner of State and Washington streets, designed by Root, Burnham and Atwood. This photograph, taken in about 1905, confirms the striking height of this pioneering skyscraper when seen it its original setting.

The Woman's Temple, Chicago, designed by Burnham & Root, constructed in 1892. Its combination of historicist Gothic and Renaissance detail made it very unlike the sleek, minimalist functionalist and almost contemporary Reliance Building.

offered by 'archaeological' analysis of the building itself. There are, for example, many early drawings of the building surviving,[3] including some relating to initial work on the ground floor and basement. But there are no drawings from Root's lifetime showing the building as a whole. It is possible this set of drawings has been lost but it is also possible that they never existed; Root may not have produced a design for the building in its entirety before his death.

On the other hand, there are certain details and structural systems incorporated or implied in Root's ground floor and basement that are pursued in the upper floors of the tower and give the Reliance much novel character and distinction. For example, the simple Gothic – as opposed to classical – motifs used in such a memorable way in the upper storeys are also found on the ground floor, where the bronze ornament designed by Root and combined with granite for shopfronts has comparable Gothic detail.

Root also used Gothic in other late works like the masonry-clad Woman's Temple, Chicago (1892) designed for the Women's Christian Temperance Union, which combined Renaissance forms with late Gothic and incorporated turrets, tall pitched roofs and the twenty-one-storey Masonic Temple, also of 1892, which reflected Root's interest in French Gothic.

The preference for Gothic rather than classical as a historic style for skyscraper embellishment is hardly surprising since Gothic – with its vertical emphasis – is far more appropriate for skyscraper design than classical buildings, that in their composition tend to the horizontal. And the groundbreaking minimalism of the Reliance Building's construction – where the terracotta panels cladding the steel frame are as narrow as possible, allowing the windows to be as large as possible – is inaugurated by the treatment of the ground floor.

However, lest one gets too carried away with the notion that the Reliance was – in all its anticipatory novelty – the last gasp of Root's creative and inventive genius, it is important to note how different the building is to Root's other near-contemporary sky-scrapers. The Woman's Temple, Chicago, which was demolished in 1926, was thirteen storeys high with massive masonry walls and heavy historicist detailing, and the Masonic Temple Building, demolished in 1939, featured a somewhat bizarre pitched roof, complete with dormer windows and framed by huge triangular gables, reflecting an idiosyncratic historicism far removed from the Reliance Building. As was usual at the time, the bulky and ornamental masonry elevations of these two buildings were not only designed to conceal the slender character of their structural frames and disguise their radical structural nature but also – by the use of visually dominant horizontal features such as cornices and tiers of dormers – to reduce the appearance of height.

All things considered, it must be concluded that it is more likely than not that Atwood was the power behind the creation of the Reliance Building's upper part; although, of course, his famed exploits at the White City reveal him to be also a great master in the design and construction of classical architecture of more or less conventional scale and proportion, as does his design of 1892 for Marshall Field's department store on State Street, virtually opposite the Reliance (see introduction).

So for Atwood, as for Root, the bold and inventive novelty, minimalism and proto-modernism of the Reliance Building is hardly hinted at in his preceding works.

The puzzle over the relationship between Root and Atwood in the design of the Reliance is as old as the building itself. In January 1895, just as the building was nearing completion, the *American Architect and Building News* noted that it was 'the last building on which the late John W. Root left the stamp of his own individuality', admired the granite-clad and generously glazed ground-floor elevations and concluded that 'it scarcely seems possible that the upper stories as they stand were not materially changed from any design Mr. Root may have made for them.'[4]

This scepticism over Root's role in the design of the upper storeys is sustained by Harboe, who, after intense research and much highly informed scrutiny of the structure, 'assumes' that even if Root conceived the Reliance as a skyscraper 'Atwood redesigned the exterior cladding and chose the material, color, and detailing of the ornament.' As Harboe explains, 'when seen in the context of his other buildings around this time it is hard to imagine he would have abandoned the heavier appearance of a substantial masonry wall for the minimal spandrels and mullions of terra cotta' that distinguish the Reliance. However, such minimalism, characterized by slender mullions and the generous use of glass to create an early form of curtain wall, is – arguably – present in the rear elevation of Oriel Chambers and the Cook Street staircase, both in Liverpool. These are structures of the mid-1860s that Root could have seen and admired (see page 46), so the minimalism and materials that characterize the upper portions of the Reliance were almost certainly well known by Root. So his authorship, although unlikely, remains a possibility.

The position with the Gothic detailing is similar. Harboe notes that 'the specific sources of [Atwood's] Gothic inspiration are not known,'[5] leaving the distinct possibility that Atwood's use of Gothic was no more than the continuation and development of the Gothic theme established by Root at ground-floor level. Why Root introduced Gothic detail and Atwood retained and developed its use is another question. Probably it was to give the Reliance Building a sense of history. Its design being so radical, both architects no doubt believed it needed the pedigree of the past to give it cultural resonance. This would have been in line with the thinking of John Ruskin – a profound influence on Root – who argued in 1849 that it was the 'unnecessary' but culturally rich 'feature' added to basic construction that raised

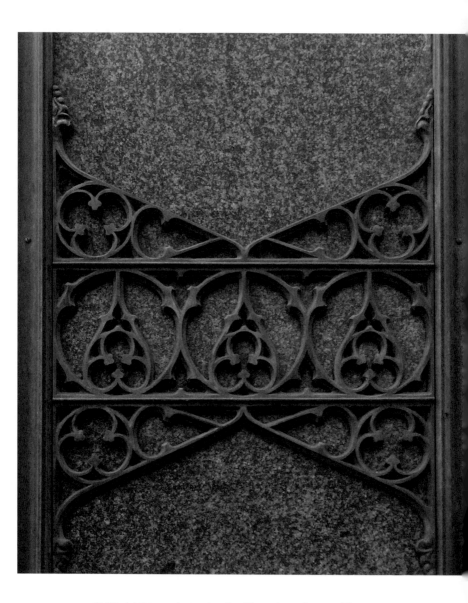

Gothic detail in metal set against Scottish granite on the ground floor
of the Reliance Building, as repaired and restored in the 1990s.

a merely utilitarian building to the status of poetic architecture. This, Ruskin believed, could be achieved by the addition of even a minimal detail of historic ornament – such as the Gothic quatrefoils moulded in the terracotta panels on the elevations of the Reliance (see image on page 188).[6]

An important clue to understanding the origin and evolution of the Reliance Building is offered by the character of its developer. William Ellery Hale was typical of the versatile entrepreneurs who rebuilt Chicago after the 1871 fire and who, within a few years, made it one of the most prosperous and architecturally most innovative cities in the world.[7]

Hale had been born in Bradford, Massachusetts in 1836 and, having started his business career as a clerk in a dry-goods store in Hartford, joined the Rock River Paper Company, based in Wisconsin. He was then aged twenty-one and this marked the start of his rapid rise. In 1862 he moved to Chicago to manage the firm's burgeoning business interests in the city and by the late 1860s he had been made a partner. He now seems to have started to turn the firm into something of a family business by bringing in his brother George W. Hale. As the same time he started to diversify his business interests by entering the Chicago building world as an investor and developer. His first building enterprise, in partnership with Lucius G. Fisher, was completed in 1867 on the southeast corner of State and Washington Streets. By chance this building stood opposite the site of the future Reliance Building. Named the Hale Building, it was a five-storey commercial building of conventional masonry, and was lost in the fire of 1871.

As with many of his contemporaries, the Chicago fire was the making of Hale because it created so many opportunities in the construction business. Initially Hale profited not by acting as a builder or developer but by providing new technology for the new generation of Chicago high-rise commercial architecture. Presumably he had observed the success of the Otis Elevator

Company, which must have had more work than it could handle making tall buildings in Chicago comfortable to inhabit. In 1872 William and George Hale founded W. E. Hale Company (later becoming the Hale Elevator Company) with the aim not just of matching the Otis firm in the design and construction of steam-powered hydraulic safety elevators but of outclassing it. In this Hale proved successful and it was in this enterprise that, according to the *Chicago Tribune*, he 'made much of his fortune'.[8]

Hale's success in the elevator business is one of the clues to the progressive nature of the Reliance Building. Its developer not only embraced the potential of modern technology, which no doubt was one of the foundations of his success in the paper manufacturing industry, but – specifically – the technology of high-rise buildings. If you are a developer who starts an elevator company then, naturally, you are going to build tall.

While Hale was consolidating his elevator business he returned to property speculation, often working in collaboration with Owen and Arthur Aldis, and in December 1882 bought, from his former business partner Lucius G. Fisher, an existing five-storey masonry-built bank building on the southwest corner of Washington and State Streets. This was the site on which the Reliance Building was to be constructed.

During this time, in the early 1880s, Hale forged his professional relationship with Burnham & Root, perhaps acting on the recommendation of Owen Aldis. Early shared projects included the nine-storey, steel-framed Rialto Building of 1886 on La Sale Street (demolished 1940) and the Midland Hotel in Kansas City (see page 203). Also, in what seems to have been his usual working method, Root nurtured Hale as a private client; he designed a house for him at 4545 Drexel Boulevard. This was a gamble because, of course, relations between the architect and client could have become very difficult if the family home failed. But, as was usually the case with Root, the gamble paid off and the house provided Hale with a happy home until his death in November 1898.

An obituary in the *Chicago Tribune* recorded that after successfully establishing his elevator company Hale had been 'engaged largely in building and promoting the "sky-scrapers" of this city'.[9] At the time of Hale's death he was best known – in the architectural world at least – for the Reliance Building. This building – in its ambitious scale, bold application of current technology and in its sleek and progressive appearance – was seen as something of a portrait of the man. What seems clear is that Hale's role in the creation of the Reliance was more than being merely the money-man. Indeed Hale was responsible for the most unusual, technologically based, aspects of the Reliance. Having acquired the site on which it was to be built Hale was confronted by several intriguing challenges. The existing masonry bank building on the corner site had an eighty-four-foot frontage to Washington – which was generous enough – but it was wrapped around by an L-shaped building, which meant that Hale's site had no alley or access to its rear or side. Clearly, servicing any building on the site would be difficult and if a skyscraper were built then, obviously, all difficulties would be magnified because the taller the building the more intense the servicing requirements.

The obvious way to make his constrained corner site viable for high-rise development was for Hale to acquire the adjoining land. But this he could not do. According to the *Chicago Inter Ocean* newspaper of 7 July 1889, the L-shaped property framing Hale's site was 'too strongly held… by Levi Z. Leiter… to give any hope of a future consolidation'.[10] So the neighbouring land and buildings were not for sale, which meant that if Hale wanted to develop his marooned corner site he had to work within its constraints. But, in the early 1880s, the biggest constraint on development was not the awkward site but the fact that the tenants of the existing five-storey building held leases to May 1894. No doubt in consultation with Burnham & Root, Hale brooded on this problem for some time and then in 1889 decided to act. The decision, as outlined on pages ooo-o, was extraordinary. By this time he had secured vacant possession of the ground floor and basement and decided that this gave him enough space to work around the existing tenants on the upper floors. They remained in place, conducting business as usual, while the upper portion of the existing building was supported on jackscrews and the ground-floor, basement and foundations were demolished and rebuilt to form a visually and technically suitable lower portion of a skyscraper.

This lower portion, constructed during 1890, was without question Root's design – executed during the last year of his life – and is most rewarding to study in some detail because it confirms that certain key elements that distinguish the upper storeys of the Reliance – constructed after May 1894 when the departure of the tenants meant the remains of the existing building could be demolished – have their origins in Root's ground floor design.

Analysis of the existing ground floor and basement, together with design and construction drawings of 1890, make Root's intentions pretty clear. There is, of course, the Gothic detailing in the bronze window surrounds (and on the granite piers) that seems to confirm that the inclusion of the same detailing above is something Atwood inherited from Root. But more significant is the general aesthetic handling of the ground floor. Glass dominates – with the building's steel structural frame clad in slivers of polished Scottish granite and bronze Gothic-style trim. Of course, large windows were nothing new in 1890s Chicago. One of the key features of Chicago School architecture (see page 81) was large and wide tripartite windows, often set in slight projections or oriels. But on the ground floor of the Reliance the handling of the wide windows and the sliver-like cladding over the structural frame is most novel and very different in feel from Root's near-contemporary skyscrapers. In these, as was typical of the time, the skeletal steel frame is concealed, even denied, by a facing of bulky and ornamented masonry or terracotta cladding. At the Reliance – in striking contrast to the Monadnock and the Masonic Temple Building – the sense of transparency is combined with a smoothness of wall plane, achieved by the use of panes of glass up 21 feet 6 inches high and 9 feet 6 inches wide divided only by slender, bronze mullions. On the ground floor of the Reliance, as on the later elevations above, the minimal nature of the steel frame and the visual potential offered by large sheets of glass is celebrated and defines the aesthetic of the building. It's now hard to be sure, but it seems possible that Root had set the pattern for maximum glazing and relatively minimalist cladding that Atwood so brilliantly developed and exploited.

The large amount of glass incorporated within the elevations of the Reliance is only one aspect of the general strategy to open the interior to as much natural light and ventilation as possible. This strategy is evident in the building's structural system, in its plan – as determined initially by Root – and in numerous details also introduced by Root. The structural system, established by Root in the lower portion of the Reliance and utilized and refined by Atwood for the upper portion, was already well established in Chicago by 1890: the structural frame was made of riveted-steel members stiffened with wind bracing, and fire-proofing was achieved by cladding the steel structural frame with incombustible materials. This type of steel frame system not only created a strong and relatively fire-proof structure but also – because loads were carried on columns and not walls – meant that elevations could have large areas of glass set between the steel columns, allowing daylight to flood inside, and the interior could be largely open and easily adaptable since internal partitions were either absent or non-structural and easily moved.

The plan of the Reliance, at ground-floor level, incorporates a narrow light well or 'open area' on Washington Street, 'prismatic lights' or glass panels in the pavement around the perimeter of

the building and light boxes below shop windows, all intended to bring natural light into the basement. In addition, white glazed tiles are used to clad basement light wells to make the most of the light that does enter. There is also a 'court' or light well at the southwest corner. This was probably planned by Root because it extended down to ground-floor level until 1901, when its lower portion was turned into a first-floor library. This light well was necessary because of the peculiar nature of the site. With buildings in different ownership abutting on the south and west sides, the well was to allow daylight and air to enter the Reliance even if high buildings were eventually constructed on the adjoining sites.

One of the most striking external architectural expressions of the quest for light is the projecting glazed bays. These might, in their form if not their details, also be Root's idea. Certainly they have echoes in earlier Root buildings; they also perhaps show the influence of Oriel Chambers Liverpool and, with their large dimensions, they are dominant features of the upper floors of the Reliance, increasing both the square footage of the floor plan and the amount of light that penetrates into the building. Harboe

An oriel form 'Chicago Window' on the Reliance Building, formed with a large sheet of fixed plate glass flanked by narrow sashes. Note also the Gothic detail on the pale-coloured terracotta cladding.

suggests that the way the bays are 'handled as an integral part of the façade... begs the question of Root's role', and concludes that they must, initially, have been Root's idea. In support of this claim Harboe refers to the opinion of the eminent architectural historian Professor William H. Jordy, who observed that the bays of the Reliance Building, 'like the bays of [Root's] Monadnock', are not 'addenda to the wall plane' but 'cling to the core shape of the building, as an undulant perimeter', suggesting 'that Root must have been responsible for this aspect of the design'.[11]

The determination to give the Reliance a light and airy interior was probably not exclusively Root's. Not only were natural lighting and ventilation key aspects of functionalist Chicago School architecture but – more specifically – a well-lit interior seems to have been part of the brief evolved by Hale. Significantly, when the Reliance was finally completed and officially opened on 15 March 1895, the *Chicago Tribune* particularly admired the light and airy interior and recorded that 'the necessity of providing ample light in each office was pointed out to the architects by Mr. Hale, and this was fully recognized by them in the making of the design'.[12] So it was Hale, as much as any other single person, who was responsible for the Reliance Building's most immediately striking feature – its generously glazed elevations with minimal areas of wall.

Unpicking the building history of the ground floor can be tricky and great caution is necessary if one attempts to demonstrate that the seeds of much of Atwood's later design lie embedded in Root's initial work. For example, the main ground-floor entrance was not constructed until 1895. This is disconcerting if one wants to present the ground floor and basement as exclusively Root's work. But there is another twist. Harboe has discovered that surviving drawings make it clear that the entrance, although constructed under Atwood's control, was in fact built to Root's design. So clearly at least one key element of Root's ground floor

OVERLEAF
The ground floor of the Reliance Building in *c.* 1895 when it served as the silk department for the Carson, Pirie, Scott & Company store.

The ground floor of the Reliance now serves as a restaurant. Note that the piers, with cores of steel, have lost their ornamental cladding and capitals.

was executed when Atwood was architect. Are there others? The attractive mezzanine is another contested area. A mezzanine does make an appearance in early drawings, where it is called an entresol, but according to Harboe's analysis it was not built; the existing mezzanine dates only from the 1920s. In addition the ground floor of the Reliance has changed much during the first hundred years of its life. Early photographs show the steel internal column clad with an octagonal shaft and sporting richly detailed capitals of Romanesque/Corinthian type. They are now very plain, almost brusquely so. The Reliance is indeed a complex building to fathom. The first tenant of the rebuilt ground floor and basement had a number of specific physical requirements that also make the building's lower two floors hard to understand, even deceptive.

The tenant initially envisaged for the retail space in the Reliance – while the basement and ground floor were under construction in 1890 – was Chas. Gossage and Company, retailers in dry goods. It already occupied the surrounding L-shaped building owned by Leiter, but evidently believed its retail business would prosper if it also occupied the commercially attractive new corner building with its light and attractive interior. Consequently, and perhaps confusingly, the basement and ground floor of the Reliance were designed with large openings connecting to Leiter's neighbouring L-shaped building.

Soon after Gossage and Co. signed a lease with Hale it was bought out by trendsetting department store Carson, Pirie, Scott & Co., who became the tenant, occupying the Reliance Building in 1891. By 1900 the department store was employing around 1,000 staff on this corner site at State and Washington Streets and in 1904 it decamped to a store at State and Madison Streets that had been designed in 1899 for another store by Louis Sullivan and was one of his last significant works.

Whether Root or Atwood was the essential force behind the

design of the Reliance Building tower, it was, as Harboe points out, with its 'taut skin of large plate glass windows and thin spandrels of white glazed terracotta… a strong departure from every other building that had come before it', because 'no previous building had exterior walls that had been reduced to such minimal expression'.[13] When officially opened on 15 March 1895, the Reliance was a breathtaking achievement that anticipated by fifty years Modern Movement towers with their 'curtain walls' of glass, such as the ninety-four-metre-high Lever House of 1950–52 by Gordon Bunshaft of SOM and the 157-metre-high Seagram Building of 1955–58 by Mies van der Rohe, both on Park Avenue, New York. The scale of the achievement was generally recognized at the time. The *Chicago Evening Journal* of 15 March 1895 declared the Reliance 'as near perfect as modern science and skill can devise',[14] while *The Economist* of 16 March 1895 called it 'the most elegant [building] yet erected in Chicago for business purposes'.[15]

Given the pioneering importance of the Reliance Building, and its reasonable claim to represent the origin of the modernist commercial tower block, it is fascinating to examine its upper portion in some detail, to see how it was engineered, how fireproofed and serviced and how it was made habitable and fit for its very specific purpose.

STRUCTURE

The Reliance was constructed during a period of rapid technological innovation when steel-framed high-rise buildings were becoming easier and quicker to construct, with less material used yet their strength increased. A key element was the introduction of rivets rather than bolts to fix steel components together. Rivets were inserted hot, and because they shrank as they cooled, they pulled the components together, making the frame more rigid so that loads were transferred more efficiently. This gave the structure added strength.

Photographs of the Reliance Building under construction show that its steel frame was surrounded by a network of scaffolding; but even so, the novel high-level steel and hot rivet construction process must have been daunting. Hale, no doubt acting with Burnham's advice, employed the George A. Fuller Company to construct the Reliance.[16]

This is most significant. George Fuller was an East Coast architect trained at the Massachusetts Institute of Technology, who had worked for architects Peabody & Stearns in New York – he was made head of their New York office in 1876. In about 1881 Fuller moved to Chicago, where in 1882 he started work as a general contractor, undertaking all aspects of construction apart from design. He prospered during the 1880s and started to specialize in steel-framed high-rise construction – notably working for Holabird & Roche on the thirteen-storey Tacoma Building (completed 1889 and demolished 1929), during which rivets were used on a large scale for the first time. So by 1890 Fuller's company was the expert in Chicago – indeed in the world – for high-rise steel-framed construction. Hale and Burnham could not have made a better choice of contractor.

The speed of the change in building technology in early-1890s Chicago is revealed by the fact that the basement and ground floor of the Reliance utilize a significantly different structural system to the only slightly later upper floors. Root, as has been made clear (see page 87), had significant engineering know-how and a liking for bold and inventive experimentation – particularly when it came to evolving foundations adequate to supporting Chicago's first generation of skyscrapers. But credit for the innovatory structure of the Reliance must, at least in part, be given to

Edward C. Shankland, Burnham & Root's office engineer, who was responsible for both phases of the building and for the use of relatively light but strong lattice steel girders. The theory was that 'an accumulation of many small rigid elements could provide the same stiffness as a few large planes of trusses'. This realization, and the subsequent adoption of the lattice girder, was, according to Thomas Leslie, 'one of the key innovations in tall building construction to emerge from Chicago in the 1890s.'[17]

The footings of the Reliance were constructed in the grillage manner already established by Root, with railroad rails set perpendicular to each other in a succession of layers and then encased in concrete, but it was probably Shankland who chose to use steel columns – H-shaped in plan – for the first phase of the Reliance. These columns are composed of lengths of Z-profile steel plates and flat steel plates riveted together to create the H-shaped column. A trifle confusingly, this type of column is usually referred to as a Z-bar column.[18]

But when the building campaign was resumed in 1894, Shankland chose to use a very different type of column, which had only recently come into use. Called the Gray column, it was also formed from steel sections, riveted together to give a diamond-pattern plan. The hollow Gray columns had great strength, with this strength enhanced by design; they were erected in two-storey sections and alternate columns were linked on every other floor to 'stiffen' the structure. The hollow nature of the columns has another great advantage beyond strength; they could also be used to contain water

Steel plates riveted together to create a form of Z-bar column, revealed in the Reliance during repairs in the 1990s.

and gas pipes that, in consequence, could be fully integrated with the structure. This was almost certainly the reason for the change of column system because the function envisioned for the Reliance – with numerous tenants, many requiring the abundant supply of fresh water and the disposal of much foul water – meant that services and pipe runs were a major issue. However, although the Gray column system seemed the ideal solution it did demand a high level of planning and co-ordination between services and construction. Obviously once the column system had been erected it would be very awkward to change, or add to, the pipe runs.

The wind bracing employed in the upper portion of the Reliance is also effectively integrated within the broad design of the building and is made compatible with the broad aim of achieving maximum transparency. Wind bracing strengthens a building against lateral movement while its floor and column system carries vertical loads. Charles Jenkins, in an article on the Reliance entitled 'The White Enameled Building' published in *Architectural Record* in March 1895, singled out the wind bracing for detailed description: '...instead of tension rods, which have been used heretofore [for wind bracing], it was determined to put plate girders twenty four inches deep at each floor between the outside columns, thus binding the columns together and transferring the wind strain from story to story on the table-leg principle.'[19] What this meant was that the bracing was located within the floor structure so as not to reduce or interrupt the generous area of glazing.

It is however important to remember that, while the Reliance's braced steel frame had a 'liberating' effect on the building's 'skin', freeing it from the need to be load-bearing and allowing it to be 90 per cent glazed,[20] the nature of its corner site meant that two of its four perimeter walls were in fact solid masonry-construction party walls.

FIRE PROTECTION AND TERRACOTTA

Fire protection was a key concern. The main strategy was to make the primary structure as fire-proof as possible. The floors, made of clay tiles springing from twelve-inch-deep steel beams, were covered with 3½ inches of cinder fill, which protected the steel beam. Within the fill were placed timber sleepers into which floorboards were fixed. In corridors, plaster and marble chip terrazzo and/or mosaic were laid on top of the cinder fill. On the ground floor, where there were larger areas of terrazzo and mosaic floor, a stronger masonry-arched structure was used to carry the greater load. The portions of the steel frame that were not protected by the cinder fill (notably the columns) were encased by porous clay or terracotta tile fire-proofing. This was the usual method at the time. The south and west ends of the building, formed by the large masonry walls that acted as fire separation from neighbouring buildings.

Related to fire protection was the decision to clad the building with incombustible terracotta panels. Terracotta cladding had, of course, been used before, but this was the first time a skyscraper was clad entirely with terracotta rather than a mix of terracotta, stone and brick. Charles Jenkins predicted in 1895, with prophetic insight, that this dominant use of 'enameled' terracotta would 'make this building stand out as a conspicuous mark in the history of architecture in America.'[21] The terracotta was glazed – or 'enameled' – largely in an attempt to render it a self-cleaning material. As *The Economist* observed in 1894, the elevation would 'be washed by every rainstorm and may if necessary be scrubbed like a dinner plate.'[22] But this simple idea did not quite work in practice, with oily soot generally proving impervious to rain. Also, the decision was taken – whether by Root, Burnham, Atwood or Hale – to colour the terracotta white so, when glazed and clean, it would sparkle in the sunlight. It is generally observed that this decision – surprising in the context of the Chicago of the time, when darker stone colours were generally favoured for exteriors – was inspired by the success of the 1893 White City.[23] The simplicity – almost neutrality – of the pristine white elevation now seems astonishing. 1890s Chicago was a vividly coloured world and such restraint must have been shocking – even after the success of the White City. Jenkins' view is interesting, and perhaps typical of more informed and thoughtful critics. He congratulated 'the architect' for his 'boldness' in breaking with the usual palette of 'dull greys, browns and reds' but hoped that the 'next enamelled building may more extensively introduce color'.[24] The quantity and quality of terracotta required was a challenge, but the material supplied by Northwestern Terra Cotta Co. was seemingly deemed acceptable. Fortunately it has proved durable and, as Gunny Harboe – who was involved with the 1990s repair of the Reliance – confirms, it has been possible to return the original terracotta to its 'original glistening beauty'.[25]

GLASS AND THE 'CHICAGO WINDOW'

Glass – as we have seen – played a crucial role, along with the glazed white terracotta, in giving the building's exterior visual punch and creating an air of novelty. Essentially, above the double-height ground floor, there are thirteen continuous bands of windows that wrap around the building to create the two elevations that are 90 per cent glass, with each band separated by far narrower bands of white terracotta, enlivened with simple Gothic detail. Each band of windows is articulated by bays, one in the centre of the building's shorter elevation, two in its longer. The bays, typical 'Chicago windows', comprise large panes of polished plate-glass (some panes as large as 10 feet 8 inches by 7 feet 7

inches) fixed in cast-iron frames and flanked by narrow timber-made sashes that form the sloping sides of the bays. The detailing of the timber sashes is also minimal, to maximize daylight entering the building. Both timber and iron window details were originally painted black, in dramatic contrast with the white terracotta.

The cast-iron frames that help to hold the glass in place also act as part of the support for the narrow terracotta mullions that separate the sheets of glass. The design of the mullions is most thoughtful. None are wide, and when extra support is required the narrow mullions are merely doubled rather than being widened. The consequence is that the soaring height of the building is emphasized. This itself was a new departure at a time when it had become usual to visually reduce a tower's lofty appearance.

A corner detail at the Reliance, showing the pale-coloured glazed terracotta cladding blocks sparkling in reflected sunlight.

Metal – notably cast iron and bronze – also plays a key role in the detailing of the interior of the Reliance. Most striking is the ornamental cast-iron staircase that makes a dramatic appearance at ground-floor level, in the entrance lobby. Although no doubt intended by Root, the design and even precise location of the staircase changed – presumably under Atwood's influence – with an early floor plan showing the staircase marked 'approved April 7 1894'. But even this does not represent the final design; it shows the staircase with some treads in the form of semicircular winders rather than with rectangular landings as built.[26] As Gunny Harboe has pointed out, except for the quatrefoil design for staircase railings, all the cast-iron components used are standard pieces from the Winslow Brothers Company. Newels and risers like those on the staircase were used in Root's Woman's Temple. This does seem to confirm that the initial design for the staircase was indeed Root's.

The iron of the staircase was given a distinctive and attractive blue-black colour and a tough durable finish by means of the 'Bower–Barff Process' that enjoyed a vogue in the last decades of the nineteenth century. The process, invented and perfected in England in the late 1870s by Frederick C. Barff and George Bower, involved heating iron or steel to around 1,000°C and then dousing with superheated steam to produce a layer of iron oxide that made the metal rust-resistant. The iron oxide layer could be increased in thickness, and durability by repeating the process. The finish became popular for aesthetic as well as practical reasons, with Bower–Barff-finished iron often used in combination with bronze or copper. The Bower–Barff iron used in the Reliance was supplied by the Orr and Lockett Hardware Company.

But the Bower–Barff process was soon found to be largely ineffective for external ironwork so, as at the Reliance, was used

almost exclusively for interior details. Harboe's analysis suggests that, in all likelihood, 'all the interior metalwork in the Reliance Building was treated with the Bower–Barff process', so the grammar of materials is pretty straightforward. Bronze for external details such as shopfronts, with painted cast iron for window frames and Bower–Barff-finished cast iron for interior details. Harboe also points out that Bower–Barff metal was used in the Rookery and the Midland Hotel in Kansas City, which suggests that Root was involved in the decision to introduce it in the staircase and for internal details in the Reliance.[27] Other Bower–Barff details in the entrance lobby include a mailbox and light fittings. That iron treated by the Bower–Barff process can stand the test of time – at least when used internally – is confirmed by the fact that much of the original ironwork survives – in good condition – on the doors of the little-altered upper floors of the Reliance Building.

ENTRANCE LOBBY AND ELEVATORS

The entrance lobby has changed over the decades as the use of the building has changed, although much of its original character was revealed and in part restored during the major and exemplary repairs of the 1990s. Originally it was a small space, but elaborate in design, with a terrazzo and mosaic floor, wall clad with a mix of multicoloured marbles and chandeliers, supplied by the Chicago Edison Company, with fittings supplied by the Garden City Chandelier Company.[28] One key feature, originally, was the cast-iron staircase; another were the cast-iron grilles of the elevator compartment. They were given a Bower–Barff finish and were described at the time as 'German Gothic in design'[29] – and they survive on a number of the upper floors.

The elevators were, of course, one of the keys to the success

The ground floor entrance corridor in the Reliance showing the elegantly and ornamentally detailed elevator grille and staircase of metal with a muted 'Bower-Barff' finish and a faint feel of the Gothic. Much was restored in the 1990s.

of a building that, in multi- and mixed commercial use, required quick, comfortable and safe communication between its many levels. Given Hale's expertise in the elevator business, tenants of the building must have expected the best of current elevator technology. If so, they were not disappointed. As the *Chicago Tribune* observed at the time of the building's opening:

> For the equipment of his own building, Mr. Hale, appreciating the value of having as nearly perfect an elevator service as possible, desired to obtain better elevators than had ever been built. This was not an easy task to accomplish because the Hale elevator already had a world-wide reputation for safety and efficiency.

The elevators, constructed by the Winslow Brothers Elevator Company (iron founders who had diversified and in 1890 bought out Hale's elevator company), were hydraulic-powered and incorporated a number of innovations. The *Chicago Tribune* noted these, and the generally significant contribution the elevators made to the beauty of the building as well as to its efficient operation: 'The four passenger elevators located close to the main entrance should be seen in order to be appreciated, [their] beautiful design… executed in iron in the inimitable way peculiar to The Winslow Bros. Co.' This is a reference to the Bower–Barff finish. But the *Tribune*'s critic was 'particularly attracted… by the construction of the safety devices.' The elevators were provided not only with:

> a safety governor, through the action of which they would be brought to a perfect stop in case of the breaking of the lifting cables, or of any part of the lifting mechanism, but also with a simple, very ingenious safety friction grips brake, through which the operator may, by the pressure of his foot… release the powerful friction brakes and immediately bring the car to a stop.[30]

The additional mechanical systems installed in the Reliance Building were also, in many cases, innovatory. There was a telephone exchange serving the tenants and the building was wired for electricity as well as being supplied with gas piping. The sanitary services, termed the 'Durham system', were also as efficient and elegant as possible. The *Chicago Evening Journal* of 5 March 1895 announced that 'all vertical risers, wastes, vent and downspouts are of wrought iron pipe, coated inside and outside while hot with coal tar varnish', and 'all pipes for carrying sewage in the ground under the building are of light cast iron' also coated with coal tar varnish.[31] Water closets were finished to a high standard. They were clad with white Italian marble on all walls and ceilings and had terrazzo floors to match those in the corridors they adjoined. There was one capacious W.C. for men and one for women located on the seventh floor (sixth floor UK style), as well as at least one smaller W.C. (some with urinals only) on each floor. At lower levels these were located off the landing on the staircase, and at upper levels in a small room just to the west of the main staircase. The heating system was the most advanced available in 1895, with hot water radiators located around the perimeter of the building, generally under each large window. There were large boilers in the basement on the west side of the building, with their main exhaust stack located just to the west of the elevator shaft. Ventilation was dependent primarily on convection for exhaust (aided by attic fans) and using open windows for supply. Since gas was not used for lighting, the need for the thorough extraction of noxious and corrosive waste fumes was not as urgent as it had been before the introduction of electric light.

The accommodation in the Reliance Building was let furnished, to a high standard, to a wide variety and large number of commercial tenants. This was not unprecedented in new developments in Chicago at the time, but in the Reliance the practice assumed its ultimate contemporary expression and was noted. The *Chicago Tribune*, in its obituary of William Hale, published on 17 November 1898, observed that he was 'probably best known as the owner of the Reliance Building', and noted that he 'evolved the idea of furnishing the offices in this building… and renting them in this way.' This was, according to the newspaper, 'a novel method' that 'proved successful'.[32]

Hale's vision, as executed by Atwood, was to divide the Reliance's thirteen upper floors (fourteen if the floor immediately below the projecting 'cornice' is included) into several 'zones', each configured and serviced slightly differently to attract different types of tenants. Thomas Leslie suggests that this preference for many tenants as opposed to a few was not Hale's original intention but his pragmatic response to the mid-1890s downturn in Chicago's economy.[33]

The *Chicago Tribune* of 16 March 1895 explains how Hale's revised system worked:

> The first floor [in UK terminology the ground floor] of the Reliance Building is occupied by Carson, Pirie, Scott & Co. The second [first] is reserved for a large retail business. The third [second], fourth [third], fifth [fourth], and sixth [fifth] are divided into sales rooms for tailors, milliners, dressmakers, jewellers, and others. The seventh, eighth, tenth, eleventh, twelfth, and thirteenth floors [sixth to seventh and ninth to twelfth floor] are devoted to the purposes of physicians, dentists, and others desiring large suites of offices. The ninth [eighth] and the fourteenth [thirteenth] floors are fitted especially for physicians and surgeons who desire office accommodations during only a few hours of each day.

This 'timeshare' approach to office rental was novel at the time, and made additionally attractive because the spaces on the ninth and fourteenth floors were well furnished, not just with sinks and hot and cold running water but with mahogany tables and chairs, and 'rich Wilton and Oriental rugs, which at once depart style and comfort to the rooms.' Other attractions were the flexibility and economy of the terms offered: 'The offices are rented at very low monthly rates for as many hours per day as the physician may desire. The rental includes use of room, furniture, light, heat, power, etc. – which averages $10 per month for use of an office one hour daily.' This, as the *Chicago Tribune* pointed out, made it possible for out-of-town physicians 'to enjoy the advantages of an office in the very heart of the city'.[34]

Gunny Harboe notes that 'the basic concept of dividing the building into zones must have been in place early in 1894' because 'the framing plans that were approved on March 2 1894 show the different stair openings to accommodate the transfer stair allowing for a more open plan on the lower floors.'[35]

Consequently the system of corridors and their treatment was of some architectural consequence in the Reliance. They had to be stylish as well as robust because they would be seen by all using the building and in much use, and it was desirable that they should, as far as possible, allow natural light to penetrate to the building's heart. The visually dominant features of the corridor at each level were the ornamental staircase and open grillage of the elevator shaft. White Carrara marble was used to clad the lower portion of the corridor walls and elevator lobbies, and for the treads of the stairs. The upper parts of the corridors were plastered and painted light pink[36] and floors were of terrazzo with marble mosaic borders. The partitions forming the walls of the corridors were made of varnished mahogany and generously glazed to allow daylight to pass through the offices around the perimeter of the building and into the corridor. To ensure privacy

for office users, obscured glass – known as 'Florentine glass' – was generally fitted in the partitions. From the practical point of view the partitions forming the different spaces had to be as lightweight as possible, and certainly not part of the building's main structure, so they could be easily adapted to accommodate changing uses or reflect the changing requirements of tenants.

A plan of a typical upper floor of the Reliance Building has been drawn by Thomas Leslie and published in his book *Chicago Skyscrapers 1871–1934*.[37] The plan is curiously complex because the numerous separate small offices, workshops or consulting rooms all had to be entered individually, with the result that no fewer than three short corridors, or entrance lobbies, had to be added to the main corridor. The result is that a significant proportion of the floor area is occupied by access space. If the floor had been fitted up for occupation by one tenant and was open-plan there would have been more lettable space. This reveals the economic consequence of Hale's decision, based on his feel for the mid-1890s commercial property market in central Chicago, to tailor the building for many diverse small businesses rather than a few affluent tenants.

White marble, pink-painted plaster walls, coloured marble chip terrazzo and mosaic floor, varnished mahogany, Bower–Barff cast iron with its dulled and burnished finish, and all illuminated with sparkling electric lights and chandeliers – the public parts of the Reliance Building interior must have been visually stunning. Again, this sense of opulence – of beauty – must have been a crucial aspect of Hale's business plan for the building.

The exterior of the Reliance was equally remarkable, and not quite like anything that had been built before. Slightly earlier Chicago skyscrapers had expressed in their design the sense of hierarchy inherited from traditional design, in which certain floors might be given emphasis, or windows grouped or placed within ornamental but functionally irrelevant arcades, to create compositions with a familiar visual harmony and reference to the past. The Rookery is a typical example. But the Reliance Building is stunningly different, and this again makes it one of the prime models for the coming age of skyscrapers, in which design was increasingly driven by the determination to honestly express function and the materials and means of construction, and make the consequences of these the prime ornament of the building rather than applied history-inspired details. Emblematic is the building's crowning cornice. Earlier skyscrapers were invariably crowned by generous cornices of more or less historic design. But the Reliance was given a terracotta cornice – little more than a horizontal slab – that derived its form from being part of the roof framing. The frieze below the cornice was implied by ornamented terracotta panels incorporating small windows or ventilation openings.

So significant is the Reliance's departure from convention that it's worth summarizing its extraordinary external characteristics. There is the large extent of the glass, of course, that gave the building a sense of transparency; the white terracotta, the minimal bronze and cast-iron detailing and the fact that no attempt had been made through design to superficially disguise the height of the building. The transparency that is now so much admired, and which gave Hale the daylight he desired, might also have given him a problem. It's possible that many at the time equated transparency, or at least wraparound glazing, with fragility. If so this could well have troubled Hale, causing him to fear that he might have difficulty finding tenants. Perhaps significantly, 1890 drawings of the building (now in the Art Institute of Chicago) refer to it simply as 'Building for W. E. Hale', but by 1894 it's called the Reliance Building. The reason for the change of name is not known, but clearly 'Reliance' suggests reassuring solidity and so could account for Hale's choice of name for his new building.

Also startling at the time the Reliance was completed was the fact that there was no attempt to disguise the repetitive nature of the plan. The external elevations of each floor are identical (apart from the first floor – US second floor – having slightly taller windows) because each floor was in generally similar use with generally similar requirements. As Harboe puts it, 'the grid-like, glass filled exterior not only expressed the building's structure, but also reflected the functional need for maximum light for the doctors, dentists, jewellers, and clothiers' who initially occupied the building.'[38] A couple of years after the completion of the Reliance Building the Chicago architect Louis Sullivan argued, when attempting to define the timeless character of well-designed architecture, that 'form ever follows function'. He could well have been thinking about the Reliance when he wrote this memorable phrase. Sullivan later explained that it was inspired by the 2,000-year-old axiom of the Roman architect Vitruvius, who declared that architecture must encompass 'firmness, commodity and delight' – meaning that it must be soundly constructed, fit for its purpose and possess poetic beauty.[39] The Reliance succeeded brilliantly on all three counts.

SPEED AND COST OF CONSTRUCTION

Also exemplary, and a demonstration of an able grasp of the potential of up-to-the-minute building technology, was the speed with which the Reliance was constructed. Evidently the inherent efficiency of 'factory'-made components – notably the steel frame – being fabricated and delivered to the site in an orderly sequence for assembly was fully utilized. The construction of the building's upper floors cannot have started on site before early May 1894 but was well advanced by 6 June 1894; a note on a drawing from that date states that 'all columns on Washington

Street and the north columns on State Street are in place.'[40] By July 1894 virtually all the steel frame was in place,[41] and on 25 August 1894, *The Economist* noted that 'no building in this city has ever been erected so rapidly', and that 'the steel frame of fourteen stories was put in place in four weeks'.[42] A sequence of dated construction photographs published by Charles Jenkins in his article, 'A White Enameled Building', confirms that by 8 November 1894 the entire terracotta façade including cornice, all the windows and the storefronts were in place, so all was completed in little more than six months.[43]

The George A. Fuller Company, which constructed the Reliance, prospered mightily and expanded its activities to include real estate development. By the time George Fuller died in December 1900, his booming company was in a position to commission D. H. Burnham and Company to design it a twenty-two-storey commercial tower, partly for its own use, on the corner of Broadway and Fifth Avenue in New York. Completed in 1902, the building was originally named the Fuller Building, but is now known as the Flatiron. As Judith Dupré points out, the Flatiron is 'Manhattan's oldest surviving skyscraper, and one of its most recognizable and famous'.[44] The Flatiron is a very direct descendent of the Reliance but, it must be admitted, it is a most odd child (see page 250).

The cost of building the Reliance is most revealing. Even if the economies of the mass production and well-planned delivery and assembly of components were brilliantly utilized to speed construction, it did not keep costs down. Evidently Hale believed that the commercial success of the Reliance depended, to a large degree, on the creation of stylish interiors, calculated to attract the right quality and quantity of tenant to pay good rents. But perhaps the specification got slightly out of hand. Articles that appeared in the early 1890s about construction costs and the cubic footage of the proposed building suggest that the initial estimate was in the range of $350,000 to $400,000.[45] But the *Chicago Daily News Almanac for 1897* lists the cost of the Reliance Building as $500,000.[46]

The manner in which Hale met this increase in costs is unrecorded but he, no doubt, took it in his stride. Certainly he remained determined to complete and manage the building. To do this he needed to get his hands on money, and he did this in a fairly conventional manner. He had initiated, but not fully completed, a building that was potentially of significant commercial value, so he used the potential value of the asset as the security to raise the cash to complete. Hale did this by selling the Reliance to Otto Young – an investor in stores and property with nearby holdings in State Street – for $480,000. Young then leased the building back to Hale on favourable terms for 198 years. This deal meant that Hale retained control of the building while also securing the money required to complete it.[47]

As the skyscrapers that came immediately after the Reliance make clear, this was a building way ahead of its time, with many of the lessons it holds not being generally applied until well into the twentieth century. When it was completed in 1895 the Reliance demonstrated – in a most remarkable manner – the application of appropriate technology to create utility combined with a desire for beauty to create accommodation that was delightful as well as practical. The Reliance was also a monument to the creation of adaptable interiors that could be open-plan or densely compartmentalized. This flexibility, the ability to adapt and to 'learn' to live in changing times, has meant that the building has evolved relatively easily from department store, physicians' consulting rooms and tailors' workshops to its current use of hotel, bar and restaurant. And then there is light – arguably the building's defining quality. Getting daylight and healthy fresh air into buildings, by means of large windows that also offered stunning prospects from tall towers, became one of the hallmarks – indeed obsessions – of twentieth-century Modernism from

1918 onwards. William Hale, John Root and Charles Atwood got there first.

But, as it happened, the structurally and artistically radical Reliance Building did not, when completed, immediately determine the direction modern high-rise commercial architecture should take. The world was not, perhaps, quite ready for the Reliance; initially the building did little more than launch a debate about the way skyscrapers should be built and how they should look. It also, along with other early high-rise buildings, led to ordinances being passed in Chicago and New York aimed primarily at fire-prevention, which controlled height and construction materials and methods (see page 259). By the late 1890s these made a building like the Reliance almost impossible to construct.

As well as its early supporters in the press and in the architectural profession (see page 198), the Reliance also had its critics. There were those who believed that a building should not only be firm and strong but should also appear so. In 1896 Barr Ferree declared in *Inland Architect* that, while the 'Reliance Building... is... the most notable attempt yet made to reduce the amount of the inclosing material to a minimum', it was in effect 'scarcely more than a huge house of glass divided by horizontal and vertical lines of white-enameled brick.'[48] Perhaps the former Burnham employee A. N. Rebori put the critics' case most succinctly in 1924 when – with the benefit of hindsight – he categorized the Reliance, when considered as a pioneer, as something of a work in progress. For Rebori, the Reliance was not 'an artistic solution of the problem, but only a statement of it', and its greatest conceptual legacy was the bold reduction of its façade to the function of mere cladding 'with no illusion of structural capacity'. In other words, the first expression – in a thorough and convincing manner – of the idea of the generously glazed curtain wall that has little structural purpose beyond its own support.[49] As it happens, this legacy alone makes the Reliance Building of supreme importance for the coming generations of skyscrapers.

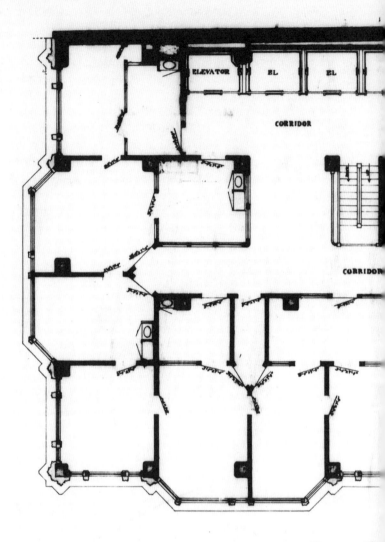

TYPICAL FL

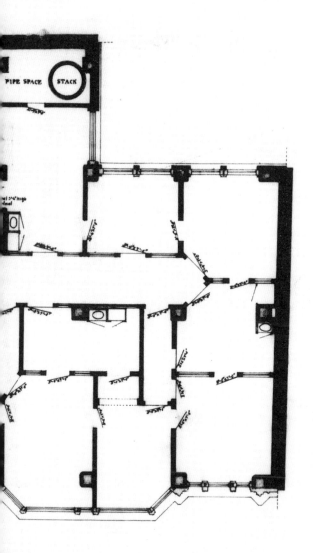

PIPE SPACE   STACK

N

RELIANCE BUILDING
FOR
W E HALE
SCALE ¼ IN = 1 FT.   D. H. BURNHAM v CO. ARCH'TS.   (40)

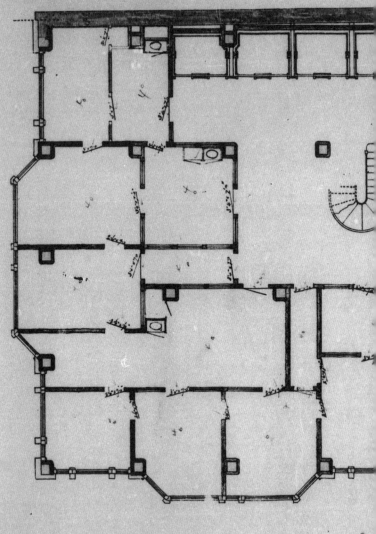

EIGHTH·F

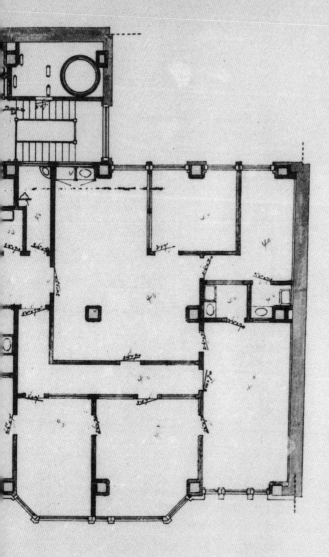

·PLAN·

·RELIANCE·BVILDING·
FOR
·W·E·HALE·
·SCALE·$\frac{1}{4}$"=1·FT·   ·D·H·BVRNHAM·ARCH'T·

⑧

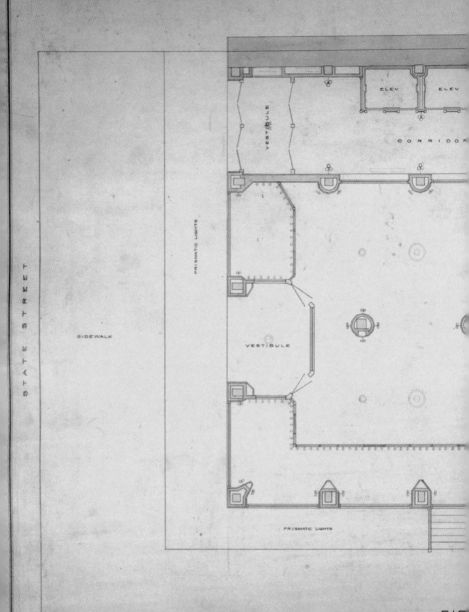

STATE STREET

SIDEWALK

PRISMATIC LIGHTS

VESTIBULE

VESTIBULE

ELEV

ELEV

CORRIDOR

PRISMATIC LIGHTS

FIR

WASHIN

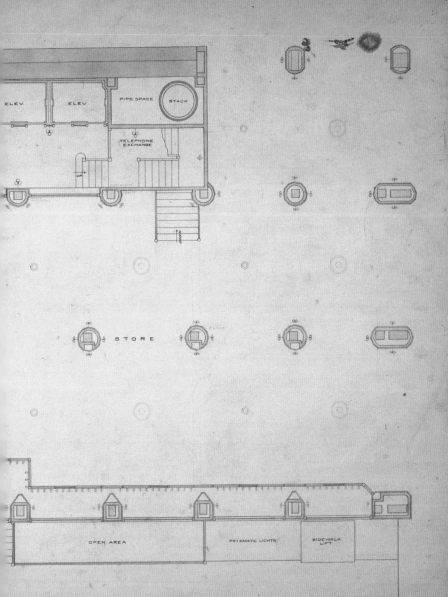

ELEV. ELEV. PIPE SPACE STACK

TELEPHONE
EXCHANGE

STORE

OPEN AREA   PRISMATIC LIGHTS   SIDEWALK
LIFT

FLOOR

STREET

ELECTRIC WIRING—
CONDUIT WIRES ON 3 WIRE CIRCUITS
SWITCHES AND CUT OUTS IN BASEMENT.

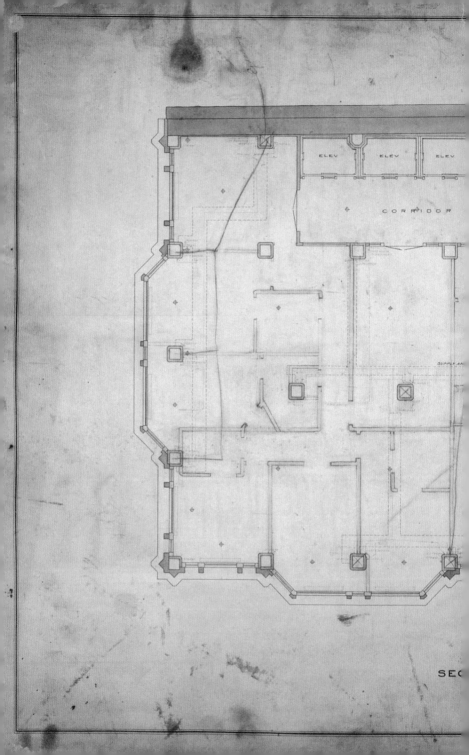

ELEV   ELEV   ELEV

CORRIDOR

SUPPLY AN

SEC

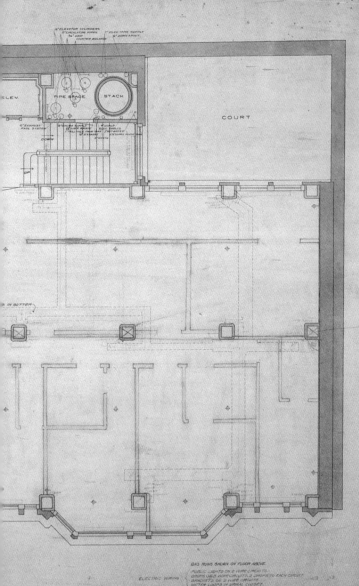

COURT

ELEV   PIPE SPACE   STACK

GAS RUNS SHOWN ON FLOOR ABOVE.

ELECTRIC WIRING

FLOOR

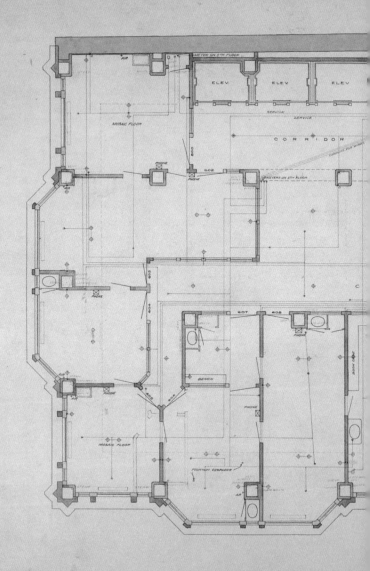

ELEV. ELEV. ELEV.

CORRIDOR

SIX

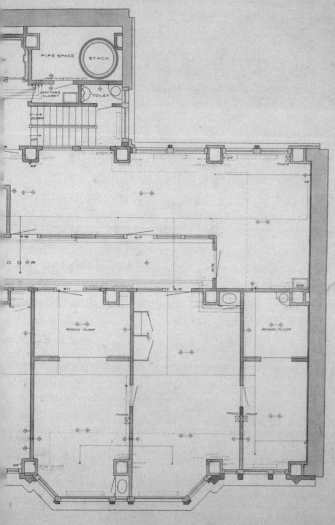

PIPE SPACE　STACK

CIRCUITS METERED ON 6TH

JANITORS
CLOSET　TOILET

DOWN

D O O R

MOSAIC FLOOR　MOSAIC FLOOR

PHONE　PHONE PHONE

GO. RUN SHOWN IN BLUE
BRACKETS FOR 6TH STORY
DROPS - 5TH
PUBLIC LIGHTS ON 2 WIRE CIRCUITS.
ELECTRIC WIRING EACH ROOM ON 2 WIRE CIRCUITS I METER.
METERS IN METER CLOSET.

OOR

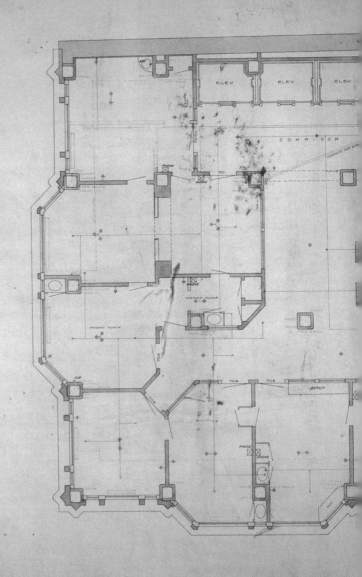

ELEV   ELEV   ELEV

CORRIDOR

701

704   705   BENCH

SE

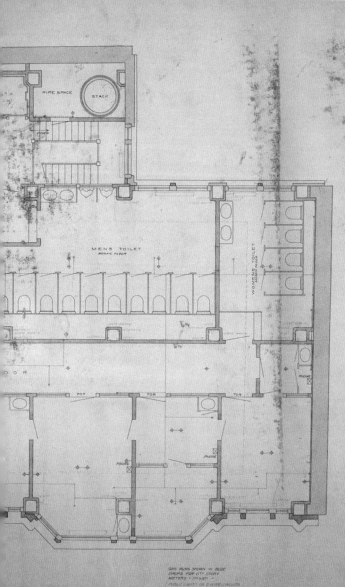

PIPE SPACE

STACK

JOHN

MENS TOILET
MOSAIC FLOOR

WOMENS TOILET
MOSAIC FLOOR

PHONE

707   708   709

PHONE

GAS RUNS SHOWN IN BLUE
DROPS FOR 6TH STORY
METERS - 7TH &8TH -
PUBLIC LIGHTS ON 3 WIRE CIRCUITS
PRIVATE LIGHTS - NEUTRAL TO
3 NEGATIVE AND 2 POSITIVE WIRES
METERS IN JANITORS CLOSETS

ELECTRIC WIRING

FLOOR

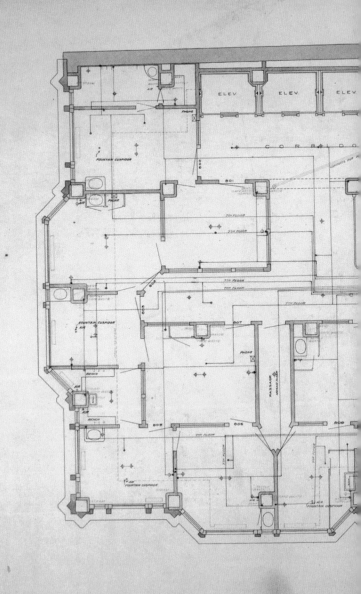

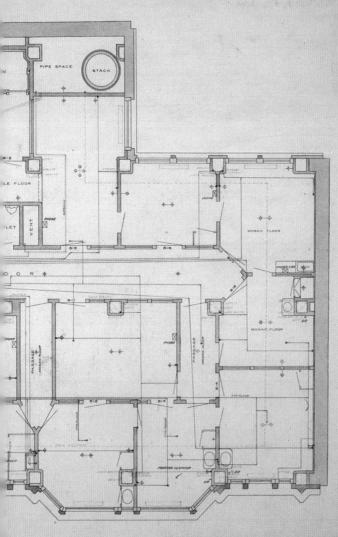

PIPE SPACE

STACK

LE FLOOR

VENT PHONE

PHONE

MOSAIC FLOOR

PHONE CUB

MOSAIC FLOOR

PASSAGE

PHONE

PASSAGE

TOY FLOOR

FOUNTAIN CUSPIDOR

GAS RUNS SHOWN IN BLUE
BRACKETS FOR 8TH STORY
ALL RUNS 1" TO 1"
METERS ON 1"

PUBLIC LIGHTS ON 8 WIRE CIRCUITS
PRIVATE LIGHTS 3 NEUTRAL TO
1 NEGATIVE AND 2 POSITIVE WIRES
METERS IN TOILET ROOM

ELECTRIC WIRING

FLOOR

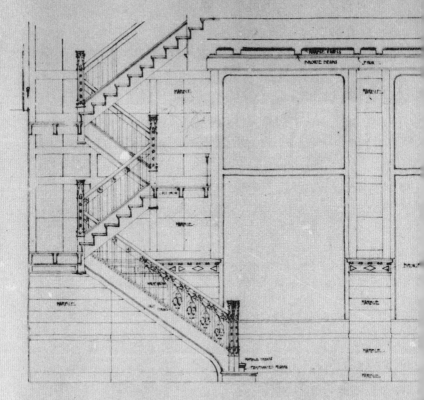

·NORTH·

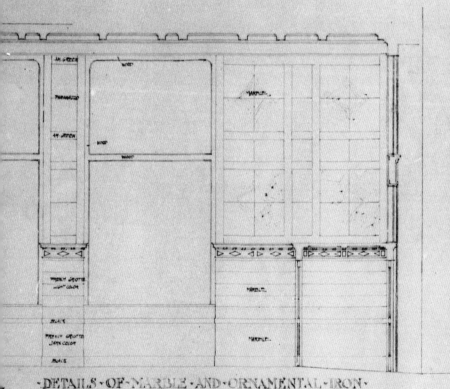

·DETAILS·OF·MARBLE·AND·ORNAMENTAL·IRON·
·RELIANCE·BLDG·FOR·W·E·HALE·
·SCALE·½·INCH·ONE·FOOT···D·H·BVRNHAM·ARCH·T·

(34)

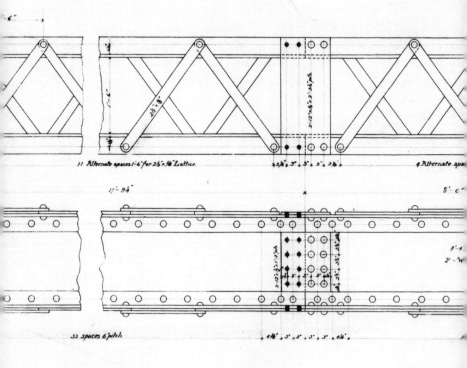

11 Alternate spaces 1'-6" for 2½"×⅜" Lattice.   ·3½· · 3" · · 3" · · 3" · ·3½·   4 Alternate spa

17'-9¾"   8'-0"

32 spaces 6"pitch   ·4½· · 3" · 3" · 3" · 3" ·4½·

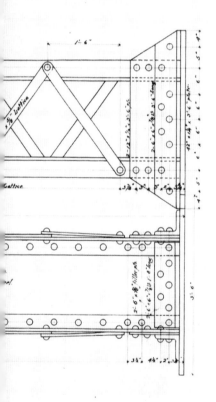

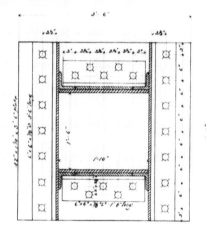

Note: All material steel.
All rivets ⅞ inch. diam.

Column C.
W. E. Hole Bldg.
Burnham and Root. Arch'ts.

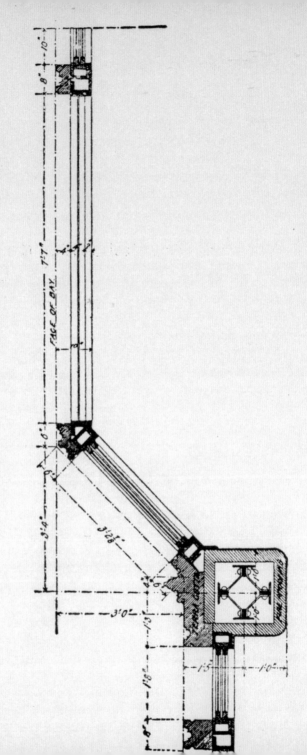

Black and white floor plans

TYPICAL FLOOR PLAN: this was presumably drawn-up during construction between 1893 and 1895, after Root's death, and during the period when Charles Atwood was the job architect.

EIGHTH FLOOR: a handwritten note states 'approved 7 April 1894', but the staircase was not in fact executed as shown, with curving winders replaced by straight flights and landings. The partition system depicted on this plan and the Typical Floor Plan is extraordinary, showing the large number of small offices and consulting rooms that Hale was obliged to create within the building's open plan.

Colour floor plans

These plans are not dated nor do they bear the architect's name. They appear to show the primary structure as built but were apparently also used to test or plan partition layouts for various floor. North is to the bottom.

FIRST FLOOR (UK GROUND FLOOR): the entrance corridor, four elevators and staircase are clearly shown, as is the open court in the south-west corner. Also note the eccentric placing of the structural columns, most strikingly with those in the centre of the State Street frontage not aligning with the row of central columns.

SECOND FLOOR: an array of partitions have been pencilled-in to create small spaces to let. Here, the open space in the south-west corner is clearly marked as a 'court'. Pink denotes brick construction, thus making the size and location of the fire-proof party walls very clear.

SIXTH FLOOR: a range of offices/ consulting rooms of generally regular form have been drawn, most with plumbed-in sinks and pipe runs indicated. According to a description published in 1895 this level was originally intended

for 'tailors, milliners, dressmakers [and] jewellers', but this plan suggests intentions had changed and it was to be occupied as the floors above – by physics and dentists.

SEVENTH FLOOR: this floor contained the largest collection of communal lavatories for the men and women using the building. This level was intended for occupation by 'physicians, dentists and others desiring large suites of offices'.

EIGHTH FLOOR: smaller consulting rooms are drawn, with much of the floor area taken up by corridors and access spaces.

Drawings

ELEVATION AND SECTION THROUGH STAIRCASE showing 'details of marble and ornamental iron'. Marked 'approved April 1894' by E. C. Shankland, Daniel H, Burnham & Company's 'office engineer'.

ELEVATION AND SECTION OF 'COLUMN C': this drawing was made before Root's death in January 1891. It is marked for the 'W. E. Hale Bldg.', so dates before the name 'Reliance Building' emerged and bears the legend 'Burnham and Root Archts.'. A handwritten note reads 'OK 4/29/90 ECS', so it was approved by the office engineer E. C. Shankland.

SECTION AND PLAN OF AN ORIEL WINDOW showing the integration of the ornamental terracotta of the Reliance Building's cladding with the steel structure. The steel column, formed with plates riveted together, is protected by fire-proofing, to which the terracotta exterior cladding is fixed.

Legacy

The reaction against the Reliance Building was immediate. The hostile response was probably based more on a failure to understand it, or appreciate its artistic or functional potential, than on downright antipathy. Some critics praised it upon completion (see page 198), but most architects and clients involved in the creation of skyscrapers in Chicago and New York in the mid-1890s rejected the minimalism the Reliance espoused and did not approve of the abandonment of history-inspired decoration that its design implied. The building profession continued to take the general view that tall buildings ought to look strong as well as be strong and that historical details represented reliability, familiarity and a sense of high culture that was good for business. The Beaux-Arts aesthetics of the 1893 White City, and their implication that Roman-Renaissance classicism was the American national style for all buildings with cultural pretensions, continued to hold sway and in Chicago and New York its exponents won the initial debate about the artistic direction skyscrapers should take. Nikolaus Pevsner observed as much in 1936 when he stated that 'after the Chicago Exhibition of 1893' there was a 'reaction against the innovations of Root'.[1] The Reliance was simply too odd and too newfangled to be readily emulated.

A few key examples from the decades immediately after 1895 make the point, and of particular interest is Daniel Burnham's own journey from the avant-garde Reliance to his later, visually more conventional, architecture. But, to confuse matters, Burnham's first major high-rise building after the completion of the Reliance suggested for a moment that the spirit of the Reliance endured and that it would have immediate and recognizable progeny. The Fisher Building, constructed on the corner of Dearborn and Van Buren Streets for Hale's former business associate Lucius G. Fisher, was designed in Burnham's office in 1893 by Charles Atwood, no doubt while enthusiasm for the Reliance project was at its peak and Atwood was still at the height of his powers. But delays and negotiations, notably to do with the height restrictions being considered as part of the Chicago's 1893 building ordinance, meant that construction of the Fisher Building did not start until 1895 and was not completed until the following year, after Atwood's death.

But this delay and Atwood's death do not appear to have materially compromised the building. It was – and remains – remarkable. Despite the city authority's growing concerns about height, the Fisher is nineteen storeys or 275 feet (84 metres) high (construction started before enforcement of the 1893 code began, so the height was something of an achievement given that the new code set a height limit of 130 feet), and the façade is generously glazed, although not quite as extensively as the Reliance. The Fisher's façades, incorporating a large number of bays, are about 70 per cent plate-glass. Each of the Reliance Building's two main elevations are about 90 per cent glazed. Consequently, the mullions on the Fisher are more numerous and the sense of solidity greater, despite the fact that the horizontal bands between the rows of windows are very narrow. Again the cladding material is terracotta, but a pale stone colour, not white. Interestingly, the history-based ornament on the Fisher is slightly more pronounced than on the Reliance. Perhaps this was due to Fisher himself. Once again the moulded details are inspired by Gothic architecture but, unlike the Reliance, the upper portion of the Fisher is rather conventional, even retrograde, and certainly somewhat fussy. The Reliance has only an implied cornice and frieze but on the Fisher both are more literally presented and, to accentuate the debt to history, the building's windows are crowned by a high-level arcade.

In its structure, however, the Fisher is more futuristic than the Reliance. The character of the site occupied by the Reliance Building – essentially an amalgamation of terraced-house plots meeting on a constricted corner site – meant that two of the building's four exterior walls are in fact constructed of thick masonry to function as fire-proof party walls. But the Fisher is different. E. C. Shankland was again the engineer and the Fisher's wind-braced riveted-steel frame rises without masonry wall support and is clad with glass and terracotta on three of its four sides (the north elevation is now obscured by a slightly taller but generally matching addition of 1906) making it not only well glazed and relatively minimal in its exterior detail but originally also – despite rising from a street frontage in the traditional manner – a virtually free-standing sculptural tower of the sort favoured in the later twentieth century.

More typical of the immediate post-Reliance period is the nine-storey State Mutual Life Assurance Company Building (now the Commerce Building) on Main Street, Worcester, Massachusetts. Completed in 1897 to the designs of Peabody & Stearns – the Boston-based architects who designed one of the

major buildings in Chicago's White City (see page 135) – it is an intriguing example of how Beaux-Arts architects built high and how negligible was the influence of the Reliance. The building has a steel structural frame but this is concealed – even denied – by the stone facing and the conventional classical composition of the elevations, which include a rusticated podium, arcades, storeys of sleek ashlar walling and a heavy crowning cornice – all in Renaissance palazzo style.

To understand why the lessons of the Reliance, and its sense of transparency and architectural minimalism, were rejected in mid-1890s Chicago in favour of visual solidity and ornamented historicism, it is necessary to place the Reliance in its contemporary context. When this is done two main reasons emerge – one obvious and direct, the other more speculative and subtle. The former has to do with the objective practicalities of the

The Fisher Building, Chicago, designed in 1893 by Charles Atwood. There is a strong family resemblance to the Reliance, but the terracotta cladding here is buff coloured not glazed white, and there is less glass and more history-inspired ornament.
Above The main door showing *putti* and a wreath of classical derivation set below Gothic detailing – all realized in terracotta.

building process; the latter concerns subjective issues of artistic taste. With the benefit of hindsight we tend to see the Reliance as the bold harbinger of the coming age of Modernist architecture, especially in its exploitation of the mostly glazed curtain wall. But in the mid- to late 1890s the Reliance was evidently perceived by most architects and critics as little more than a curiosity, a passing whim and certainly not a significant prototype. As Thomas Leslie points out, it is now 'tempting to see… curtain-wall structures [like the Reliance and Fisher Buildings] as precursors of their twentieth century counterparts, but these experiments were not as prescient as they might appear… The synthesis of the self-braced frame and curtain wall', essentially an outer 'skin that was draped over the frame rather than integrated with it… was remarkably short-lived in Chicago', and for Daniel Burnham the momentary experiment 'was quickly abandoned [when] this formulation… became problematic'.[2] Some of the problems were partly prosaic – there was, for example, a sharp rise in the price of plate-glass – but some were more profound. The Fisher Building had just escaped the new Chicago building codes, but later skyscrapers in the city could not.

BUILDING CODES AND
LEGISLATION AGAINST BUILDING HIGH

During the 1890s architecture increasingly became subject to political control as opinion divided over the role of skyscrapers in cities. Their construction was undoubtedly important for the business community and for urban building entrepreneurs, but what about the city as a whole? Two main issues emerged: 'tall buildings increased fire problems, and their bulk deprived neighbouring lots and streets of sunlight and fresh air'.[3] It was primarily these two concerns that were reflected in the 1893 Chicago Building Ordinance and its subsequent revisions. The rules regarding the height of buildings reveal the intensity of the business and political lobbying provoked by the ordinance.

In 1893 the maximum height was fixed at 130 feet or ten storeys. This was perhaps somewhat arbitrary, and was certainly beyond the height that could be reasonably reached by fire ladders. This arbitrary quality made the regulation vulnerable to lobbying from the construction and business community. In 1896 the height limit was raised to 155 feet but counter-lobbying saw it reduced, in 1898, back to 130 feet. In 1901 it was raised once again, this time to 180 feet, and in 1902 to 260 feet.[4] In Chicago the interests of business, in the end, prevailed but only because firefighting techniques improved and because it was generally accepted that related building legislation made tall structures less combustible or liable to risk. Notably, the code limited the size of bay windows, increased the thickness of fire-proof cladding and required that external walls, whether load-bearing or not, be increased in thickness and solidity the higher they rose. Together these requirements severely limited the potential for glazed curtain walls. By 1903 window frames had to be made of incombustible materials, which put paid to the 'Chicago window', with its timber sashes flanking a large sheet of fixed plate-glass. By the first decade of the new century it was legally impossible in Chicago to construct a building like the Reliance – and in New York the evolving building codes were even more onerous.

THE 'SKYCOLUMN' AESTHETIC

The more subtle reason for the neutering of the Reliance model is the emergence of an aesthetic theory for the design of skyscrapers that could, by promoting a more visually solid-looking form of architecture, accommodate the safety controls of the codes. In 1896 this emerging taste was given powerful voice by the Chicago-based Louis Sullivan. Sullivan viewed himself as an artist-architect, had admired John Root as a man after his own heart (see pages 94–5) and, despite being awarded a significant commission for the 1893 World's Columbian Exposition, had developed a vengeful loathing for his patron Daniel Burnham and an even more powerful hatred for the Beaux-Arts classicism the Exposition had championed. Always happy to spread his architectural preferences through popular journalism, Sullivan wrote an article for the March 1896 edition of *Lippincott's* magazine. Entitled 'The Tall Office Building Artistically Considered', the article is now famous because it included a phrase – 'form ever follows function' – that was to become a mantra for early-twentieth-century Modernism.

But more specifically Sullivan put forward a theory, visual rather than technical, in a bid to explain what skyscrapers – the new building-type of the age – should look like. For him high-rise buildings were exclusively commercial buildings. In the 1890s Sullivan, like most of his contemporaries, had yet to fully comprehend – let alone visualize – the residential tower. That still lay in the future. He started by asking his readers rhetorically 'What is the chief characteristic of the tall office building?' and answered by making the obvious point that 'it is lofty'. But what Sullivan meant by this question is perhaps not so obvious and certainly gets to the point of skyscraper design. For him, architects should embrace the artistic and emotive potential of loftiness and not try to disguise it by means of visual ruses. As he put it, 'this loftiness is to the artist-nature [the skyscraper's] thrilling aspect... It must be tall, every inch of it tall. The force and power of altitude must be in it... every inch a proud and soaring thing, rising in sheer exultation that from bottom to top it is a unit without a single dissenting line.'

This reads, perhaps, as if it was written with the Reliance Building in mind, where no attempt had been made to visually disguise the structure's height. But Sullivan goes on to envisage a very different type of high-rise composition. He started to give visual form to his theory by observing that 'certain critics, and very thoughtful ones, have advanced the theory that the true prototype of the tall office building is the classical column, consisting of base, shaft and capital – the molded base of the column typical of the lower stories of our building [containing plant or shops], the plain or fluted shaft suggesting the monotonous, uninterrupted series of office-tiers, and the capital the completing power and luxuriance of the attic.'

It might seem paradoxical that Sullivan – the trenchant critic of Beaux-Arts classicism – should tolerate the notion that the skyscraper, the architectural epitome of the modern age and product of new technology, should take the three-part form of a classical column. But there was logic behind Sullivan's apparent inconsistency. And this logic was founded on his famed phrase that 'form ever follows function'. This, he asserted, was the 'law' taught by nature. 'Where function does not change form does not change.' But when function changes then, according to this theory, form must also change. The application of this natural law 'readily, clearly and conclusively' demonstrated, to Sullivan's complete satisfaction, meant that 'the lower one or two stories [of a skyscraper] will take on a special character suited to the special needs, that the tiers of typical offices, having the same unchanging function, shall continue in the same unchanging form, and that as to the attic, specific and conclusive as it is in its very nature, its function shall equally be so in force, in significance, in continuity, in conclusiveness of outward expression.' And thus, concluded Sullivan, if this logic were followed, 'the design of the tall office building [would take] its place with all other architectural types made when architecture, as has happened once in many years, was a living art.' This line of reasoning inspired – or certainly underpinned – the birth of the 'skycolumn' – a tripartite composition with base, shaft and top of differing forms reflecting their different functions – that was to define skyscraper design well into the twentieth century.

Even before Sullivan wrote this article he had designed a skyscraper that revealed his thinking and tested his theory. The Wainwright Building in St Louis, Missouri, was conceived by Sullivan when he was working with Dankmar Adler, and completed in 1891. It is ten storeys high, of steel-frame construction clad with red brick, has a ground floor of distinct design created to accommodate the specific requirements of a department store, tiers of repetitive office floors above and a top-floor attic treated as an entablature and embellished with exquisite swirls of the naturalistic ornament, made of terracotta, that Sullivan was then evolving to replace the conventional Gothic or classical repertoire of decoration.[5] This naturalistic ornament, in the form of foliage, offers another clue to Sullivan's thinking. The column was one model for the skyscraper but another was the plant, which Sullivan saw as the natural prototype for the design of buildings of any height. The ground floor was to visually root the building to the site, with the repetitive office floors representing the stem and the ornamented upper storeys and cornice being the analogy for the plant's crowning and beautiful blossom.

Despite the absence of familiar classical details the Wainwright Building – with its tripartite composition evoking the divisions of a classical column or the divisions of a Roman temple elevation into podium, columns and entablature – has a powerful classical presence. Indeed, it is generally regarded as a pioneer of the palazzo style that dominated skyscraper design in the years immediately after the completion of the Reliance Building. Such was the success of the Wainwright Building that, many years later,

The Wainwright Building, St Louis, Missouri was conceived by Louis Sullivan when he was working with Dankmar Adler and completed in 1891 – a pioneer of the tripartite 'skycolumn' aesthetic.

Frank Lloyd Wright called it the 'very first human expression of tall steel office building in architecture'[6] (and see page 135). This is of course an odd description, but presumably means that, while not the first steel-framed high-rise office building, this was the first that Wright believed was architecturally successful, with its success lying in what he considered to be Sullivan's 'human' touch. For Wright, it seems, Sullivan's solution for the design of skyscrapers, rooting them in the natural world, gave them a human dimension and cultural connections and in consequence made them an acceptable building-type. Many clearly felt the same because the model offered by Sullivan – developed significantly in 1896 by his thirteen-storey Prudential (now Guaranty) Building in Buffalo, New York State – quickly became the standard solution, and did much to put the Reliance Building in the shade.

It was perhaps Sullivan's increasing bitterness towards Burnham, provoked largely by Burnham's businesslike approach to architecture and his promotion of 'foreign' Beaux-Arts classicism as America's national style (see page 127), that spurred him to promote a rival 'artistic' and 'human' solution for the design of high-rise office blocks. It must have given Sullivan some considerable satisfaction to see his arguments prevail. But, ironically, as they did his architectural practice went into eclipse while Burnham's became increasingly successful. The bleak lesson seems clear: when it comes to commercial architecture the exigencies of profit – the ethic of the businessman – must always prevail over the artist.

Skyscrapers designed soon after the completion of the Reliance show how dominant the tripartite skycolumn or palazzo style had become. Sullivan did not of course invent the tripartite division of skyscraper composition, with horizontal tiers of differing form reflecting the building's different functions. Indeed, Burnham and Root's 1887 design for the Rookery in Chicago, for example, can be characterized as tripartite. But Sullivan did refine and demonstrate the approach with his Wainwright Building, evangelized it with his writings, gave voice to the emerging fashion for the palazzo approach and succeeded in giving the skyscraper, to use Wright's analogy, a 'human expression'.

The 'skycolumns' that followed after the Reliance could be more or less classical in their details, and traditional in the choice of materials with which they were faced and ornamented and in the relationship between window and wall. Most architects went for full-blown classicism and preferred to clad steel frames with generous amounts of masonry and to design windows of more or less conventional shape and size. Peabody and Stearns' 1897 State Mutual Life Assurance Company Building in Worcester, Massachusetts is, with its classical detail, a typical example of the popular palazzo-style skyscraper. The American Surety Building, located at 100 Broadway, New York, was constructed between 1894 and 1896, before Sullivan published his seminal article in *Lipincott's* magazine, and so can be taken as evidence that Sullivan was reflecting rather than creating a national architectural taste.

The American Surety Building was originally twenty-one storeys in height, and its granite façades clad a steel frame. This was novel at the time in New York because it was only in 1892 that the city's building codes were changed to allow the primary structural frame to be of metal, not masonry. The thinking behind the building's design was summarized by its architect, Bruce Price, as 'a campanile with four pilaster faces, the seven flutes [of each pilaster face] being represented by seven rows of windows.'* As with the 'skycolumn' envisioned by Sullivan, Price's American Surety Building has a visually distinct base or podium that incorporates giant Ionic columns, a stack of repetitive office floors above (but with the lower two given emphasis by the use

---

* In the early 1920s the building was enlarged, which involved widening it from seven to eleven windows, compromising its pilaster analogy.

of cornices), and is capped by a complex 'capital' six storeys high that includes Corinthian pilasters and is terminated by a classical cornice and attic. Another early and arresting New York example of the classically detailed 'skycolumn' is the steel-framed and brick- and terracotta-clad Park Row Building (now 15 Park Row), which was completed in 1899 to the designs of R. H. Robertson. Rising twenty-nine storeys and 119 metres high, the tall and slender Park Row Building has a generously glazed podium, then rows of repetitive office floors embellished by tiers of giant pilasters and engaged columns and is topped by four corner cupolas. The building originally contained 950 separate offices accommodating around 4,000 workers.

ENTER THE FLATIRON

Soon after the American Surety Building and the Park Row Building were completed Daniel Burnham started design work, probably at some point early in 1901,[7] on a building that was to become his most famous work and which reveals, with dramatic clarity, the architectural journey he had taken since the Reliance and Fisher Buildings were completed only five and six years earlier. The Fuller Building, on Broadway and Fifth Avenue, was commissioned by Harry S. Black of the George A. Fuller Company – the builders of the Reliance – to serve as their New York headquarters and named after the company's founder George Fuller, who had died in December 1900. It has since become known as the Flatiron Building (see image page 252). Burnham, being very busy with projects of national significance – notably the Senate-sponsored improvements to Washington[8] – quickly handed the project to one of his staff architects, Frederick P. Dinkelberg.

This was an intriguing choice. Dinkelberg knew Charles Atwood and through him had met Burham, who in 1892 or 1893 hired him to work on the Chicago Exposition. So Dinkelberg and Burnham went back quite a way and – more significantly perhaps – Dinkelberg had known Atwood when in his prime and as a Burnham and Co. employee had even perhaps worked on the Reliance Building. But if that were the case, and if it was Dinkelberg who worked up the form and details of the Flatiron Building, then Atwood and the Reliance seem to have been far from his mind. When completed in 1902 the Flatiron was the epitome of the classicized skycolumn or palazzo style. It rises twenty-two storeys and is of steel-frame construction, but its stone and terracotta cladding creates a massive impression, the proportion of glazing is relatively small and the window sizes and their proportions, and their relationship to areas of wall, are fairly conventional. And, crucially, it is of the tripartite 'skycolumn' form promoted by Sullivan – with a visually if relatively subtly distinct podium, then fifteen more or less identical floors of offices, topped by multi-storey composition forming an 'attic' or 'capital' capped by a cornice. The detailing throughout is classical. Any lingering loyalty Burnham or Dinkelberg might have had for Atwood's radical Reliance prototype has clearly gone – eclipsed by ever more onerous building codes and by the increasing popular and professional affection for the tripartite, classicized, ever-so-solid-looking column in the sky. But the Flatiron does possess one key characteristic in common with the Reliance and the Fisher buildings that puts it at odds with many contemporary New York towers and makes it look like a slice of Chicago embedded in the Big Apple.

The Reliance Building aspired, but didn't quite manage, to be a free-standing tower rising from the pavement edge. This is the visual impression it creates but the constraints of its awkward corner site worked against it. The Fuller Building was virtually

a free-standing tower and the Flatiron certainly is – a soaring, three-dimensional prism-like sculptural form rising majestically in space, with its shard-like shape a brilliant utilization of its unusual triangular plot created by the fact that Broadway wanders diagonally across the city's 1811 orthogonal grid. This free-standing form was the Chicago ideal. In New York things were done differently. Downtown Chicago and New York north of Houston Street were monuments to the right-angular gridiron plan. But in Chicago all was a little more relaxed than in New York, where the grid of the 1811 Commissioners' plan ruled with a ruthless and repetitive regularity. When the city blocks, with their only very small variations in size, were gradually built upon during the first three-quarters of the nineteenth century, all was well; the terraced plots each block was divided into sprouted terraced brownstone houses and buildings of conventional and generally uniform size. Then New York was, more or less, like any European gridiron classical city. But when skyscrapers started to be built in numbers during the last decade of the nineteenth century something started to happen, and continued to happen for years to come, and gradually but increasingly there were those who thought that what was happening was wrong.

Initially new high-rise buildings merely ousted brownstones, and at first the dramatic consequences were generally appreciated for their visually thrilling novelty. But potential problems with skyscrapers were soon identified. A skyscraper rising on one site could inhibit a similar development on the adjoining site. Was this equitable, and was it even legal? Clearly the development of high-rise buildings on a tight urban grid, within which neighbouring plots of land were under different ownership, had to be managed most carefully, and to protect not only the rights of landowners but also of city dwellers as a whole. As the 1893 Chicago code made clear, although skyscrapers could possess commercial and artistic benefits they also had the potential to

The Fuller Building, New York, now better known as the 'Flatiron', designed by Frederick P. Dinkelberg and Daniel Burnham and completed in 1902. Cutting edge in structure and technology the Flatiron is a prime example of the steel-framed and classically detailed palazzo tower.

create profound, anti-social, problems by becoming frightful fire hazards and by casting shadows over neighbouring buildings and raising the population density of the areas in which they stood to an uncomfortably high level. The Flatiron captures the moment when popular and professional perceptions of the commercial skyscraper in New York started to change.

At first the Flatiron was applauded for its audacious scale. Typical was the reaction of the *Architectural Record*. It observed jauntily in 1902 that, 'there was nothing left to be done in New York, in the way of [achieving] architectural altitude [because] the architect of the Flatiron... has succeeded in accomplishing that difficult feat. This building is at present quite the most notorious thing in New York, and attracts more attention than all the other buildings now going up put together.'

The same year the *New York Tribune* recorded that, 'since the removal last week of the scaffolding... there is scarcely an hour when a staring wayfarer doesn't by his example collect a big crowd of other staring people... No wonder people stare! A building 307 feet high presenting an edge almost as sharp as the bow of a ship... it is well worth looking at.'

The gogglers included H. G. Wells, who in 1906 admitted, in *The Future of America: A Search After Realities*, that 'I found myself agape, admiring a sky-scraper, the prow of the Flat-iron Building... ploughing up through the traffic of Broadway and Fifth Avenue in the afternoon light.' But it was the architectural photographer Alfred Stieglitz, who made some of the earliest and most striking images of the Flatiron, who was most succinct in his praise of the building: '...it is the new America. The Flat Iron is to the United States what the Parthenon was to Greece.'

But even as the plaudits flew the popular mood was starting to move against skyscrapers. They were invariably commercial in use and thus increasingly perceived as little more than money-making machines that operated for the benefit of the few at the expense of the majority of citizens. Henry James captured the cynical attitude of many New Yorkers, and anticipated evolving sentiment, when in 1907 he wrote in *The American Scene*: 'Skyscrapers are the last word of economic ingenuity... the thousand glassy eyes of these giants of the mere market.'[9]

In 1908 the newly founded Committee on Congestion of Population in New York decided enough was enough. The Singer Building, on Liberty Street and Broadway, forty-seven storeys high and reaching a height of 186.5 metres, designed by Ernest Flagg, had just been completed (it was demolished in 1968); the Metropolitan Life Insurance Building, on Madison Avenue, fifty storeys and 213 metres high and designed by Napoleon LeBrun and Sons, was nearing completion; and plans had just been unveiled for a sixty-two-storey tower, designed by Daniel H. Burnham and Company, for a site on Broadway.

In fact, by the time the Singer Building was designed, developers and their architects had come up with their own series of responses to the growing number of high-rise critics in New York. And the solutions they proposed were to give New York skyscraper development a very distinctive form. In Chicago towers tended to rise from the entire area of the building plot available, as did some early New York skyscrapers such as the Park Row Building. But in New York developers and their architects rapidly evolved a different approach. They came up with the idea of amassing a number of brownstone plots and then building a tall block over the entire site, usually with a conventional street frontage rising from the pavement edge, but with the tower itself rising on only a portion of the site. This was the dominant characteristic of the Singer Building, which took the form of a twelve-storey block rising from the pavement edge, with the forty-seven-storey square-plan tower rising from one of its corners. The tower, covering only about a quarter of the plot area, was topped in most picturesque manner by a dome and cupola. The entrance lobby of the building was also intensely historicist, furnished with columns and domes. This form and internal finish rapidly became the New York model. The tower of the Metropolitan Life Insurance Building was similarly disposed and – most whimsically – modelled on the campanile of St Mark's Square, Venice, while the sixty-storey Woolworth Building, on Broadway, designed by Cass Gilbert and built between 1910 and 1912, rose in stages to peak with a 241-metre-high neo-Gothic, pinnacled tower.

But these schemes, in which slim towers occupied only a small proportion of the development site, still did not satisfy the members of the Committee. They proposed that the city should revise its building codes to limit the height and number of skyscrapers and advocated 'zoning' to restrict tall buildings to certain districts or raising a special – and theoretically inhibiting – land tax on skyscrapers.[10]

The Committee did not stop the sixty-two-storey Daniel H. Burnham and Company skyscraper on Broadway. It didn't have to because the juggernaut ground to a halt of its own accord. But to get an idea of the megalithic feel of the Burnham design it is only necessary to contemplate the Oliver Building on Smithfield Street, Pittsburgh, which was built to Burnham's design between 1908 and 1910. Although a relatively modest twenty-five storeys, its stone and terracotta cladding and relatively small windows, and its oblong-plan 'skycolumn' composition – including a massive cornice – give it an oppressive feel. It's not only a long way from the Reliance but also, in its ponderous presence, a long way from the witty and elegant Flatiron.

But the project that in 1913 replaced the abandoned Burnham Broadway design was almost as daunting. Known as the Equitable Building, it took the form of a 164-metre-high forty-storey tower rising from a site little more than an acre in area (4,000m square) and contained 1.85 million square feet of offices. Despite hardening

The Oliver Building, Pittsburgh, Pennsylvania, built to Daniel Burnham's design. In its solidity and massiveness it makes an odd last gasp for a man who played such an instrumental role in the making of the avant-garde Reliance Building.

public and political opinion in New York against skyscrapers, the Committee failed to halt this project. With hindsight we can now see it was fighting a battle that was impossible to win. New York was the rapidly expanding financial heart of the nation and the fact that the city was constrained by being located on a rocky island made the rise of the commercial tower inevitable. If the city could not expand sideways, it had to go upwards – and the geology of Manhattan made this relatively easy.

The Equitable Building rose, Chicago-style, as a single tower but with its massive size disguised somewhat by giving it an H-shaped plan, so that from some angles the building looks like two identical towers, which are in fact connected by a cross-wing. The echo of a Chicago connection is perhaps explained by the fact that the tower's architect, Ernest R. Graham, had worked in Chicago for Burnham & Root and then, after Root's death, for Daniel H. Burnham and Company on the design of the World's Columbian Exposition. After Burnham's death in 1912 Graham took over the company and thus inherited this commission.

Graham's professional origins suggest the possibility that the Equitable Building might mark a return to the model of the Reliance. In fact, beyond being a single tower, it does not. The building was instead given the by then standard neoclassical trim and was composed in the tripartite skycolumn manner with its steel frame clad, in somewhat funereal manner, with Colorado white marble.

Although the construction of the towering Equitable Building could not be stopped, its completion in 1915, when its greedy scale and blighting shadows became painfully apparent to all, led to a significant change in New York planning law. Ernest Flagg had already argued, and demonstrated with the Singer Building, that a skyscraper's height could be mitigated if it occupied only a small proportion of the site and thus – tall but slender – did not cast all its neighbourhood into perpetual shade. So in 1916, in the wake of the Equitable Building and following Flagg's lobbying, the city passed its first zoning ordnance, which among other things controlled the bulk, and therefore the design, of skyscrapers. The ordinance stated that a skyscraper's total floor area could not be greater than twelve times the size of its plot area – and if a developer wished to build higher than twelve storeys then they must – as Flagg had done – build on only part of the potential building plot, or reduce floor areas as the building got higher. This led to the creation of the tiers of set-backs that give many New York skyscrapers of the 1920s and 1930s such a distinct profile.

HIGH-RISE: FIRE AND POLITICS

An event took place, just before construction of the Equity Building started, that also had a profound and lasting influence on the way in which skyscrapers were designed and occupied in the United States – and ultimately around the world. On 25 March 1911 fire broke out on the upper floors of the ten-storey Asch Building, located on Washington Place, Greenwich Village, New York. This was the first serious fire, leading to multiple deaths, in a metal-framed skyscraper and demonstrated that the building codes – despite their increasing focus on solid construction aimed at preventing the outbreak and spread of fire in high-rise buildings – could still not prevent disaster. The essential problem was that the codes ignored the human factor, and thus did not anticipate or mitigate the ruthless practices that might be followed by some irresponsible high-rise landlords or tenants.

The Asch Building had been constructed in 1901 in the standard steel-framed and masonry-clad palazzo style, but with a larger proportion of glazing than was then usual. Like most such metal and masonry structures of the time, built in accordance with increasingly safety-conscious building codes, the Asch Building was regarded as fire-proof. This, together with its large windows, made it an attractive location for the garment industry, then flourishing in and around Greenwich Village. The textile trade used potentially flammable materials and processes and employed a workforce requiring as much daylight as possible to execute its meticulous labour. Consequently the top three storeys of the building were crammed with many workers – mostly poor Italian and Jewish immigrants – employed by the Triangle Shirtwaist Factory, a typical rag-trade enterprise that operated without much regard to the safety or working conditions of its employees.

Tragically, if predictably, the interior of the building proved to be far from fire-proof, and when disaster struck 146 garment workers were killed. The fire, horrendous as it was, proved edifying. It spread quickly because the flammable materials being used were stacked within the building with scant or no regard for fire-prevention, and the victims died in a number of ways, with many deaths not the direct consequence of being burned or of smoke inhalation but of overcrowding, inadequate means of escape and ventilation or criminally irresponsible business practices that rapidly led to murderous panic.

At the time the fire broke out most doors to the staircase and fire escape were locked because the management wanted to prevent workers from taking unauthorized breaks or from pilfering merchandise; those who made it to the staircase found it dark and treacherous. It was soon packed with a confused and hysterical mob, some of whom were trampled to death. The fleeing proprietors of the company used the elevator to escape from the top floor but the fire prevented it ascending to pick up more people. Many of those trapped by the fire threw themselves down the lift shaft. Others preferred to jump rather than burn and soon bodies littered the sidewalk. Those who did manage to reach the external fire escape found it woefully inadequate. It stopped a considerable distance from the ground, could not be extended downwards and finally collapsed as the crowd trapped on it jostled and steadily increased in number. The firefighters, when they arrived, could do little to save people trapped on the upper floors. Their ladders could reach only to the sixth floor, while the fire raged on the eighth floor and above, and the press of bodies on the staircase – both living and dead – made rapid ascent by rescuers in large number impossible.

The structure itself survived the fire and today, now named the Brown Building, is used in part by New York University. In 1991 it was designated a National Historical Landmark. So the building codes did, in fact, protect the fabric of the building and, by preventing structural collapse, did presumably save lives. But creating a fire-proof structure very evidently did not deal with all the dangers of fire. The lesson was clear: high-rise buildings, even when their structure was fire-proof, could when occupied or used in the wrong way turn into death traps – and the higher they were more deadly they could become.

Some of the causes of the disaster were the result of violations of existing legislation –for example water hoses were faulty – and the owners were charged with criminal negligence and subsequently sued by members of the victims' families. But other causes revealed gaps in legislation covering the occupation of high-rise buildings. For example, there was no official limit to the number of people occupying each floor, and while in a low-rise building overcrowding could be dangerous, in skyscrapers without adequate means of escape it could prove catastrophic. And the staircase – lawfully built without landings, refuges or adequate lighting – turned out to be a death trap.

The fire also had significant political consequences that helped to change labour practices in American cities and the way in which skyscrapers were occupied. Around 100,000 people attended the victims' funeral march through Manhattan. This gave the tragedy considerable political potential, rapidly mobilized by the International Ladies' Garment Workers Union (ILGWU), which had been founded in 1900 and which, boosted by the popular sympathy following the fire, quickly became one of the largest and most powerful unions in America. Rose Schneiderman, a socialist labour leader and ILGWU member, addressed a public meeting in early April 1911 that was intended to memorialize the dead. But emotions and anger were still very high and the meeting rapidly became a political rally at which culprits and causes were identified – and these included structures like the Asch Building. Schneiderman told the audience that she 'would be a traitor to these poor burned bodies if I came here to talk good fellowship' and then informed it that the union had 'tried you good people of the public and we have found you wanting'. Her position was that society was to blame for the tragedy because it had not done enough to protect poor immigrant garment workers – Schneiderman herself was Polish-born – and, in particular, had allowed them to be packed into 'firetrap structures that will destroy us the minute they catch on fire'.[11]

Legislation was overhauled after the fire, but the focus was not on beefing up skyscraper construction and physical fire barriers but on ensuring that adequate means of escape were provided and protected and that the occupation of high-rise buildings was better managed to ensure safety. These included the introduction of mandatory fire drills, periodic fire inspections that included the testing of fire hoses, the installation of sprinkler systems, exit directions, fire alarms, doors designed to swing in the direction of emergency exits from a building and safe staircase design. Broadly speaking, the 1911 fire led directly to the creation of the modern, safety-conscious, skyscraper interior.

The next stage in the story of the skyscraper came from the east – from the Old World. Until the early years of the twentieth century the development of high-rise architecture had been an exclusively North American affair. Its origins, however, lay in Europe with late-eighteenth-century iron-framed buildings such as Marshall, Benyon and Bages's flax mill of 1796 in Ditherington, England (see page 75), and inspiration was drawn from other European examples of large-scale iron and steel construction. Gustave Eiffel's tower in Paris, rising 324 metres (roughly equivalent to an eighty-storey building), was, of course, an astonishing demonstration of the delight of height and of how it can be achieved. The tower, fabricated from wrought-iron components riveted together, was also very well known in the States, particularly in Chicago, because it formed the main architectural feature of the Paris *Exposition Universelle* of 1889. It was this fair that set the standard for the Chicago World's Columbian Exposition of 1893 and which Burnham strove to surpass.

There were other European exemplars, such as London's Crystal Palace of 1851 – conceived by Joseph Paxton – that revealed the speed, beauty and relative economy that it was possible to achieve by using mass-produced cast-iron components and large amounts of sheet glass, then only recently developed. The people of New York were impressed enough by the Crystal Palace to build their own version in 1853 – also named the Crystal Palace – in what is now Bryant Park, near the site on which the New York Public Library was later constructed. It housed an 'Exhibition of the Industry of all Nations' – clearly inspired by the London model – that included the first public presentation of Elisha Otis's safety elevator. The New York Crystal Palace did not last long. It was rapidly destroyed by fire in 1858 and, with its sudden and speedy end, acted as a solemn reminder that iron and glass construction was no more fire-proof than timber and masonry.

These European models demonstrated that height and the use of new materials – cast iron, wrought iron and large panes of sheet glass – could be aesthetically and functionally pleasing. But they were not inhabited high-rise structures. Nothing in late-nineteenth-century Europe could seriously compete against – certainly could not surpass – America's office skyscrapers.

But in the early decades of the twentieth century things changed – and with a vengeance. Perhaps it was due to the horrors of the First World War. The men who fought and survived seemed transformed, ideas burned bright, the world had to change and no obstacles – after the nightmare of trench warfare – seemed insuperable. This worked for good and for ill. One man changed – fatally and bitterly – by his wartime experiences was Adolf Hitler. Others affected were the architects Ludwig Mies van der Rohe and Walter Gropius. While Hitler, who promoted ponderous neoclassical architecture as his totalitarian house-style, set in train a regime of nationalist, militarist and racist politics that was to end in catastrophe, van der Rohe and Gropius – who both served, like Hitler, in the German army as enlisted men – became founding fathers of Modernism. The architecture they developed – the polar opposite to Hitler's – embraced the potential offered by technology and made the design and construction of high-rise architecture one of Modernism's key projects in its bid to realize a utopian new world, in which the overcrowded and diseased city of the nineteenth century was to become a place of light and space.

In Europe Berlin took the lead when, in 1921, the city sponsored a competition for the design of a skyscraper for a riverside site near Friedrichstrasse. The project, intended to inspire a debate about the future of the city and to represent Berlin's determination to throw off the gloom of Germany's recent defeat, proved compelling. There were 140 entries and great interest from the public as well as from architects and artists.

Skyscrapers as emblems of urban identity, of rebirth and of a belief in the benign nature of progress had been part of Europe's avant-garde artistic imagination since the very early years of the twentieth century. Peter Behrens, a Berlin-based architect and industrial designer with a utilitarian and technology-driven approach to design, had been entranced by skyscrapers and in 1912 declared that 'a germ of a new architecture – was inherent in the high-rise commercial architecture of New York.'[12] But more significant and sweeping was the support of the Italian futurist movement. The futurists ultimately evolved a somewhat sinister vision that included the glorification of the machine, war and violence and saw the high-rise tower – megalomaniac in scale and boldly functional in design – as symbolic of the technology-driven and ruthlessly reorganized cities of the future. The futurists' leading tower visionary was the Italian Antonia Sant'Elia, who, between 1912 and 1914, designed abstract and expressionistic towers inspired by skyscrapers in Chicago and New York but intended as egalitarian homes for workers rather than as offices. Part of his Città Nuova project, these tower designs were no more than demonstrations of ideas but the power of their imagery made the schemes highly influential. Sant'Elia himself built nothing significant, which was no doubt at least partly due to the fact he joined the Italian army in 1915 – seemingly intent on putting futurist militaristic theories into practice – and was killed in action in 1916.

This obsession with towers forms part of the artistic context for the Berlin competition and, to a degree, explains an extraordinary design that, viewed in hindsight, can be seen as epoch-making. It was the work of Ludwig Mies van der Rohe. The competition site was roughly triangular, or crystal-shaped, and this might have inspired Mies to conceive his scheme as a 'Crystal Tower', with its expressionistic crystalline form – a symbol of purity and renewal – enhanced by the proposal to clad the steel frame with a curtain wall made almost entirely of glass, or certainly with non-glass elements kept to an absolute minimum.

The design was, in part at least, inspired by Paul Scheerbart's polemical and futuristic 1914 publication *Glasarchitektur*, which, among other things, made the point that 'an iron skeleton is of course indispensable for glass architecture', noted that 'America is… the chief country for impressive giant buildings', promoted Bruno Taut's glass house, shown at the 1914 Werkbund Exhibition in Cologne, and concluded that 'the new glass environment… glass culture… will completely transform mankind.'[13] Another publication Mies must have known was Bruno Taut's *Alpine Architecture* of 1918, which, intended as a 'hymn of praise to the magnificence of the world', included drawings of crystal-form mountain peaks of intensely architectural appearance.

Also inspirational for Mies were, predictably, the skyscrapers of Chicago and New York, with perhaps Daniel H. Burnham and Company's triangular-plan Flatiron Building playing a decisive role. This is supported, in most opportunistic manner, by a photograph taken at the Berlin opening of the First International Dada Fair on 30 June 1920 that shows Johannes Baader – the sensationalist Dada performance artist – directing Mies' attention to the cover of *Neue-Jugend* of 17 June 1920, which featured a photograph of the Flatiron.[14] According to Terence Riley and Barry Bergdoll, the Flatiron, 'with its prismlike shape and restrained stone façade', was an 'heroic monolith' that presented

The 'Crystal Tower' designed in 1921 by Ludwig Mies van der Rohe for an ideas competition for a site on Friedrichstrasse, Berlin. It took the potential offered by the steel frame and minimalist glass curtain wall of the Reliance to new heights.

itself 'as the first structure in an outscaled city of the future for which it established… the rule'. As such it seemingly inflamed Mies' imagination; his own crystalline glass tower also 'conjured up a new, visionary city of giants'.[15]

Particularly moving for Mies were photographs of skyscrapers under construction. Then, as he explained in 1922, the 'bold constructive thoughts' are revealed, and 'the impression of the high-reaching steel skeleton is overpowering'. He also emphasized that 'the novel constructive principles of these buildings' only 'comes clearly into view if one employs glass for the no longer load-bearing exterior walls'.[16] At least one critic has made the connection between Mies' glass and steel tower project of 1921 and the Reliance Building. Sigfried Giedion – an early champion of Modernism and the first secretary-general of the movement's think-tank, the Congrès International d'Architecture Moderne (CIAM) – observed in his polemical *Space, Time and Architecture* of 1941 that the innovative Mies tower had 'nevertheless… been anticipated by the Reliance Building', and suggested that the Chicago building was not just 'an incentive for fantasy' but 'an architectonic anticipation of the future'.[17]

Unprecedented in its minimalism and the extent of its glazing, Mies' Crystal Tower hovered on the edge of what was, in 1921, structurally feasible.[18] But this did not matter because it was a response to what was only an ideas competition and construction was never an option. The scheme, with its eerie ethereal quality, lived primarily as a compelling photomontage, a type of almost surreal presentation made popular by the Dada movement,[19] but this was enough for it to play a significant role in the debate about how the skyscraper ought to look. Indeed, for some breathless critics the design is evidence that Mies 'invented a new architecture' and that the tower 'pointed the way towards the modern skyscraper that has come to define the very essence of the 20th century city around the world'.[20]

WALTER GROPIUS
AND THE GLAZED CURTAIN WALL

While Mies' epoch-defining scheme was being discussed, a former colleague of his made a highly significant contribution to the debate about the city of the future and high-rise design. In early 1911 Mies had been working in the Berlin office of Peter Behrens, the architect with a fascination for the skyscraper and who in 1908 gave his masonry- and concrete-built AEG Turbine Hall in Berlin a spectacular glass curtain wall. Also in the office, for four months from late 1910, was Le Corbusier. Walter Gropius, who joined in 1908, had just left. Behrens – dedicated to utility, structural logic, the integration of all elements of a building and the utilization of technology – was a key inspiration for these men who, between them and in the following decades, did much to provide Modernist architecture with a theory, a philosophy, the means to give its aims tangible and compelling architectural form and – most important – an exemplary body of work.

1921 was a significant year for all three men. Mies, of course, staked his claim as a visionary designer of glass-skinned skyscrapers. Walter Gropius had, for two years, been master of the Bauhaus School of design and building and the institution was going from strength to strength in pursuit of its all-enveloping social and artistic mission. Gropius, at the height of his powers, was about to design a building for the Bauhaus that was the culmination of years of architectural reflection and practice. It would be his masterpiece. The origin of this seminal building lay in a three-storey factory building Gropius had designed, in 1911 and before the trauma of war, in Alfeld, Germany for the Fagus shoe company. It was to be, in several ways, epoch-making. Clearly inspired by Behrens' AEG Turbine Hall, the building, according to the historian Nikolaus Pevsner, 'for the first time' included 'a complete façade… conceived in glass'. Also, as Pevsner pointed out, 'thanks to the large expanses of clear glass, the usual hard separation of exterior and interior [was] annihilated.'[21]

For the American critic Henry-Russell Hitchcock the factory was 'the most advanced piece of architecture built before the war', and its praises were sung by the Modernist historian Sigfried Giedion, who particularly admired the internal glass walls that made it a 'simple and... humane interpretation of the office'. Giedion also praised the two-storey 'model' factory and office building that Gropius had designed in 1914 as part of the Cologne Werkbund exhibition, notably because of its glass elevation, simple, well-lit interior and spiral staircases – entirely enclosed in glass – that seemed 'like movements seized and immobilized in space'.[22]

This transparency, open and adaptable plan and the ambiguity between exterior and interior space, noted by Pevsner and Giedion, became key aspects of later twentieth-century glass-walled architecture, notably the skyscrapers designed by van der Rohe. Gerrit Rietveld in the Netherlands explored some of the spatial ideas of the Fagus factory in 1924 when he designed the Rietveld Schroder House in Utrecht. But it was Gropius himself who took the factory's architecture to the next stage when, in 1925, he designed the Bauhaus's new four-storey building at Dessau.*

Minimal, entirely functional, with a logical and open plan; Gropius gave the Bauhaus building in Dessau one entire elevation of glass, essentially a minimally detailed curtain wall, attached to but projecting beyond the load-bearing concrete frame. For Gropius, by this time, elevations had become nothing more than 'simple curtains... screens stretched between the upright columns of the frame-work to keep out rain, cold, and noise.'[23] The generously glazed Bauhaus building was quickly followed by

---

* Giedion righty states that this building had been 'foreshadowed' by the Fagus factory.

the idiosyncratic Maison de Verre in Paris. Designed in 1928 by Pierre Chareau with Bernard Bijvoet, it was a hymn of prayer to contemporary technology, materials and flexible planning and featured a façade clad entirely with glass blocks.

LE CORBUSIER

In 1921, Le Corbusier was also just about to achieve international recognition. As a Swiss national he had not been obliged to serve during the First World War, and understandably had chosen to avoid the bloodbath. Instead he undertook architectural research and theoretical studies, taught a little and took on some modest architectural commissions. But in 1922, in the wake of Mies' Crystal Tower, Le Corbusier caught public and professional attention by the publication of his project for the 'Ville Contemporaine'. In 1921 Mies had envisaged one skyscraper with a fully glazed curtain wall. In his project for the 'Contemporary City' Le Corbusier envisaged two dozen sixty-storey towers, of steel-frame construction and cruciform plan, set in parkland, and each encased – Mies fashion – in curtain walls of glass. Le Corbusier had experimented with cruciform skyscrapers, later known as 'Cartesian skyscrapers', as early as 1919 as a means of building high and wide towers that also allowed natural light to enter their inner spaces.

The Ville Contemporaine, in which uses were segregated, and the automobile venerated as a practical and potentially life-enhancing object, was intended to house three million people, many within the largely residential skyscrapers. These generously glazed skyscrapers were, perhaps, unlikely objects to take centre stage in Le Corbusier's Ville Contemporaine because much of his earlier architectural research and practice had been concerned with low-rise, reinforced concrete-built houses, such as the 1922 version of his mass-produced 'Citrohan House' that introduced what became his leitmotif – the piloti or concrete column – into his work. Evidently the shimmering imagery of Mies' Crystal Tower had proved impossible to resist.

From 1930 onwards Mies and Le Corbusier developed their respective projects in most fascinating ways with the architecture, notably the skyscrapers, of Chicago and New York playing key roles. Mies, whose professional and personal life were thrown into confusion and then turmoil by the rise of the Nazis, left Germany in 1938 for the United States. He had taken a long time to make the move. The Bauhaus, of which he was the last director, was closed by the Nazis in 1933. Mies came under 'criminal investigation' by the Gestapo and commissions dried up. Gropius, also under increasing pressure, fled to England in 1934 and then in 1937 made his way to the United States. But Mies hung on. Indeed, he even tried to come to an accommodation with the Nazi regime when, in August 1934, he agreed to add his signature to a 'proclamation' in support of Hitler circulated shortly before the national referendum that the Nazi regime had organized to legitimize its unlawful seizure of power.* Finally, when it became absolutely clear that he had no professional future in his homeland, Mies left, virtually abandoning his family and long-time lover Lilly Reich.

Soon after his arrival in the United States Mies was appointed director of the department of architecture at the Armour Institute of Technology based in Chicago, which in 1940 became the Illinois Institute of Technology (IIT). This appointment gave Mies the opportunity to become intimately acquainted with Chicago's innovative skyscrapers, including the Reliance Building with its generously glazed curtain wall. Walter Gropius had, meanwhile,

---

* This action was probably a response to continuing intimidation but was to haunt Mies in later years. See Hochman, *Architects of Fortune*, pp. 217–20, 313.

established himself at the Harvard Graduate School of Design, becoming chairman of its department of architecture in 1938. He and Mies had little contact and, in contrast with Mies, Gropius was happier to focus on teaching and domestic or utopian design, avoiding larger commercial commissions.

Le Corbusier expanded the Ville Contemporaine project and represented it in 1930 as the 'Ville Radieuse', although not in book form until 1933. This revision envisaged a city – roughly modelled on an abstracted form of the human body, rigidly zoned and with uses segregated – that sought to provide homes with a human quality within an open and well-ordered urban environment. Once again skyscrapers and tall housing blocks, inspired by early Soviet-era collective housing, were to play a key role. He also travelled to the United States to study high-rise cities, arriving in New York in 1935. The city had long fascinated him, and he appears to have been mesmerized by New York giants like the forty-storey Equitable Building of 1915, which he apparently admired despite its neoclassical trim and the marble cladding over its steel frame. Certainly he illustrated it – apparently with approval – in the 'Architecture or Revolution' chapter of his book *Vers une Architecture*, published in 1923, along with the observation that the world was in a 'critical period... a moral crisis' and that 'things have changed; and changed for the better'.[24]

Yet Le Corbusier found New York as a city profoundly disturbing. In 1924 in *Urbanisme* (*City of Tomorrow*) he had condemned New York from afar for its canyon streets formed by a riot of closely packed skyscrapers rising from the pavement edge. It was for him a place of 'only confusion, chaos and upheaval' and as for beauty, as far as Le Corbusier was concerned it had 'none at all' because beauty 'has order as its basis'.[25] After his visit, impressed by the energy and silhouette of the city, he termed it a 'fairy catastrophe'. For Le Corbusier cities of towers did not have to be like New York – places of shadow and cacophony, of luxury

OVERLEAF
The Unité d'Habitation in Marseille, France, constructed from 1947–52 to the designs of Le Corbusier. It offered a utopian dream of urban living to be realized in ruggedly detailed steel-reinforced concrete.

in stark contrast to overshadowed slums – and these evils could be avoided if, by building tall, the required high density could be achieved while allowing space for large areas of parkland around each tower, in the manner proposed in the Ville Radieuse. *The City of Tomorrow* includes Le Corbusier's 'Voisin' scheme for rebuilding parts of central Paris as a city of towers rising from parkland, all set within a ruthless grid. In the book he included a photograph of the Flatiron, rising on the busy junction of Broadway and Fifth Avenue, close to neighbouring high-rise blocks, and captioned it '…the exact opposite of what the "Voisin" scheme proposes for Paris.'[26]

In 1933 many of the urban and architectural theories expressed by Le Corbusier in his Ville Radieuse were endorsed by the Modernist community by being codified in the 'Charter of Athens' drawn up by the Congrès International d'Architecture Moderne, at the time a highly influential body that ultimately did much to form opinions among the succeeding generation of architects and town planners. So the residential skyscraper entered the repertoire of urban forms and, for good or ill, helped to characterize post-war reconstruction in Europe's wrecked cities. But the war itself threw Le Corbusier's career into disarray, just as it did for Mies and Gropius, even though – inadvertently – it created opportunities for his theories to be applied and, initially at least, to flourish. During the early 1940s, when the axis powers and their vassal states were in the ascendancy and appeared to be undefeatable, Le Corbusier lobbied the Italian fascist dictator Benito Mussolini and the French collaborationist Vichy government to adopt his urban theories for proposed new towns. Le Corbusier knew, of course, that lobbying the German authorities – among whom Hitler's taste for overblown, stern and mechanistic neoclassism had taken root – would be futile whereas the Italian fascists, at least in the early days, had promoted rationalist Modernism.[27]

When the war ended the truly serious parts of Mies' and Le Corbusier's careers began. They both proved to be astonishing survivors, and both embraced high-rise architecture – although with significantly different architectural expressions.

Mies, while teaching at the IIT, became the lead figure in what is now termed the Second Chicago School, and the principles of this school were no less than Modernism's basic tenets, as forged during the previous thirty years or so: buildings should be a response to the site and brief, and utilize the potential of innovative building technology truthfully expressed in the rational and minimalist spirit of functionalism and utility. These tenets also included the belief that buildings should possess a high degree of flexibility in their design to allow changes in use and to aid repair, upgrading or adaptation, and that mechanized production processes should be harnessed when possible to allow – for artistic as well as economic reasons – the prefabrication of repetitive components. Some of these tenets were explored in Mies' Crystal Tower project, which itself was, to a degree, rooted in the first Chicago School and in the Reliance and the Flatiron buildings in particular.

In Europe just after the war Le Corbusier pursued an architectural direction that veered away from the steel-framed, glass curtain-walled skyscraper prototype. For artistic and economic reasons he continued his love affair with reinforced in situ cast concrete – often 'roughly' handled and with timber-mould marks left in place or exaggerated to create a powerful if somewhat raw surface texture. This Béton Brut, or tough-looking rough-cast concrete finish, reminiscent of utilitarian industrial buildings and fortifications, possessed a rugged beauty that was, seemingly, a direct expression of the material and manner of construction. It soon spawned a cult-like following and launched what became known as 'Brutalist' architecture. Utilizing Béton Brut building techniques, Le Corbusier developed the mixed-use high-rise slabs that had featured in the Ville Radieuse to create self-sustaining communities. These slabs included 'internal streets' to act as access corridors and even shopping malls. The supreme example is the slab-shaped Unité d'Habitation in Marseille. Twelve storeys high, and supported on piloti of oblong tapering shape, the Unité was constructed between 1947 and 1952 and provides over twenty flat-types (many split-level) for 1,800 inhabitants as well as shops and cafes along internal corridors, a clinic and – in emulation of Soviet collective housing projects such as Moisei Ginzburg's 1928-built Narkomifin in Moscow – a rooftop crèche, running track and sports facilities.

MIES VAN DER ROHE
AND THE HIGH-RISE CURTAIN WALL

In Chicago, while Le Corbusier was labouring to make his visionary architecture a reality in the South of France, Mies created a skyscraper architecture that is a true child of the Reliance Building. The degree of this dependence is speculative – Mies never publicly acknowledged the directness of the debt – but it is striking. The first built expression of his vision was 860–880 Lake Shore Drive, a pair of twenty-six-storey apartment blocks built between 1949 and 1951 – exactly when the Unité d'Habitation was under construction.

These two projects present wonderfully complementary aspects of the same vision. The Unité is of massive, concrete construction, with many direct references to history or precedent (for example, the deep-set windows with coloured reveals evoke the vernacular architecture of North Africa), there is symbolic if abstract ornament (notably the 'modulor' man – an anthropometric scale of proportions used in the Unité and cast in concrete at ground-floor level) – and the building is tall but also long and narrow.

The Mies apartments in Chicago are steel-framed, minimal in their fully glazed curtain walls and without obvious ornament or overt reference to history. But their location, as free-standing sculptural objects on the edge of the vast Lake Michigan, enjoying stunning prospects and fresh air, achieves one of the ideals of Le Corbusier's Ville Contemporaine. Also in line with Le Corbusier's thinking are the exposed columns around the buildings' perimeters, which not only echo the colonnades of Greek temples, and thus bestow on the towers a strange if most indirect pedigree of the past, but also correspond to Le Corbusier's column-like piloti.

These two Miesian towers are full of fascination, not least as demonstrations of the evolution of some of the ideas underpinning the design and construction of the Reliance Building and as tangible expressions of Mies' long-held architectural theories. His Crystal Tower of 1921 imagined the glass-clad and steel-framed skyscraper and in 1933 he explained the theory and potential of such towers: 'glass walls alone permit the skeletal structure its unambiguous constructive appearance and secure its architectonic possibilities.' These, Mies asserted, 'are genuine building elements from which a new, richer building art can arise.'[28] Unspoken by Mies, but apparent, is a debt to Gropius's glazed curtain-wall buildings of the immediate pre-First World War and inter-war periods. Gropius's buildings were low-rise but, from the constructional and aesthetic points of view, they were trailblazers in the evolution of glass curtain wall architecture.

Given Mies' high claims, the generously glazed curtain wall of the Lake Shore Drive Apartments is of particular interest. In theory, a curtain wall is a skin draped over the primary structural frame of a building and not significantly integrated with it, and does little – from the structural point of view – beyond supporting its own weight. The glass, iron, timber and terracotta

curtain wall of the Reliance Building realizes much of this aim and derives much of its beauty from the true way in which it expresses its materials and manner of construction. In the curtain walls in the Lake Shore Drive Apartments, Mies moved beyond the purely functional into the philosophical realm of how truth is best expressed. A moment's contemplation of the curtain walls reveals not only the dramatic extent of the glazing but also the fact that the areas of glass are divided by steel mullions of I-section profile. These enliven the elevation, like Gothic ribs or in an almost theatrical Baroque manner, casting shadows when the sun shines. They are modelled by raking light and they save flush glass elevations from potential blandness.

Are these mullions strictly – functionally – necessary? Mies is famed for embracing the notion, when designing architecture for functional excellence or emotional impact, that 'less is more' – a phrase he seems to have picked up from the mid-nineteenth-century British poet Robert Browning.[29] But in fact these mullions are – despite their visual message – structurally insignificant, even superfluous. At the very least, the role they play could be achieved in a more minimal fashion. In an interview in 1960 Mies explained that a structure is 'logical' when it is 'the best way to do things and express them'.[30] So these mullions are responses not, primarily, to structural or practical necessity but to a greater truth than that of pure function. They represent an artistic truth.

Peter Carter, who studied under Mies at the ITT from 1957 and then worked in his office until 1971, explained this permutation of the curtain wall in some detail in his 1974 publication, *Mies van der Rohe and His Work*. That he did so is not surprising. The I-section mullions are visually striking – if somewhat puzzling – not least because this can be seen as a structurally retrograde move. As early as 1922 Mies had made it clear that the full artistic and functional potential of steel-frame construction could be realized only when glass exterior walls were no longer part of the 'load-bearing'

860–880 Lake Shore Drive, Chicago, is a pair of epoch-making glass curtain-walled residential towers built from 1949–51 to the designs of Ludwig Mies van der Rohe.

structure. But in the Lake Shore Drive Apartments the 'skin' of the curtain wall and the primary structure were designed to be, to some extent, integrated. Essentially the curtain wall is formed within the main structural frame and not independent of it.

Attempting to explain this perhaps surprising turn of events, and to reconcile the visual with the actual 'truth' of the structure, Carter offers an insider's view. He notes that the glass in the elevations of the apartments is set between the elements forming the structural frame and not in front of them causing the structural frame and glass infill to be structurally united with, in the process, 'each element losing part of its particular identity in the process of establishing a single architectural statement.'[31] So curtain wall and structural frame were merged to create greater architectural unity, with the mullions – little more than slivers of steel – playing the key role in this 'statement' because they are masquerading as a structural frame of astounding minimalist elegance.

Also, as part of this masquerade, the mullions are in fact attached to the main structural frame so that – contrary to Mies' visionary theory of 1921 – the glazed skin of the apartments is not free from the load-bearing structure. This was due, at least in part, to building codes that required the true steel frame to be protected by – and thus partly concealed behind – fire-proof material. In fact, at the practical level, the mullions mask the junctions of the glass 'modules' forming the windows but also mark the locations of the vertical elements of the main structural frame.[32]

With what is almost a sleight of hand – and in a brilliantly pragmatic manner – Mies managed to reconcile two seemingly conflicting views of the curtain wall that arose in the 1890s. On the one hand was the view that it should be independent of the main structure and, relieved of a major structural role, do no more than support itself so that it can be lightweight and generously glazed – as with the Reliance Building. On the other hand was the view that the curtain wall should not only be strong, but also look reassuringly strong and solid. As we have seen, the growing preference for the latter after the completion of the Reliance Building compromised the former vision. With the almost entirely glazed curtain wall of his Lake Shore Drive Apartments, visually stiffened as they were by the rows of structurally unnecessary steel mullions, Mies achieved both aims.

THE SEAGRAM BUILDING

A few years later, in New York, Mies developed the ideas embodied in the Lake Shore Drive Apartments to achieve a new level of architectural elegance. The thirty-eight-storey Seagram Building on Park Avenue, designed and built between 1954 and 1958, is a sleek glass office tower, seemingly free-standing as Le Corbusier promoted in his Ville Radieuse, placed not in parkland but set back from Park Avenue on the edge of a plaza. Although relatively small this plaza, complete with oblong pools and with a surface continuing within the ground floor of the tower – thus in Gropius manner dissolving the boundary between exterior and interior – permitted the Seagram to rise as a sculptural object in its own very specific space and to enjoy and offer superb urban prospects. This plaza and tower relationship was especially striking when the scheme was completed. In 1977 Ludwig Glaeser, then curator of the Mies archives in the Museum of Modern Art, observed that 'there is no precedent for the configuration of the Seagram plaza in the work of Mies van der Rohe', while Phyllis Lambert – a highly significant figure in the creation of the Seagram – could only liken it to the parvis in front of a cathedral.[33]

Once again, I-section mullions were employed and, once again, they are structurally fraudulent. Mies would, no doubt, have preferred the steel frame of the tower to be honestly exposed to make the building's structure its greatest ornament but – once again – building codes intervened. As in Chicago, these required that structural steelwork be protected by fire-proof material such as concrete on the basis that steel, in intense heat and when in a confined space, can fail. So, with the true structure of the tower masked, Mies – as in the Lake Shore Drive Apartments – used non-structural I-section mullions, here bronze-toned, to visually suggest the tower's structure. And the slender mullions are more deftly handled than in the Chicago towers, so the impression is enhanced that the structural frame is more minimal than it actually is. At a casual glance, the tower appears to be formed with a network of impossibly minimal columns. It is not, of course, but for most the trick works brilliantly.

The differences between the skins of the Seagram and the Chicago towers were due in part to the fact that the glazed curtain wall had been developed significantly since the completion of the Lake Shore Drive Apartments and most of these developments had taken place in New York. First there was the thirty-nine-storey slab-form United Nations Secretariat that, completed in 1952, forms a key part of the UN enclave on Manhattan. Conceived in 1947, this enclave was created to the designs of Oscar Niemeyer and Le Corbusier working as consultants to the lead architect Wallace K. Harrison. The story of the making of the enclave is complex, not least because Niemeyer, later the key architect from 1956 for the new city of Brasilia, was inspired by Le Corbusier's urban planning and architecture but – on this project – differed significantly with Le Corbusier over planning strategy and design.

Le Corbusier attempted to dominate proceedings by producing his own comprehensive scheme for the entire site at an early stage and by encouraging Niemeyer to become his acolyte rather than his opponent. Harrison persuaded Niemeyer to stand his ground and finally the pair's differing designs were fused to produce the

The Seagram Building, New York, completed in 1958 to the designs of Ludwig Mies van der Rohe. The Seagram is the ultimate expression of the high-rise architectural adventure launched in Chicago by the Reliance Building over sixty years earlier.

existing group of buildings. Forced marriages rarely end happily, and there was some bitterness on Le Corbusier's part because ultimately Niemeyer's planning strategy for the site was chosen over his. But the Secretariat – essentially Niemeyer's design – turned out to be an object lesson in Modernist design and was the first fully glazed curtain-walled high-rise in New York, with its skin sleeker than that of Mies' towers in Chicago. Also completed in 1952 was Lever House, on Park Avenue, a twenty-four-storey block of offices designed by Gordon Bunshaft of SOM. Its form was highly influential, with a block of offices rising off a wider, two-storey podium supported on columns and including a plaza, garden and generous reception and public areas. The curtain wall on the tower was designed in highly minimal manner, with heat-resistant glass of striking blue-green colour framed by stainless steel mullions and spandrels. It was similar to that on the UN Secretariat and was executed by the same contractors.

The changed context for the design of curtain walls evidently stimulated Mies and his team and they rose to the challenge. Working closely with him on the Seagram were the client's daughter Phyllis Lambert, who had secured Mies the commission and ultimately became director of planning, and architect Philip Johnson. He became Mies' partner for the project and was largely responsible for interior design, but between 1955 and 1957 was the sole legal author of the Seagram because the New York Chapter of the American Institute of Architects, in a bizarre and petty-minded manner, 'refused Mies authorization to practice his profession on the pretext that he did not have a university diploma.'[34]

On the Seagram Building the curtain wall projects, in cantilever fashion, from the structural frame of steel fire-proofed with concrete, with the I-section mullions marking the cantilevers and the junctions between panes of glass forming the windows.[35] This cantilever principle – absent in the Lake Drive

Shore Apartments but explored in tentative manner by Mies in his Esplanade Apartment Building in Chicago of 1953–56 – ensured that 'the skin was inherently separate from the structural frame', allowing it to be wrapped around the building so that, with no significant structural role, it could be almost entirely glass.[36] Artistically, explains Lambert, this meant the building could 'be treated as a volumetric whole, a monolithic unit' with the use of tinted glass helping to 'secure the effect'.[37] The introduction of the tinted glass was highly significant, doing much to determine the appearance – even character – of the building. Tinted glass can be somewhat sinister, suggesting that there is something to hide within this monument to the corporate world. But it also increases the number of ways in which the building can be perceived. In certain conditions it can look transparent, in others monolithic with its tinted glass set within a darkened bronze frame, or it can – as a prismatic display of images – reflect the world around it, while at night it is luminescent with a warm glow.

But the seeming inconsistencies and contradictions of the Seagram's curtain wall continue to perplex, puzzle and even infuriate. The main bone of contention remains architectural 'truth' and the way the construction of the wall appears to undermine Mies' declared dedication to structural logic. What ultimately is to be made of the fact that the implied honesty of the expressed structure of the Seagram is in fact a charade, a piece of almost Baroque theatre? Typically, Jean-Louis Cohen notes that the 'frame of H-shaped mullions [more correctly, perhaps, I-shaped mullions]… stops flush with the [steel] corner columns, which are themselves sheathed in a layer of concrete and a skin of metal… Belaying any pretense of structural "honesty" the same façade formula continues on the upper service level, with its concrete infill.'[38]

But for others this complexity and contradiction, the consequence of Mies' practical, pragmatic and poetic approach to the realization of his functionalist architectural vision, is the Seagram's greatest quality. In 1999 Herbert Muschamp, the distinguished architecture correspondent of the *New York Times*, declared the Seagram 'the millennium's most important building' and noted that 'the business of civilization is to hold opposites together', which 'goal', he suggested, 'has been rendered here by Mies with a serenity unsurpassed in modern times.'[39]

Beside its curtain wall the Seagram faced other structural and artistic challenges that echo those faced by Root and Atwood just over sixty years earlier in Chicago. As was the case with the Reliance Building, the Seagram's steel structure needed bracing to resist lateral movement. This was achieved by constructing concrete floors to add weight and by stiffening the structure by creating an elevator and service core incorporating diagonal steel braces. The core also played a role in creating a simple and flexible interior because with lift and services combined in the centre of the building, floors could be open-plan, or divided as required by lightweight partitions.

This flexibility and adaptability of plan related to a tenet of Modernism that Mies held dear. Architecture – if truly functional – had to possess the machine's capacity to be repaired, updated if possible and if not then, as with any redundant machine, be discarded, without undue emotion. The best way to give a building enduring life and to ensure that it provided long-term value for money was not just to build it well, but to make sure it had a form that was flexible in the way in which it could be used, and thus ensure that it could adapt to survive. This meant that Mies did not absolutely agree with the Modernist tenet, articulated in prophetic manner in 1896 by Louis Sullivan, that 'form ever follows function' (see page 21). This was too simplistic. As Peter Carter explains, Mies 'believed that functional requirements may, in time, change while form, once rigidly established, cannot easily be modified'. What this meant, in practice, is that

Mies chose structural systems suitable for a broad, rather than a narrow or specific range of functional requirements 'to achieve flexibility and to allow freedom for future modifications'.[40] The wisdom of Mies' thinking is surely confirmed by the fact that the Seagram survives, largely unchanged in form despite changes of ownership and – to a degree – of function.

THE SPIRIT OF THE RELIANCE BUILDING RETURNS TO CHICAGO

After the completion of Lever House and the Seagram Building the combination of steel frame with glass curtain wall became a standard form for commercial towers in cities around the world. Naturally the repetition, often for inappropriate sites and realized in diluted and somewhat unthinking manner, devalued the formula. At its most negative the sleek glass-clad skyscraper, once a symbol of artistically progressive architecture, has come to represent energy-guzzling corporate greed and environmental profligacy. Certainly, as far as sustainability goes, glass curtain walls can be a challenge because, by their nature, they tend to create interiors that get cold in winter and warm in summer and which require costly systems of environmental controls. But in Chicago the form was developed, in spectacular and architecturally positive manner, in a seemingly never-ending quest for height. The John Hancock Center was completed in 1969 and, at a height of 343.7 metres, was then the tallest building in the world outside New York. To achieve this height its architect Bruce Graham of SOM and its structural engineer Fazlur Rahman Khan radically rethought the principles of framed construction. Khan came up with the 'tube' structural system, which not only has greater strength than conventional framing but uses less

material and so is cheaper to build, makes less environmental impact, allows for the creation of more interior space and permits architects to design skyscrapers in a greater variety of shapes. The tubular system also permits the frame to be made of steel, reinforced concrete or a combination of both. The Hancock Center, containing offices and flats, has powerfully expressive elevations that feature a series of X-shaped frames – one stacked upon another – which reveal that the structure's surfaces are in fact part of its 'tubular' structural system.

The same design team of architect and structural engineer produced the Sears Tower (now named the Willis Tower), which, when completed in Chicago in 1973, at a height of 442.1 metres was, for a quarter of a century, the tallest building in the world. The Sears Tower is formed of a vertical series of nine square 'tubes' that, from the structural point of view, are each essentially independent buildings.

The potential of Khan's 'tubular' system – which in theory is capable of achieving infinite height – led in the 1970s to a rebirth of skyscraper construction. But the new generation of skyscrapers, achieving greater heights than ever before, did face new problems. When buildings reach extreme heights it is not only huge lateral movement caused by wind hitting the building's large surface areas that has to be dealt with; the buildings themselves oscillate. An innovation in skyscraper design had been the introduction of large-scale 'tuned mass dampers' – made in concrete or steel and housed in the upper portion of the towers – that, like vast pendulums, move in opposition to the oscillations and thus create equilibrium. One of the earliest uses of a damper is in the 279-metre-high fifty-nine-storey Citygroup Center on Lexington Avenue, New York. Completed in 1978 to the designs of Hugh Stubbins and engineer William LeMessurier, the tower – now famous for a hasty and initially secret stiffening of the wind-bracing system just after completion – incorporates

The cutting edge skyscraper returns to Chicago: the Willis Tower, completed in 1973 to the designs of Fazlur Rahman Khan and Bruce Graham of SOM. The tower took the steel framed and glass clad high-rise in a breathtaking new direction.

a damper that weighs a massive 400 tons.[41] So the architectural adventure – to build tall with elegance, comfort and safety – that started in Chicago in the 1880s continues to reach new heights. And the Reliance Building – with its generously glazed non-load-bearing curtain wall and minimalist detailing – has in the long term proved to be the most enduring and inspiring pioneer of skyscraper design. Sigfried Giedion, who in 1941 called the Reliance the 'architectonic anticipation of the future', has been proved right.[42]

But the journey of the Reliance has been strange. Having been initially disregarded in its own city and own country, where its almost unornamented appearance and abandonment of historic prototypes meant that it was too far ahead of the prevailing tastes of the time, it soon entered – and inspired – the imagination of the European avant-garde. And then from Europe its imagery, given additional meaning by being incorporated into visionary theories about the architecture and cities of the future, returned to its native shore. Here much of its early promise was realized, with the Seagram Building arguably forming the logical end to a line of architectural enquiry that had been launched by the Reliance over half a century earlier. But the Seagram proved, of course, to be another starting place, and has ultimately confirmed the glass-skinned super-high tower as the supreme expression of steel or reinforced concrete-framed skyscraper architecture. It is safe to say that the glazed curtain-walled towers that now rise around the world as emblems of the technologically driven twenty-first century are, to a significant degree, direct heirs to the extraordinary skyscraper that John W. Root, Daniel H. Burnham, Charles B. Atwood and William E. Hale created in Chicago during the closing years of the nineteenth century.

Notes

2 JOHN WELLBORN ROOT: ATLANTA, LIVERPOOL AND NEW YORK

1   Shelby Foote, *The Civil War*, Vol. 2 (Pimlico, London 1992), pp. 938–9.

2   David J. Eicher, *The Longest Night* (Pimlico, London 2002), p. 697.

3   Harriet Monroe, *John Wellborn Root: A Study of His Life and Work*, 1896 (Prairie School Press edition, 1966), pp. 7–8.

4   Ibid.

5   Ibid, p. 7.

6   Thomas G. Dyer, *Secret Yankees: The Union Circle in Confederate Atlanta*, (The Johns Hopkins University Press, Baltimore), 1999, 2001, p. 60.

7   Franklin M. Garrett, *Atlanta and Environs: A Chronicle of its People and Events*, Vol. 1 – 1820s–1870s (University of Georgia Press, 1954, 1969 facsimile edition), p. 439.

8   Monroe, p. 3.

9   Monroe, pp. 7–8.

10   Eicher, p. 707.

11   Monroe, p. 8.

12   Eicher, p. 714.

13   Ibid.

14   Ibid. and *From Atlanta to the Sea*, edited memoirs of William T. Sherman, edited and introduction by B. H .Liddell Hart (Folio Society, London, 1961), p. 104.

15   *From Atlanta to the Sea*, pp. 110–27 for this and many other pungent and pithy statements from Sherman on the siege of Atlanta and the treatment of the city's fabric and citizens after its surrender.

16   Monroe, pp. 8–9. Garrett records an order issued on the 5th September 1864 by the commander of the Union Provost Guard that 'all families now living in Atlanta, the male representatives of which are in the service of the Confederate States… will leave the city within five days.' Confederate General Hood sent a note to Sherman claiming that the 'unprecedented measure… to expel … from their homes and fireside the wives and children of a brave people' was 'studied and ingenious cruelty' that 'transcends… all acts ever brought to my attention in the dark history of this war.' Sherman's riposte was to charge Hood with being a hypocrite. See Vol. 1, 1954, p. 640, 641–2.

17   See Garrett, Vol. 1, 1954, pp. 655–9 for a description of the ruins of Atlanta as published in the *Atlanta Intelligencer* of 22nd December 1864, 'Atlanta as Sherman left it'.

18   Monroe, p. 9.

19   Ibid.

20   Ibid, p. 10.

21   Ibid, p. 8.

22   Ibid, pp. 10–11.

23   Ibid, p. 11.

24   Ibid.

25   Donald Hoffmann, *The Architecture of John Wellborn Root*, (Johns Hopkins University Press, Baltimore & London, 1973), p. 4.

26   Monroe, p. 12.

27   Thomas Browne, *Religio Medici*, 1642, section 16; *The Oxford Museum, The Substance of a Lecture by Henry W. Acland*, James Parke & Co. (Oxford, 1867), p. 13.

28   Monroe, pp. 12–13.

29   Hoffmann, p. 4.

30   Monroe, p. 14.

31   Ibid, pp. 15–16.

32   Hoffmann, pp. 4–5.

33   Sarah Bradford Landau, *P. B. Wight; Architect, Contractor and Critic*, (Art Institute of Chicago, Chicago), 1981.

34   Monroe, p. 23.

3 'CHICAGO: 1871–1891

1   Monroe, pp. 23–4 of 1966 edition.

2   Ibid, p. 24.

3   Ibid, p. 25.

4   Ibid.

5   Erik Larson, *The Devil in the White City* (Doubleday, 2003), pp. 20–1.

6   Monroe, p. 130.

7   Larson, p. 21.

8   Louis H. Sullivan, *The Autobiography of an Idea*, foreword by Claude Bragdon, (Press of the American Institute of Architects, New York, 1926), pp. 285–6.

9   Larson, p. 22.

10   Monroe, p. 49.

11   Larson, p. 22.

12   Ibid.

13   Monroe, p. 169.

14   Charlotte Gere with Lesley Hoskins, *The House Beautiful: Oscar Wilde and the Aesthetic Interior* (Lund Humphries, London, 2000), p. 88.

15   Kevin H. F. O'Brien, 'The House Beautiful': a reconstruction of Oscar Wilde's American lecture, Victorian Studies, vol. 17, no. 4 (Indiana University Press, January 1974), pp. 395–418; Gere and Hoskins.

16   George Eliot, letter to John Blackwood, 5 November 1873, quoted in Denis Donoghue's *Walter Pater: Lover of Strange Souls*, New York, 1995, p. 58.

17   Essay included in *Intentions*, 1891; quoted by Gere, p. 14.

18   *Mr Oscar Wilde's Lectures, Seasons 1883–4*, p. 5.

19   *New York Herald.* Quoted in Wilde's Lectures.

20   Gere and Hoskins, p. 88.

21   Ibid., pp. 88 and 92.

22   Norman Page, *An Oscar Wilde Chronology*, (MacMillan, Boston, 1991).

23   Gere and Hoskins, p. 92.

24   Ibid.

25   *Mr Oscar Wilde's Lectures, Seasons 1883–4*, p. 5.

26   Kevin H. F. O'Brien, *Oscar Wilde in Canada, an apostle for the arts* (Personal Library, 1982), p. 114.

27   Gere and Hoskins, pp. 88–9.

28   Oscar Wilde, *Impressions of America*, 1906, p. 3; *The Philosophy of Dress*, 1885.

29   Larson, p. 25. However, in 1900 a 'map of the business centre of Chicago' states that skyscrapers are from '12 to 21 stories' high.

30   T. Gunny Harboe, *Reliance Building Historic Structures Report* (McClier Preservation Group), p. 1.

31   Larson, pp. 24–5.

32   Donald L. Miller, *City of the Century: The Epic of Chicago and the making of America*, (Simon & Schuster, New York, 1996), p. 319; Aldis studied at Yale University and in the early 1890s started to acquire first editions, primarily by American authors, with the ambition of including with each one a letter from the author referring to the title of the volume. He left his collection to Yale where it is maintained as a separate collection known as the Yale Collection of American Literature. Root and Aldis must have had a relationship that reached far beyond the bounds of construction and real estate.

33   Ibid., p. 320.

34   Ibid., p. 319.

35   *Chicago Tribune*, 25 February 1885, p. 15.

36   Larson, p. 25.

37   Monroe, p. 114.

38   Larson, pp. 24–5.

39   Monroe, pp. 114–15.

40   Ibid, p. vii.

41   Harboe, p. 2.

42   Larson, pp. 25–6.

43   Harboe, p. 1.

44   Monroe, p. 63.

45   A. W. N. Pugin, *True Principles of Christian or Pointed Architecture* (Henry Bohn, London, 1853), p. 1.

46   John Ruskin, *The Seven Lamps of Architecture* (George Allen, Kent, 1889), p. 9.

47   Larson, p. 30.

48   Charles Moore, *Daniel H. Burnham, Architect, Planner of Cities*, vol. 2, (Houghton Mifflin, Boston, 1921), p. 147.

49   Larson, p. 29.

50   Ibid.

51   Information thanks to Gunny Harboe; *Chicago Tribune*, 7 July 1889, p. 9.

52   Monroe, pp. 141–2.

53   Ibid.

4 THE 'WHITE CITY

1   Information thanks to Gunny Harboe, see *Inter Ocean*, vol. xviii, 2 March 1890, p. 10.

2   Carl W. Condit, *The Chicago School of Architecture*, (The University of Chicago Press, Chicago, 1964), p. 111.

3   Alexis de Tocqueville, *Democracy in America*, part 1, 1835; part 2, 1840.

4   Ibid, part 2, p. 36.

5   Norman Bolotin and Christine Laing, *The World's Columbian Exposition: The Chicago's World's Fair of 1893*, (University of Illinois Press, Chicago), 2002, p. 1.

6   Oscar Wilde, *Impressions of America*, 1906.

7   Ibid., p. 3; *The Philosophy of Dress*, 1885.

8   The Godwin Bursary 1893. Report on the Columbus Exposition at Chicago 1893 by the holder Banister F. Fletcher ARIBA, MS copy in RIBA Library 725.91. 73 (C) (043) – X079 257).

9   Monroe, p. 218.

10   Ibid, p. 219.

11   Monroe, p. 220 of 1896 edition.

12   Louis Willie, *A City Circled by Parks: Forever open, clear and free*, (University of Chicago, 1991), p. 54.

13   Monroe, p. 221.

14   Ibid.

15   Ibid, pp. 221–2.

16   Ibid, p. 222.

17   Ibid, p. 224.

18   Ibid, p. 221.

19   Erik Mattie, *World's Fairs*, (Princeton Architectural Press, 1998), p. 88.

20   Sullivan, p. 285.

21   Banister Fletcher, Godwin Bursary report, MS copy, pp. 3–4.

22   Banister Fletcher's report – completed in late December 1893 – includes photographs, drawings and many sketches of construction details, particularly of the metal roofs of the Exposition halls. The largely handwritten report is lodged in the library of the Royal Institute of British Architects in London. The RIBA administered the Godwin Bursary. See: 'The Godwin Bursary 1893. Report on the Columbus Exposition at Chicago 1893 by the holder Banister F. Fletcher ARIBA' (RIBA Library 725.91. 73(C) (043) – X079 257.

23   Banister Fletcher, p. 4.

24   Monroe, p. 225.

25   Mattie, p. 88, 97.

26   Hoffmann, p. 230.

27   Sullivan, pp. 285–92.

28   Banister Fletcher p. 9

29   Moore, p. 40 of 1968 edition.

30   Mattie, p. 89.

31   Moore, pp. 40–1 of 1968 edition.

32   Ibid.

33   Ibid.

34   Ibid.

35   Ibid.

36   Mattie, pp. 88–9.

37   Fletcher, p. 10.

38   Moore, p. 43.

39   Sullivan, *Autobiography of an Idea* (1926), p. 320.

40   Ibid., p. 320

41   Moore, p. 44 of 1968 edition

42   Monroe, pp. 262–3.

43   Miller, p. 382; Larson, p. 107.

44   Mattie, p. 89.

45   Moore, pp. 44–5 of 1968 edition.

46   Moore, p. 45 of 1968 edition.

47   Mattie, p. 89.

48   Frank Lloyd Wright, 'The Tyranny of the Skyscraper', in *Modern Architecture*, (Princeton University Press, 1931), p. 85.

49   Bolotin and Laing, p. 44.

50   Moore, p. 46 of 1968 edition.

51   Ibid.

52   Hoffmann, p. 220. Letter from Burnham to Homer Saint-Gaudens in *The Reminiscences of Augustus Saint-Gaudens* edited by his son Homer, 2 vols (New York, 1913), vol. ii, p. 66.

53   Moore, p. 50 of 1968 edition.

54   Mattie, p. 89.

55   Moore, p. 47 of 1968 edition.

56   Banister Fletcher, p. 4.

57   Ibid., p. 6.

58   Ibid., p.8.

59   Ibid.

60   Ibid.

61   Ibid.

62   Judith Dupré, *Skyscrapers* (Black Dog and Leventhal, New York, 1996), p. 22.

63   Ibid., p. 11.

64   Ibid.

65   Mattie, p. 96.

66   DUP Blue Print, p. 16.

67   Mattie, p. 96.

68   *Engineering* magazine, August 1892.

69 *Lippincott* magazine, March 1896, pp. 403–9.

70 Mattie, p. 97.

71 Miller, p. 502.

72 Ibid.

73 Jeanne Madeline Weimann, *The Fair Women: The Story of the Woman's Building, World's Columbian Exposition* (Academy Chicago, Chicago, 1981).

74 Candace Wheeler, *Yesterdays in a Busy Life* (Harper Brothers, New York, 1918), pp. 253–4; see also Amelia Peck and Carol Irish, *The Art and Enterprise of American Design*, (Metropolitan Museum of Art, New York, 2001).

75 Judith Paterson, 'Harriet Monroe' in *Dictionary of Literary Biography*, (Gale, Detroit, 1990), pp. 226–34.

76 *The Columbian Ode*, Harriet Monroe, W. Irving Way & Co., Chicago, 1893, commissioned by the Joint Committee on Ceremonies of the World's Columbian Exposition, delivered on 21 October 1892 'before an audience of more than one hundred thousand persons, during the dedicatory ceremonies in the building for the Manufactures and Liberal Arts.'

77 Monroe, p. 242.

78 Ibid, p. 243.

79 Ibid, pp. 243–4.

80 Ibid, p. 242.

81 Sullivan, pp. 324–5.

82 *Lady Windermere's Fan*, Act III, Oscar Wilde, first performed in February 1892 in London.

83 Sullivan, p. 323.

84 Moore, p. 45 of 1968 edition.

85 *Chicago Tribune*, 14 January 1893, p. 6.

86 Miller, p. 531.

87 Moore, p. 86 of 1968 edition.

88 Hoffmann, p. 220.

89 Banister Fletcher 1893 report.

90 Moore, p. 74 of 1968 edition.

91 Miller, p. 532; Linda Dowling, *Charles Eliot Norton, The Art of Reform in Nineteenth-century America*, (University of New Hampshire Press, 2007).

5 THE RELIANCE BUILDING

1 Joanna Merwood-Salisbury, *Chicago 1890* (University of Chicago Press, 2009), p. 98.

2 Harboe, pp. ix, 2.

3 Ryerson and Burnham Archive, Art Institute of Chicago.

4 Harboe report, p. 8; *American Architect and Building News*, vol. xlvii, no. 996, 26 January 1895.

5 Ibid.

6 Ruskin, p. 9.

7 Miles I. Berger, *They Built Chicago*, 1992, pp. 49–58.

8 *Chicago Tribune*, 17 November 1898, p. 7.

9 Ibid.

10 *Chicago Inter Ocean*, vol. xviii, 7 July 1889, p. 18.

11 William H. Jordy, *American Buildings and Their Architects: The Impact of European Modernism in the Mid-twentieth Century*, Vol. 3 (Doubleday, New York 1976), p. 61.

12 *Chicago Tribune*, 16 March 1895, p. 8.

13 Harboe.

14 The *Chicago Evening Journal*, 15 March 1895, p. 5.

15 *The Economist*, vol. xiii, 16 March 1895, p. 301. Thanks to Gunny Harboe for bringing my attention to these quotes.

16 Harboe, p. 28.

17 Thomas Leslie, *Chicago Skyscrapers 1871–1934*, (University of Illinois Press, Chicago, 2013), pp. 69–71, 91; Joseph Kendall Freitag, *Architectural Engineering, with Especial Reference to High Building Construction* (John Wiley & Sons, New York 1895), p. 276 in 1907 edition.

18 Kendall Freitag *Architectural Engineering, with Especial Special Reference to High Building Construction* (John Wiley & Sons, New York; Chapman & Hall, London, 1907).

19 Charles E. Jenkins, 'A White Enameled Building', *Architectural Record*, vol. iv, January–March 1895, p. 302.

20 Thomas Leslie, *Chicago Skyscrapers, 1871–1934* (University of Illinois Press, Chicago, 2013), p. 93.

21 Charles E. Jenkins, 'A White Enameled Building', p. 299.

22 *The Economist*, vol. xiii, 25 August 1894, p. 206.

23 For example see Judith Dupré, p. 22.

24 Charles T. Jenkins, 'A White Enameled Building', *Architectural Record*, vol. iv, 1896, p. 302.

25 Harboe, p. 10

26 Harboe, p. 14.

27 Harboe, p. 15.

28 *Chicago Evening Journal*, 13 March 1895, p. 5.

29 *Ornamental Iron*, vol. ii, May 1895, p. 92.

30 *Chicago Tribune*, 16 March 1895, p. 8.

31 *Chicago Evening Journal*, 5 March 1895, p. 5.

32 *Chicago Tribune*, 17 November 1898, p. 7.

33 Leslie, p. 91.

34 *Chicago Tribune*, 16 March 1895, p. 8.

35 Harboe, p. 13.

36 Ibid., p. 15.

37 Leslie, p. 91.

38 Harboe, p. 3.

39 Marcus Vitruvius Pollio, *Ten Books of Architecture* (De architectura), *c*. 30 BC, Book I Chapter 3. Morris Hicky Morgan renders 'utilitas', 'firmitas' and venustas' as 'durability, convenience and beauty' in his 1914 translation, p. 17 of 1960 Dover edition.

40 The Reliance Building, Drawing no. 39, D. H. Burnham and Co., 6 June 1894; Harboe, p. 7. Charles E. Jenkins, 'A White Enameled Building', *Architectural Record*, vol. iv, 1895, pp. 303 and 305 states that 'the architect and contractors had the material all ready to go up, and on May 1st [1894]... a projecting platform had been built' to demolish the existing storeys and commence work on the upper portion of the Reliance.

41 Joanna Merwood-Salisbury, p. 98.

42 *The Economist*, vol. viii, 25 August 1894.

43 Jenkins, p. 300, 301, 304–6.

44 Dupré, p. 25.

45 Harboe, p. 27; *The Economist*, vol. 3, 1 March 1890, p. 229; *Ornamental Iron*, May 1895.

46 *Chicago Daily News Almanac for 1897*, p. 448.

47 Berger, p. 57.

48 Thomas Leslie, *Chicago Skyscrapers 1871–1934*, pp. 92–3; Barr Ferree, 'The Modern Office Building', in *Inland Architect and News-Record*, vol. xxvii, no. 1, May 1896, pp. 34–8; Jenkins, p. 299.

49 A. N. Rebori, 'Work of Burnham & Root', *Architectural Record*, vol. xxxviii, no. 1 July 1915, pp. 33–168, p. 66, quoted in Leslie, *Chicago Skyscrapers*, pp. 92–3. Rebori wrote the obituary on 'Louis H. Sullivan', in *Architectural Record*, vol. 55, no. 6, June 1924, pp. 586–7; Leslie, pp. 92–3.

6 LEGACY

1 Nikolaus Pevsner, *Pioneers of the Modern Movement: from William Morris to Walter Gropius*, (Faber & Faber, London, 1936), p. 166. Subsequent editions were titled *Pioneers of Modern Design*.

2 Leslie, p. 98, 99–100.

3 Ibid., p. 100.

4 Ibid.

5 As explained in his article 'Ornament in Architecture' published in *Engineering* magazine in August 1892.

6 Lloyd Wright, p. 85

7 Charles Moore, *Daniel H. Burnham Architect Planner of Cities* (Da Capo Press, New York, 1968), p. 213.

8 Ibid., pp. 127–40.

9 Henry James, *The American Scene*, an account of journeys through the United States in 1904 and 1905, sections first published in various journals and in book form in 1907.

10 Benjamin C. Ward was a co-founder in 1907 of the Committee, its first executive secretary and in 1909 he published *An Introduction to City Planning: Democracy's Challenge and the American City*, which set out the problems as perceived by the Committee and suggested solutions based on a worldwide study of cities with pressures similar to those of New York.

11 Pamphlet including speech entitled 'We have found you wanting' quoted in Leon Stein (ed.), 'Out of the Sweatshop: the Struggle for Industrial Democracy', Quadrangle/New Times Book Company (New York, 1977), pp. 196–7.

12 Peter Behrens, *Berlins dritte Dimension*, ed. Alfred Dambitsch, (Berlin, Ullstein, 1912), pp. 10–11; Terence Riley and Barry Bergdoll, *Mies in Berlin* (Museum of Modern Art, New York, 2001), p. 363.

13 Paul Scheerbart, *Glass Architecture*, ed. Dennis Sharp (Praeger, New York, 1972), pp. 42, 56, 63.

14 Riley and Bergdoll, p. 106.

15 Ibid., p. 44.

16 Mies van der Rohe, *Frülicht 1.* no. 4 (1922), p. 124, quoted in Fritz Neumeyer, *Artless Word: Mies van der Rohe and the Building Art* (MIT Press, 1991), p. 240.

17 Sigfried Giedion, *Space, Time and Architecture* (Harvard University Press, 1967), pp. 387–8.

18 Elaine S. Hochman asserts that 'the technology to build it [was] not yet in existence' in her *Architects of Fortune: Mies van der Rohe and the Third Reich* (Weidenfeld & Nicolson, New York, 1989), p. 10.

19 The set of photomontages and charcoal sketches were probably produced in 1922, for publicity purposes, and not included in the 1921 Berlin exhibition of competition entries. One of the images was later donated by Mies van der Rohe to the Museum of Modern Art in New York. See Riley and Bergdoll, pp. 325–7.

20 Hochman, p. 10

21 Nikolaus Pevsner, p. 214.

22 Henry-Russell Hitchcock, 'Catalogue of the 'Modern Architecture' exhibition at New York Museum of Modern Art, 1932, p. 57; Giedion, pp. 482–6.

23 Ibid, p. 482; Walter Gropius, *The New Architecture and the Bauhaus* (London, 1937), pp. 22–3.

24 Le Corbusier, pp. 251–2.

25 *Urbanisme* was translated into English by Frederick Etchells and published in 1929 as *The City of Tomorrow and Its Planning* (The Architectural Press, London, 1971), p. 51.

26 Le Corbusier, p. 288

27 Hochman, pp. 141–2, 312.

28 Mies van der Rohe, unpublished MS. 13 March 1934, quoted in Neumeyer, p. 314.

29 Robert Browning, *Andrew del Sarto*, 1855, '…yet do much less, so much less… Well, less is more…. There burns a truer light of God…' The other famous Mies phrase – 'God is in the details' – has no recorded source and, as Franz Shulze points out, 'no one… ever heard him say it. Flaubert wrote 'Le bon Dieu est dans le détail' and perhaps Mies, if he uttered the phrase, was quoting Flaubert. *Mies van der Rohe: A Critical Biography*, p. 281.

30 Moises Puente, *Conversations with Mies* (Princeton University Press, New York, 2008), p. 31.

31 Peter Carter, *Mies van der Rohe at Work* (Phaidon, London, 1974), pp. 45–6.

32 See sections though wall of Lake Shore Drive Apartments in *Mies in America*, ed. Phyllis Lambert, Canadian Centre of Architecture, Montreal, 2001, illustration 4.214. The H-section structural steels are cased in concrete and plaster, and faced with an external skin of metal onto which the I-section mullions are fixed directly. Other I-section mullions cover the metal plates into which adjoining sheets or window glass are housed.

33 Catalogue to 1977 exhibition *The Seagram Plaza: Its Design and Use* (Museum of Modern Art, New York), quoted in S*eagram: Union of Building and Landscape* (Phyllis Lambert, April 2013).

34 Jean-Louis Cohen, *Ludwig Mies van der Rohe* (Birkhauser, Berlin, 2007), p. 141. Franz Schulze in *Mies van der Rohe: A Critical Biography* states that it was the New York Department of Education that told Mies he did not have a licence to practise architecture and would not be granted one until he passed an examination after showing proof of the equivalent of a high school education. Mies' friends duly obtained Mies' education records from Germany and the examination was waived, pp. 280–1.

35 See floor and wall sections in *Mies in America,* ed. Phyllis Lambert, illustration 4.216.

36 Lambert, *Building Seagram,* pp. 49–55.

37 Ibid.

38 Cohen, pp. 143–4. This perhaps slightly confusing criticism is explained by Franz Schulze in *Mies van der Rohe: a critical biography* (University of Chicago Press, 1985), p. 270: 'To brace the lofty but slender profile of the building against wind force, shear walls were installed in the north and south faces of the spine. These two elements, though constructed of concrete, were clad in Tinian marble then covered, yet again cosmetically, with a network of mullions and spandrels that imitated the treatment of the other walls. These devices were hardly true to Mies' purported devotion to logic and clarity.'

39 Herbert Muschamp, 'Opposites Attract', *New York Times* magazine, 18 April 1999.

40 Carter, p. 37.

41 'The 59 story crisis' by Joseph Morgenstern, *New Yorker* magazine, 29 May, 1995, p. 45.

42 Giedion, pp. 387–8 of 1967 edition.

Index

All buildings are in Chicago
unless otherwise specified.
NY is New York.

Acknowledgements

I would like to thank the following people for their help in the conception, writing and the production of this book. First and foremost to Neil Belton for inviting me to publish a book with Head of Zeus and for accepting The Reliance Building as the focus for a book on skyscrapers and, as usual, to my agent Charles Walker for his skill and advice; to T. Gunny Harboe for making his research on the Reliance Building available and for sharing – in a most generous manner – his insights and knowledge, and for taking me on a tour around the building; to Geoffrey Baer, a Chicago-based architect and broadcaster – for his enthusiastic help, and to Tim Samuelson of the Chicago Cultural Center for information about late-nineteenth-century Chicago and its leading architects – particularly Daniel Burnham and Louis Sullivan. I'd also like to thank The Ryerson & Burnham Library, based in the Art Institute of Chicago, for its assistance in compiling images for this book. The library of the Royal Institute of British Architects in London for making available the Banister Fletcher notes on the World's Columbian Exposition held in Chicago in 1893, and to Georgina Blackwell for steering the book through production to publication in a most deft and expert manner.